Policies Against Fraud and Cybercrime:

Strategic, Legal, and Technological Approaches

Ricardo Marcão
https://orcid.org/0000-0003-3277-3078
ISLA Santarém Polytechnic University, Portugal

Vasco Ribeiro Santos
https://orcid.org/0000-0002-3535-9377
ISLA Santarém, Portugal & GOVCOPP, Portugal

Nuno Mateus-Coelho
https://orcid.org/0000-0001-5517-9181
Lusófona University, Portugal

IGI Global Scientific Publishing
Publishing Tomorrow's Research Today

Vice President of Editorial Melissa Wagner
Director of Acquisitions Mikaela Felty
Director of Book Development Jocelynn Hessler
Production Manager Mike Brehm
Cover Design Jose Rosado

Published in the United States of America by
IGI Global Scientific Publishing
701 East Chocolate Avenue
Hershey, PA, 17033, USA
Tel: 717-533-8845 | Fax: 717-533-7115
Website: https://www.igi-global.com E-mail: cust@igi-global.com

Library of Congress Cataloging-in-Publication Data

Names: Marcao, Ricardo, 1987- editor | Santos, Vasco, 1986- editor | Mateus-Coelho, Nuno Ricardo, 1981- editor
Title: Policies against fraud and cybercrime : strategic, legal, and technological approaches / edited by Ricardo Marcão, Vasco Santos, Nuno Mateus Coelho.
Description: Hershey, PA : IGI Global Scientific Publishing, 2026. | Includes bibliographical references and index. | Summary: "This book aims to bridge theory and practice by presenting a diverse range of perspectives on combating fraud and cybercrime"-- Provided by publisher.

Identifiers: LCCN 2025042337 (print) | LCCN 2025042338 (ebook) | ISBN 9798337359922 hardcover | ISBN 9798337359939 paperback | ISBN 9798337359946 ebook
Subjects: LCSH: Computer crimes--Prevention--Case studies | Computer crimes--Government policy--Case studies
Classification: LCC HV6773 .P65 2026 (print) | LCC HV6773 (ebook)
LC record available at https://lccn.loc.gov/2025042337
LC ebook record available at https://lccn.loc.gov/2025042338
British Cataloguing in Publication Data
A Cataloguing in Publication record for this book is available from the British Library.

Table of Contents

Foreword ix

Preface xi

Chapter 1
Volatile Evidence: Memory Forensics in Digital Investigations 1
Roshni Pandey, Gujarat University, India
Kiranbhai R. Dodiya, Gujarat University, India
Parvesh Sharma, Gujarat University, India
Kapil Kumar, Gujarat University, India

Chapter 2
Cybersecurity and Human Rights in South Asia: A Legal and Governance Perspective Through Case Studies 55
Abhilash Aggarwal, Rai University, India

Chapter 3
AI-Driven Fraud Analytics: Proactive Strategies for Detecting Emerging Cybercrime Patterns 97
R. N. Ravikumar, Marwadi University, Rajkot, India
S. Aarthi, Marwadi University, Rajkot, India

Chapter 4
Email-Based Privilege Escalation Attack Detection in Cloud Environments Using Machine Learning 135
B. Sreedevi, SASTRA University, India
S. Barathi, Srinivasa Ramanujan Centre, India

Chapter 5
The Rise of Deepfake Fraud: Legal Challenges and AI-Driven Detection Strategies 161
Kaveri Sharma, Turon University, Karshi, Uzbekistan
Yunfei Li, Department of Business Sciences, University Giustino Fortunato, Benevento, Italy
Ubaldo Comite, Faculty of Economy, Department of Business Sciences, University of Calabria, Italy

Chapter 6
The Evolving Cyber Threat Landscape in India: Trends and Implications 197
Pallavi Kudal, Balaji Institute of International Business, Sri Balaji University, Pune, India
Rahul Waghmare, Balaji Institute of International Business, Sri Balaji University, Pune, India

Chapter 7
Policies Against Fraud and Cybercrime: Strategic, Legal, and Technological Approaches........ 217
Radha Ranjan, Amity University, Patna, India
Ankit Kumar, Sandip University, Sijoul, India
Shagufta Parween, Chaitanya Bharathi Institute of Technology, India
Naveen Nandal, JIMS, India
Anupam Sinha, Amity Law School, India
S. Srinivas Kumar, Jain University, India
Bhoopathy Rajan, Sree Rama Engineering College, India

Compilation of References 265

About the Contributors 297

Index 305

Detailed Table of Contents

Foreword ix

Preface xi

Chapter 1
Volatile Evidence: Memory Forensics in Digital Investigations 1
Roshni Pandey, Gujarat University, India
Kiranbhai R. Dodiya, Gujarat University, India
Parvesh Sharma, Gujarat University, India
Kapil Kumar, Gujarat University, India

Volatile evidence in system memory (RAM) has become vital in digital forensics, capturing live data such as active processes, network sessions, cryptographic keys, and malware fragments often absent from disk analysis. Its transient nature makes memory forensics essential for reconstructing attacks, uncovering sophisticated intrusions, and exposing anti-forensic tactics. This chapter examines key acquisition and analysis techniques, emphasizing challenges of volatility, scalability, and data integrity. It also explores advanced applications—like AI-driven anomaly detection, blockchain-based chain-of-custody, and quantum-safe approaches—positioning memory forensics as a cornerstone of next-generation digital investigations.

Chapter 2
Cybersecurity and Human Rights in South Asia: A Legal and Governance Perspective Through Case Studies 55
Abhilash Aggarwal, Rai University, India

South Asia, encompassing countries like India, Sri Lanka, and Bangladesh, has witnessed rapid digital growth, driven by high mobile penetration and the adoption of digital financial services. As of December 2024, India alone had 970 million internet subscribers, with a 54% annual data consumption growth rate, while Bangladesh reported 50% household internet penetration. However, this digital transformation has been accompanied by a surge in cyberattacks, posing significant challenges to governance, human rights, and privacy. This chapter examines three major cyberattacks in South Asia, the 2022 AIIMS ransomware attack in India, the 2023 Sri Lankan government cloud system attack and the 2016 Bangladesh Bank heist, through a legal and governance lens, analyzing their implications for human rights and privacy. By providing descriptive and historical analyses, the chapter aims to contribute to the discourse on cybersecurity, ethical considerations and human rights in the region.

Chapter 3
AI-Driven Fraud Analytics: Proactive Strategies for Detecting Emerging Cybercrime Patterns 97
R. N. Ravikumar, Marwadi University, Rajkot, India
S. Aarthi, Marwadi University, Rajkot, India

Fraud and cybercrime are evolving rapidly, exploiting technological diversity and human vulnerabilities. Traditional detection systems are reactive and limited against sophisticated threats such as phishing, deepfakes, and insider fraud. This chapter explores AI-driven fraud analytics as a transformative approach to predict, detect, and prevent cyber threats in real time. It highlights how machine learning, deep learning, natural language processing, and graph analytics collectively improve anomaly detection, fraud prediction, and decision speed. Case studies from JPMorgan Chase (2024) and Airtel (2025) demonstrate AI's practical efficiency, achieving up to 96% accuracy and reducing fraud recurrence by 38%. The chapter also addresses ethical and regulatory issues, emphasizing explainability and data privacy. Finally, it proposes a roadmap for AI integration into national and organizational fraud prevention strategies, promoting resilience, accountability, and sustainable digital security.

Chapter 4
Email-Based Privilege Escalation Attack Detection in Cloud Environments Using Machine Learning 135
B. Sreedevi, SASTRA University, India
S. Barathi, Srinivasa Ramanujan Centre, India

Cloud computing offers scalable data access and operational efficiency but introduces serious security challenges—most notably, privilege escalation attacks where insiders gain unauthorized administrative control. This project presents a machine learning-based system to detect such attacks through email analysis. Email content is transformed into numerical features using vectorization techniques. Several classifiers including Random Forest, KNN, SVM, XGBoost, and LightGBM are trained on a labeled dataset to differentiate between safe and malicious emails. An ensemble voting classifier ensures higher accuracy and reduces false positives. The system performs real-time detection and generates alerts for suspicious activities, thereby enhancing cloud security against internal threats.

Chapter 5
The Rise of Deepfake Fraud: Legal Challenges and AI-Driven Detection Strategies 161
Kaveri Sharma, Turon University, Karshi, Uzbekistan
Yunfei Li, Department of Business Sciences, University Giustino Fortunato, Benevento, Italy
Ubaldo Comite, Faculty of Economy, Department of Business Sciences, University of Calabria, Italy

Deepfake technology, enabled by advanced AI models like GANs and diffusion networks, has created a new frontier of digital fraud. Its misuse spans financial scams, executive impersonation, political disinformation, and reputational sabotage, producing media nearly indistinguishable from reality. Legal systems remain fragmented and reactive, with inconsistent definitions, weak penalties, and difficulties in establishing liability among creators, platforms, and AI developers. The global spread of deepfakes complicates enforcement, while regulators must balance intervention with freedom of expression. This paper analyzes comparative legal responses in the European Union, United States, India, and China, alongside technological defenses such as AI classifiers, blockchain verification, and biometric tools. It advocates for harmonized laws, stronger detection, and corporate accountability to confront evolving risks.

Chapter 6
The Evolving Cyber Threat Landscape in India: Trends and Implications 197
Pallavi Kudal, Balaji Institute of International Business, Sri Balaji University, Pune, India
Rahul Waghmare, Balaji Institute of International Business, Sri Balaji University, Pune, India

India's rapid digital transformation, driven by fintech, e-governance, and smartphone penetration, has created vast opportunities but also heightened cyber risks. A 278% rise in state-sponsored attacks and incidents reported by 83% of organizations makes India one of the most targeted nations. Threats are evolving—from Ransomware-as-a-Service and state-backed espionage to supply chain exploits and disinformation campaigns. Systemic vulnerabilities such as outdated infrastructure, weak regulations, talent shortages, and poor cyber hygiene amplify risks. Businesses suffer financial and reputational losses, governments face threats to critical infrastructure, and citizens encounter identity theft and fraud. Combating these challenges requires stronger public-private partnerships, AI-driven detection, resilient infrastructure, legislative reforms, and widespread cyber literacy. Building cybersecurity talent and awareness is vital to mitigate human-factor risks. India's digital future is promising, but securing it demands collaboration, innovation, and proactive defense is essential.

Chapter 7
Policies Against Fraud and Cybercrime: Strategic, Legal, and Technological Approaches.. 217
Radha Ranjan, Amity University, Patna, India
Ankit Kumar, Sandip University, Sijoul, India
Shagufta Parween, Chaitanya Bharathi Institute of Technology, India
Naveen Nandal, JIMS, India
Anupam Sinha, Amity Law School, India
S. Srinivas Kumar, Jain University, India
Bhoopathy Rajan, Sree Rama Engineering College, India

In an age of rapid digitisation, fraud and cybercrime have transformed into intricate risks affecting individuals, enterprises, and governments. The expansion of e-commerce, online banking, and mobile payments has heightened hazards like ransomware, identity theft, phishing, and money laundering, with anticipated losses estimated at USD 10.5 trillion per year by 2025. This paper presents a comprehensive framework that integrates strategic policies, robust regulatory measures, and cutting-edge technologies—AI, machine learning, blockchain, and behavioural analytics—to identify and mitigate fraud. It analyses international rules (e.g., GDPR, CCPA, EU AI Act, FATF AML) and transnational collaboration, supplemented by case studies from the banking, e-commerce, and governmental sectors. Challenges such as adversarial AI, algorithmic bias, and disconnected response systems are tackled, with resilience techniques encompassing adversarial training and privacy-preserving analytics.

Compilation of References 265

About the Contributors 297

Index 305

Foreword

The accelerating digital transformation of the global economy has ushered in an era marked by unprecedented opportunities, and unprecedented risks. As societies integrate artificial intelligence, cloud computing, blockchain infrastructures, and hyperconnected communication systems into daily life, fraud and cybercrime have expanded in both scale and sophistication. Threat actors now exploit diverse technological vectors, from volatile memory and cloud-based authentication loopholes to deepfakes, supply chain vulnerabilities, and AI-driven attack automation. These developments expose critical gaps in existing legal, governance, and investigative frameworks, demanding a multidimensional approach to safeguarding individuals, institutions, and states.

Policies Against Fraud and Cybercrime: Strategic, Legal, and Technological Approaches responds to this urgent need for interdisciplinary dialogue. Bringing together contributions from researchers and practitioners across computer science, cybersecurity, digital forensics, law, governance, and financial technologies, the volume offers a comprehensive examination of contemporary cyber threats and the policies designed to counter them. The chapters illuminate not only the mechanisms of attack and exploitation but also the evolving landscape of defense, ranging from machine-learning-powered detection to blockchain-secured evidence management, and from human-rights protections in cyberspace to the international harmonization of cyber regulations.

By uniting technical, legal, organizational, and ethical perspectives, this book emphasizes the necessity of integrated strategies and coordinated policymaking. The contributors demonstrate that addressing cybercrime is not merely a technical challenge but a societal imperative requiring resilience, accountability, and global cooperation. It is our hope that the insights presented here will support researchers, policymakers, practitioners, and students in understanding the complexities of modern cyber threats and in shaping robust, forward-looking frameworks for digital security.

This volume ultimately demonstrates that combating fraud and cybercrime requires harmonizing strategic policy design, rigorous legal frameworks, and advanced technological innovation. By examining emerging threats and forward-looking solutions, it provides a multidimensional resource for shaping secure and equitable digital societies.

Fábio Branca
Feedzai, Portugal

Preface

As digital ecosystems expand, fraud and cybercrime have become increasing threats that undermine trust and inflict significant financial and reputational damage on organizations worldwide. Combating these risks requires a multifaceted approach that blends strategic planning and advanced technological solutions. From implementing cybersecurity policies and regulatory compliance measures to leveraging artificial intelligence (AI) for threat detection, organizations must adopt adaptive strategies to safeguard their operations.

Policies Against Fraud and Cybercrime: Strategic, Legal, and Technological Approaches explores the policies and practices designed to combat fraud and cybercrime. This book examines the tools, frameworks, and legal instruments used for prevention. Covering topics such as cybercrime, AI, and fraud, this book is an excellent resource for academicians, policymakers, cybersecurity professionals, and legal experts.

CHAPTER OVERVIEWS

Chapter 1: Volatile Evidence Memory Forensics in Digital Investigations

This chapter explores the central role of volatile memory evidence in modern digital forensics. The authors examine acquisition and analysis techniques essential for reconstructing live system states, uncovering sophisticated intrusions, and countering anti-forensic strategies. Advanced methods including AI-driven pattern recognition, blockchain-secured chain-of-custody, and quantum-resistant approaches, are discussed as integral to next-generation investigative capacities.

Chapter 2: Cybersecurity and Human Rights in South Asia – A Legal and Governance Perspective

Through detailed case studies – India's 2022 AIIMS ransomware attack, Sri Lanka's 2023 government cloud breach, and the 2016 Bangladesh Bank heist – this chapter analyzes how accelerating cyber risks intersect with governance challenges, privacy rights, and ethical responsibilities. It situates these incidents within broader legal and regulatory developments in South Asia.

Chapter 3: AI-Driven Fraud Analytics – Proactive Strategies for Detecting Emerging Cybercrime Patterns

This chapter provides a comprehensive look at AI-enabled fraud analytics, emphasizing proactive detection of complex threats such as phishing, deepfake-enabled schemes, and insider attacks. Drawing from industry case studies, it discusses accuracy gains, ethical considerations, and a strategic roadmap for deploying AI within organizational and national security frameworks.

Chapter 4: Email-Based Privilege Escalation Attack Detection in Cloud Environments Using Machine Learning

Centering on insider threats in cloud infrastructures, this contribution outlines a machine-learning system designed to identify privilege escalation attempts through email analysis. By comparing multiple classifiers and introducing an ensemble model, the chapter presents a high-accuracy, low-false-positive approach to strengthening cloud security.

Chapter 5: The Rise of Deepfake Fraud – Legal Challenges and AI-Driven Detection Strategies

This chapter examines the emerging risks posed by deepfakes across financial, political, and social domains. It critically compares legal responses in the EU, US, India, and China and assesses advanced countermeasures including biometric verification, blockchain media authentication, and AI-based classifiers. Recommendations stress harmonized legislation and platform accountability.

Chapter 6: The Evolving Cyber Threat Landscape in India – Trends and Implications

This chapter chronicles the rapidly changing cyber risk environment in India, highlighting trends such as ransomware-as-a-service, state-sponsored espionage, and supply-chain exploitation. The authors stress the importance of public-private partnerships, AI-based threat detection, improved infrastructure, and education policies to address systemic vulnerabilities and human-factor risks.

Chapter 7: Policies Against Fraud and Cybercrime – Strategic, Legal, and Technological Approaches

The concluding chapter synthesizes global technological, regulatory, and strategic developments shaping modern cybersecurity policies. It evaluates international frameworks such as GDPR, CCPA, FATF AML guidelines, and the EU AI Act, identifying challenges including adversarial AI and algorithmic bias. The authors propose integrated defense strategies leveraging AI, blockchain, behavioral analytics, and cross-sector collaboration to build resilient, adaptive fraud-mitigation ecosystems.

Chapter 1
Volatile Evidence: Memory Forensics in Digital Investigations

Roshni Pandey
https://orcid.org/0009-0006-4379-4906
Gujarat University, India

Kiranbhai R. Dodiya
https://orcid.org/0009-0001-9409-7303
Gujarat University, India

Parvesh Sharma
https://orcid.org/0000-0002-0245-5186
Gujarat University, India

Kapil Kumar
Gujarat University, India

ABSTRACT

Volatile evidence in system memory (RAM) has become vital in digital forensics, capturing live data such as active processes, network sessions, cryptographic keys, and malware fragments often absent from disk analysis. Its transient nature makes memory forensics essential for reconstructing attacks, uncovering sophisticated intrusions, and exposing anti-forensic

DOI: 10.4018/979-8-3373-5992-2.ch001

tactics. This chapter examines key acquisition and analysis techniques, emphasizing challenges of volatility, scalability, and data integrity. It also explores advanced applications—like AI-driven anomaly detection, blockchain-based chain-of-custody, and quantum-safe approaches—positioning memory forensics as a cornerstone of next-generation digital investigations.

1. INTRODUCTION

To examine digital forensics today is to examine real-time, memory-centric investigations, probing for ephemeral digital traces. Of all media of digital evidence, random access memory (RAM) is the most elusive, most fragile, yet most vivid in capturing real-time events. The very notion of volatile data exists as long as the plummeting systems are powered, harbouring vital intel of the executed processes, the in-situ network sessions, the ephemeral encryption keys, and the overt actions of the users, which otherwise cease to exist post system shutdown. The Omnipresence of capturing evidence during a critical security incident is rare, yet in abundance. Fatefully, while capturing sensitive data in a decisive moment of time, evidence is the most volatile. For as long as cyber Investigation Forensics has existed, more focus has been based on pieces of non-volatile data (log files, a complex digital filing system, a copy of a hard drive, and other myriad digital Integration sheets). More Forensic Fileless Malware struggled far more than APTs(Mehmood, 2023a). However, as technology advanced, cyber forensics started focusing more and more on real-time evidence. Bridging the most critical gap in modern cyber investigations is memory forensics. The chapter analyses volatile memory from legal, technical, and forensic angles. It examines fundamental aspects, types of volatility, acquisition methods, analytical paradigms, and the evidential integrity paradox. The chapter advocates the need for greater standardisation of policy and practice, coupled with the deployment of technology like artificial intelligence, to process the vast quantities of digital data characteristic of contemporary technologies. They argue that forensics of the volatile memory is crucial for investigators, cybersecurity professionals, and law enforcement who need to gather and understand the ephemeral data that cybercriminals leave behind in today's digital world.(Hamid & Rahman, 2024a).

1.1 volatile vs. non-volatile memory: distinguishing characteristics

During the active state of the central processing unit (CPU), volatile memory holds data necessary for interaction with hardware. It is helpful for real-time computation as long as the supply of electricity is maintained. In contrast, its contents are lost permanently when an electric supply is turned off, which renders it unsuitable for long-term retention. The two dominant types of volatile memory, Dynamic Random Access Memory (DRAM) and Static Random Access Memory (SRAM), focus on speed and low latency.

Non-volatile memory retains stored data, unlike volatile memory, which is lost when an external power supply is disconnected. Examples of this kind of memory include Read-Only Memory (ROM), Solid-State Drives (SSD), and Flash memory. These types of memory provide storage that is slower than volatile memory.

Knowing the differences enables the forensic examiner to select the most effective strategy for collecting evidence. Heuristic, disk-based techniques can provide insight into the events of the past, while volatile processes reveal the present.(Mittal & Vetter, 2016). This can be a crucial difference when determining the current state of a system during the investigation of an intrusion or for reconstructing an attack timeline.

1.2. Types of Volatile Evidence in Digital Investigations

In the world of digital forensics, investigators split volatile evidence based on its susceptibility to changes and loss. Supporting the order of the volatility model (IEEE Guidelines for Evidence Collection, 2021), the most time-sensitive bits of information must be captured first. Common categories of evidence include:

1. Highly Volatile Evidence, which is lost the moment an electronic device is powered off. This data, which exists in the physical memory or system caches, includes:
    1. Running processes and services
    2. Screen and clipboard contents
    3. Network connections
    4. Active encryption and session tokens

These artefacts are lost in volatile memory and can be framed as disappearing with the device. There are specialised evidence collection and computer forensic tools known as Belkasoft Live RAM Capturer and DumpIt, designed to collect and systemise this information.

2. Moderately Volatile Evidence. Partially persistent, retrievable from logs or registry hives. Includes:
    1. All login and logoff events and related security logs.
    2. Documents or images recently opened.
    3. Recently attached USB devices.
    4. Web browser caches or email folders.

While some remnants may be intact after reboots, timestamps or accompanying details may be changed, eroding evidentiary value.

3. Possibly Volatile or Time-Sensitive Evidence. Traditionally recoverable post-mortem, but may deteriorate over time, for example, directory listings, file metadata, and installed-application inventories.

These valuable shards of evidence may undergo more efficient and productive analysis when captured and catalogued in a systematic framework. Such structuring preserves evidence integrity and lessens information loss during immediate response activities.(Nyholm et al., 2022a).

1.3 The Forensic Value of Volatile Memory

What stands out about the feature of memory is capturing the execution of activities in real time. More often than not, real-time accounts are stored in a volatile memory.

1. User and Process Snapshots: System and user profiling can further extend to reconstructing processes, services, and sessions that are active during the selected observation period.
2. Networking: Sets of dormant commands and session logs predict the network behaviour during inactivity periods of host docking.
3. Probes: Memory or fileless malware can take the form of executables, coding shells, injection artefacts, and grabber executors.
4. Shredded Credentials: Volatile memory has physical tokens, superkeys, and other powerful cryptographic objects waiting to be redeemed, which are tethered to memory and weakly guarded.
5. Satin Application: Unnecessary user documents, contextual information, and snippets of discourse can be included in the evidence presented in a court of law.(Zhang et al., 2023)

Figure 1. Value of volatile memory

Taken collectively, these artefacts can tell a narrative, identify blunders, and indicate purpose, all of which are necessary and invaluable for both legal and commercial purposes.

1.4 Juridical Importance and Related Case Laws in India

With the rest of the world, India too aims unthinkingly at understanding the worth of, and does, administrative electronic evidence in a more or less coherent fashion. Several so-called "first" cases initiated the formative stage of development with respect to electronic documents.

1. •Anvar P.V. State 2014 enhanced the collection of 'primary' digital evidence to the level of 'unitary' primary digital documents and augmented the collection of digital evidence to the level of primary, but does so with augmented collection and primary evidence, whereby primary evidence, in corpus, is the level beyond foundation or base evidence."• Arjun Panditrao Khotkar V Kailash Kushanrao Gorantla (2020) – Reiterated that the certificate is non-negotiable, should the original electronic source not be made available.

2. •S. Selvi V State of Karnataka (2010) – Attempted to reconcile the right to privacy, which is enshrined in Article 21 of the Constitution, with the need of the state to conduct a digital amnesia interrogation.
3. •Nirav Modi PNB Fraud case 2018 – Abstracted the significance of forensic exploration within ephemeral caches for elucidating intricate financial deceit(*Anvar P.V. v. P.K. Basheer (Supreme Court on Electronic Evidence) - Info. Technology Law*, n.d.).

These cases exemplify that whilst the impact of memory forensics can be profound, the elusiveness of its records is preserved subject to admissible proof of unbroken methodological shift and custody control.

1.5 Aim and Scope of this Chapter

This chapter seeks to achieve the following aims:

1. Describe the nature of volatile evidence, its value, and its level of importance in a digital investigation.
2. Outline acquisition techniques, making the distinction between live and post-mortem.
3. Assess forensic frameworks and tools. Include both open source and commercial alternatives.
4. Discuss legal, ethical and technical issues, especially regarding the Indian context.
5. Provide case studies and fictional scenarios where the investigations are based on testimony and memory.
6. Discuss automation, the integration of artificial intelligence, and blockchain for audit in future forensic directions.

This structure sets the foundation for the chapter, highlighting volatile memory as a critical component in the world of forensics and a key element in dealing with new wave threats.

2. THE NATURE AND SIGNIFICANCE OF VOLATILE EVIDENCE

Volatile evidence is time sensitive and, therefore, complex in nature. Within computer systems, data that vanishes upon powering off the computer is termed volatile. Such data exists in the RAM and includes system buffers, CPU registers, and various caches like GPU memory and NIC ephemeral memory. Since these data are extremely easily replaced, the acquisition effort should focus more on the speed and accuracy of the collection.

2.1 Comprehending Volatility Order in a Forensic Setting

According to the Order of Volatility Principle (OoV), an investigator must capture between the head and the tail of a piece of data as a primary step. Each successive layer of the process tables, caches, temporary files, and disks, in that order, exhibits varying degrees of promptness and persistence. This principle achieves a compromise between the forensic completeness of an investigation and the massive evidentiary reliability that such an investigation would have to bear. Capturing volatile live memory imposes an immediate, acute risk of allegations regarding the state that is live and being memorised. This is, however, a very reasonable allegation to make. To hold the state, forensic investigators use read-only and write-neutral devices alongside other tools that are 'footprint' reduced to prevent collateral damage(Nyholm et al., 2022b).

2.2 Volatile Data Captured from RAM

Active volatile data, which includes the following, is increasingly being captured through contemporary forensic suites.

1. Active Network Connections – Identifying and capturing the channels of data being sent and accessed in real time.
2. Processes and Drivers that Are Active – Identifying and capturing processes and drivers that are malicious injections or unauthorised, rogue modules.

3. Registry Snapshots – Capturing temporal keys and system configurations that are registries.
4. Handles of Files and Memory-Mapped Files– Identifying and seizing files and 'resources' that were active. Cached Credentials and Encrypted Keys– Keys that allow for defeating volumes and protected accounts.

Take memory carving, for instance. It not only reconstructs broken or partially broken files. Carving memory and other sophisticated methods are critical for investigating memory-resident malware and other compromises that happen in real-time, such as ransomware and internal and external active network intrusions.

The forensic value of evidence is not only restricted to detecting malware. It also helps in real-time operations, such as slips of documents, net fraud, and investigations of insider threats. Forensic investigations are capable of supplying volatile memory data as circumstantial evidence to testify to digital presence or user intent and prove the activity timeline. (Mehmood, 2023b).

2.3 Ethical and Operational Considerations

Most of the time, the awareness and defence of espionage or surveillance are more of shielding the subjects, such as tracking communications of employees, passwords, encryption and firewalls. The law warrants that investigators are bound to specific rules to avoid breaching privacy. The act of transferring the subject is to record, document, and provide an immediate hash, which is further processed with write-blocking to ensure the chain of custody is admissible and transparent.

3. ACQUISITION OF VOLATILE EVIDENCE

The acquisition of volatile evidence is the most crucial and sensitive segment of any digital investigation. Because volatile data is lost when there is an interruption and power is turned off, the investigator has to follow particular procedures and ethical boundaries to maintain the integrity of the evidence. A rational acquisition not only ensures that the evidence is trustworthy but also guarantees that the index is an accurate and unmodified mirror of the system in real-time.

3.1 Principles of Volatile Data Acquisition

According to IEEE Guidelines for Evidence Collection and Archiving 2021, the order of volatility (OoV) has to be observed. This method provides the data in collection order, beginning with the most time-sensitive and ending with the least.

1. CPU registers and cache – In order of volatility, from fastest to nanosecond levels, strategised acquisition is recommended to be captured using optimised technology in any possible way.
2. Routing tables, ARP cache, and process tables – Demonstrates and provides insight into the internal workings of the hypervisors as well as networking subsystems and the process states of the system.
3. System memory (RAM) – Contains live processes, drivers that are in use, keys in cryptography, and information captured in a session.
4. Temporary file systems – contain files that are structured as swap files, page files, and volatile data the application is working on.
5. Non-volatile disks, peripherals, and systems – Contains the Files, configurations, and data that are stored for an extended period of time.

Every action must be recorded accurately, along with command line input and timestamps, as well as where and what data are to be obtained, so as to ensure that this process complies with procedure and legal standards later on. The structure still maintains a hierarchy, in which the first things to be remembered, and most often the most crucial, the wispiest are captured.(Sandvik et al., 2022).

Figure 2. Principles of volatile data acquisition

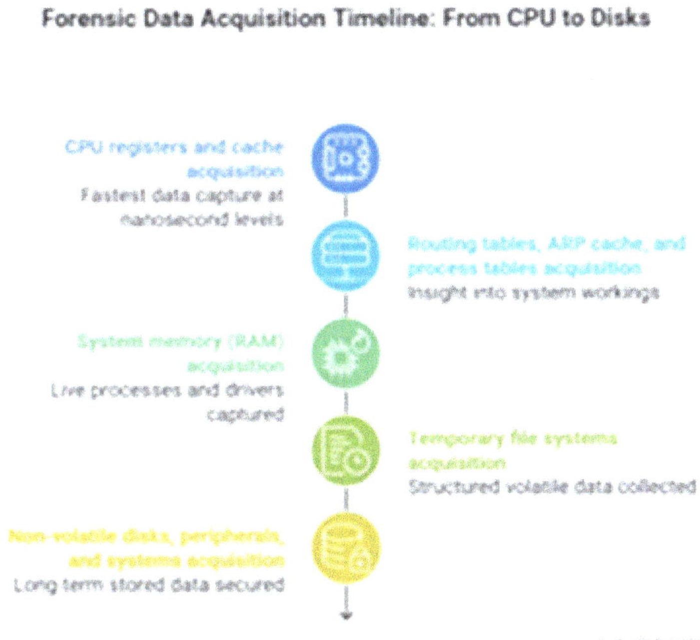

3.2 Issues with the Acquisition of Ephemeral Information

The complexities inherent in memory capturing are often disregarded.

1. Sending State Change: The act of capturing data modifies what is stored in the memory. The acquisition software takes memory and fetches and modifies a portion marked as an insignificant region.
2. Involuntary Loss of Memory: Volatile evidence is destroyed with any sudden cessation of power or an instantaneous shutdown with evidence within the circuitry.
3. Equipment Diversity: A single system with numerous forms of memory, which includes the processor cache, graphic processor, random access memory, network buffers and with the acquisition tools, must be circuitry aligned.

4. Encapsulation and Virtualisation: The method layers on top of or below a structured computer system, and a segment of random access that is encrypted, requires super-level tools that are usually below the hypervisor.
5. Obstruction to the Capture: Attackers are willing to use techniques such as the cold boot counter or the wiping of memory to counter capture techniques.

For these reasons, the process of obtaining data and evidence via live acquisition should only be performed by professionals, and proof of tools with a verified cryptographic seal should be submitted along with command logs as part of the chain of custody records, vital for court acceptance. (Oliveri & Balzarotti, 2025).

3.3 Acquisition in Comparison to Evidence Collection in Real-Time

Each technique is separated by a different system of working, where evidence acquisition in real-time and evidence collection are both prominent.

3.3.1 Live Acquisition

Live acquisition p.52 One of the methods of collecting evidence is live acquisition. It is used when the system of interest is still working, which is why it is beneficial when trying to acquire ephemeral information, such as encryption keys, processes, or network connections. It has the following advantages:

1. Acquisition of volatile information, such as live RAM sessions.
2. Immediate understanding of the action that is taking place.
3. Observation of malware in real time.

On the other hand, live acquisition is just as valuable for the investigator as it is harmful due to the contamination it brings. Any action taken during the process will invariably change the evidence. In order to execute these processes in the most proper way possible, most investigators use self-contained executables that are saved onto trusted portable devices.

Common commands/tools used:

1. Netstat, arp, ipconfig and other similar commands are used for meshing networks.
2. Pslist is used to capture and record running processes while in engagement.
3. Memory imaging is usually done through the use of DumpIt, Belkasoft Live RAM Capturer, nd WinPmem.

3.3.2 Dead Acquisition

Dead acquisition is the opposite of live acquisition, because it is done when the system is off or has been safely shut down. It focuses more on evidence that can be acquired and saved onto a hard drive, as the evidence is non-volatile. It focuses on the images that are stored on the hard drive, the configuration files, and the registry hives. Because the environment is static, the forensic soundness is beneficial and poses a lot less risk of alteration.

However, this approach fails to reconstruct certain fleeting aspects that are critical to contemporary research (e.g., injected shellcode or the live keys used to encrypt data). Consequently, investigators routinely combine both techniques, performing a rapid live capture full mesh imaging to obtain a full capture sufficient for the investigation.(*A BEST PRACTICE APPROACH TO LIVE FORENSIC ACQUISITION MM Grobler 1, SH von Solms*, n.d.).

3.4 Tools and Frameworks for Memory Imaging

The success of memory forensics analysis is primarily determined by the imaging systems and their accuracy and imaging quality. Below are selected frameworks used in the field:

3.4.1 Belkasoft Live RAM Capturer

The tool by Belkasoft is provided with 32 and 64 intermediate kernel partition drivers, which function under the highest privilege level for capture, even from the most protected processes, thus with memory capture processes, files with .mem extension are produced, which can be later analysed using Belkasoft Evidence Centre, thus establishing a direct relationship for RAM-based artefacts with the disk.

3.4.2. FTK Imager

AccessData's FTK Imager is a multipurpose application that conducts bit imaging and the acquisition of forensically sound images, which includes the preservation of unallocated and slack space. Maintaining hash values for the images assures image integrity. Although FTK Imager is not capable of natively examining RAM dumps, it is possible to analyse the images using Volatility and wxHexEditor later.

3.4.3 DumpIt

DumpIt is a memory imaging tool capable of achieving one-hundred per cent bit-for-bit memory imaging from USB and providing complete memory imaging in a matter of seconds. Its singular form of memory imaging makes it user-friendly, and it is preferred in case of a need for rapid-response operations.

3.4.4 Mandiant Memoryze

Mandiant, a section of FireEye, created Memoryze to support the retrieval and disassembly of a fully configured virtual machine. It is capable of acquiring all processes, drivers, and system memory of the virtual machine in real-time. In the same interface, analysts can also monitor and analyse processes to find hidden or injected code and rootkits.

3.4.5 WinPmem

WinPmem is the primary memory acquisition tool and was originally part of the Rekall Framework. It also allows users to place memory dumps via kernel-mode drivers. WinPmem has been designed to work seamlessly with Volatility 3 and is compatible with most memory structures from Windows 10 and 11.

3.4.6 Hardware-Assisted Solutions

In forensics, hardware devices capable of hardware direct memory access (DMA), like the PCIe Leech, can externally capture memory from a system. These solutions are ideal because they eliminate a majority of the risks associated with software contamination(Rzepka et al., 2025).

However, these solutions do require a point of access and hardware expertise.

Figure 3. Memory forensic tools overview

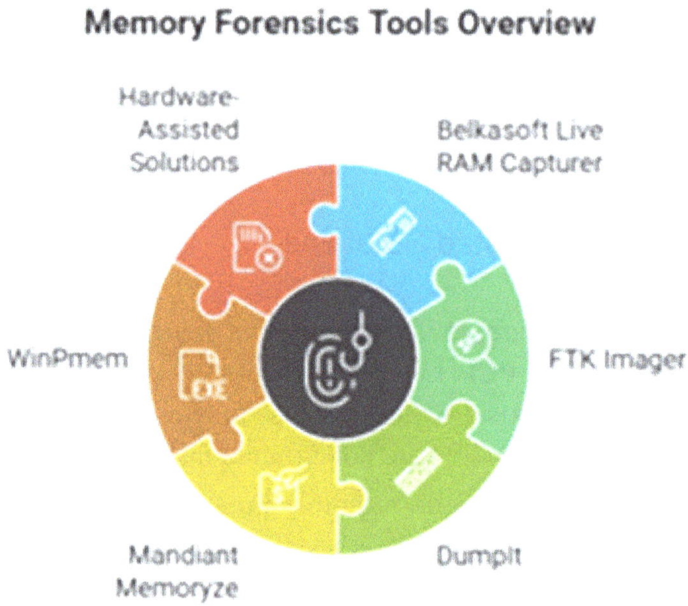

3.5 Best Practices for Evidence Preservation

To avoid infringements of laws as well as logical infringements, barriers to logical violations need to be identified. This approach ensures the evidence recollected will be evidence.

1. Capture and Save Everything: Capturing the operators of the devices used, the version of the tool in use, the account used, the essence of the tool used, and the time of acquisition, belongs to you.
2. Employ Write-Blocked Media: These media can be used to stop any changes to the original evidence.
3. Hash Verification: Making MD5/SHA-256 hashes pre- and post-imaging and making sure the values agree verifies integrity.

4. Secure Storage: Captured and stored images should be in an encrypted, controlled-access storage and premises.
5. Chain of Custody: Every acquisition, through analysis, is signed by all active loggers, ensuring the time records are kept.
6. Environmental Robustness: Do not expose sensitive data to temperature or electromagnetic disruptions, which may compromise integrity.

Adhering to all the aforementioned principles ensures that all processed memory data can be used in court. In India, this is governed by Section 65B of the Evidence Act and, in the U. S., by Rule 902(14) of the Federal Rules of Evidence.(Bernardo et al., 2024a).

4. MEMORY FORENSIC ANALYSIS TECHNIQUES

With the acquisition complete, all attention shifts to the phase of interpretation. Memory analysis attempts to analyse stored binary data and reconstruct artefacts that provide system states, combined with attempts to attribute responsibility for the behaviour deemed as malicious.

4.1 Foundations of Memory Analysis

The RAM in systems captures elements of both 'kernel space' and 'user space' data. Analysis involves the process of discerning and resolving multiple process structures, thread hierarchies, registries, network sockets and positions in time. About memory image analysis, these stages are of great importance:

Verification, Profile Identification, Artefact Extraction, Causation with Timeline Reconstruction, and Documentation Creation.

Almost all modern memory analysis and forensics revolve around two tools: Rekall and the Volatility Framework.

These two tools are equipped with unique features and plugins, providing endless capabilities to support multiple file types and operating systems.

These include: Volatility plugins, which allow tailored searches for specific information formatted as commands.:

1. pslist – obtains the current list of processes.
2. dlllist – lists the active and loaded DLLs.
3. malfind – finds code insertion irregularities.
4. netscan – identifies network connections.

With Volatility 3, the installation and use of a specific operating system profile became obsolete, and automation was improved.

1. Rekall:

Originating from Volatility, Rekall's main characteristic is its speed as well as its focus on scalability. It also provides a distinctive feature of proactive YARA-rule signature-based malware exclusion and memory carving advanced filters for enhanced efficiency.

2. Redline:

A Windows-based system with a Graphical User Interface, Redline is a triage tool that simplifies the examination of processes, registries, and network connections for devices like routers and switches.(Bernardo et al., 2024b).

4.3 Remote connections and collecting connected artefacts

Artefacts and evidence contingent on the network and stored in the volatile memory can indicate exfiltration, peer connections, remote commands, and control channels. Analysts apply the plugins like sockscan, netscan and connscan to gather:

1. Remote and local IP addresses.
2. Protocols and related process control numbers.
3. Process Identification.

The communication trail can also be confirmed using the firewall or IDS logs. In some cases, volatile memory was the only artefact that captured the command-and-control IP an attacker was using live, before this IP disappeared from all external logs.

Any volatile memory often contains highly sensitive cryptographic materials that cannot be recovered otherwise. For instance, in devices that are protected with BitLocker encryption, the Volume Master Key (VMK) and the Full Volume Encryption Key (FVEK) are temporarily stored in Random Access Memory (RAM). Investigators can also recover cryptographic keys from the dumps using keyword searches (for instance, "External Key") and analysing the metadata in context. The phenomenon of cold boot attacks, and the tools like the BitLocker plugin of Volatility, or dedicated hex viewers, demonstrate that even in a powered-off system, RAM can almost instantaneously retain some form of cryptographic keys that aid in partial booting, through what is referred to as cold boot experiments.

It has now become clear why memory forensics is becoming more critical; many viruses today operate entirely in Random Access Memory (RAM).

- Conficker Virus is a nasty piece of malware which, for purposes of spreading, is known as a worm.
- Nash is a network application that can perform live scans on certain hidden and secured areas of memory.
- Remote Forensics Tools: These tools are designed for investigators to perform remote system access quickly and affordably.
- MemProcFS: This application allows users to virtually 'mount' memory images as file systems. In addition, users are able to graphically interact with RAM fragments and artefacts in a more accessible way.

The tools provide evidence of compromise: suspicious threads, hooks, and injects, which are hidden and protected from a standard disk examination. Analysts can reassess baselines and implants to distinguish between harmless and dangerous operations.(Пташкін et al., 2021).

4.4 The Influence of Automation, Machine Learning, and Artificial Intelligence in Memory Analysis

Considering the amount of memory available, scanning through all of it physically becomes a challenge. Integrating AI and machine learning with memory forensics automates workflows to detect anomalies, artefact clustering, defensive and offensive attack patterns, and predictive compromise to predict breaches and automate memory forensics processes.

Memory analysis with Artificial Intelligence is facilitated by the use of supervised learning, whereby the algorithm is trained with labelled datasets about normal versus malicious processes, unsupervised clustering in which algorithms detect and categorise anomalous behaviours of processes, and Natural Language Processing, which enables the generation of coherent and concise summaries from the synthesised information.

The optimised profiling and allocation of hybrid memory systems consisting of volatile DRAM and Non-Volatile Memory (NVM) is Artificial Intelligence-driven. Access latency and energy cost are optimised through programmable profiling, which dynamically surfaces anomalous data patterns, and programmable profiling allows for the automated detection of anomalous data usage patterns. This automation enhances the precision of the outcome and lowers the time to complete the tedious tasks, resulting in improved efficiency.(Tageldin & Venter, 2023).

4.5 Reporting and Interpretation

The outcome of forensic investigations should be presented for easy defence in court. Typical reports contain the following sections.

1. Executive Summary: Overview of the objectives and key outcomes.
2. Methodology: Description that details the processes followed to perform the acquisition and subsequent analysis.
3. Findings: Outlined artefacts, processes, relationships, and user accounts.
4. Interpretation: Integration of logical reasoning with the analytic artefacts and conjectures.

5. Forensic process: Preservation of hashes, administering the tools used, and documentation of the procedural steps for the workflow(Karie et al., 2019).

5. CHALLENGES AND LIMITATIONS IN MEMORY FORENSICS

Service, memory forensics has not missed the attention of technical, legal and operational concerns. While conducting investigations and attempts at truth confirmation in evolving settings, they deal with issues such as data volatility, jurisdictional grey areas, or hostile vandalism of the data sets under examination.

5.1 Data Volatility and Ephemerality.

The data that does not persist in the long term in memory and is not archivable is the most difficult to store and, at the same time, the most easily destructible. Volatility. This captures the evidence of what a person's computer is doing at a precise moment in time. This is done in a conception of evidence that ceases to exist and is in danger of disappearing and falling beneath the threshold of perception as power is lost. Acquisition is a term used in the operational environment. It sets in motion a train of events memory which, in turn, sets in motion a train of events that, in turns, sets in motion, and memory will tumble, or collapse, or give birth or spin or rejuvenate into one of the proven or memory states system. To counter the effects of distortion, practitioners do use forensically low-impact acquisition devices. Even then, some measure of contamination is a certainty. Thus, to ascertain the context of something and something else, the date and time of the capture are crucial. This goes for the techniques as well as the context of the analysis. This is important as a future reference to all the documentation, which should also reside within the analysis that is coherent and well-structured. The size of modern RAM modules provides another added layer of complexity. Servers require between 64 GB and multiples of terabytes of memory. Dumping such massive amounts of data requires extensive data pipelines and high-performance forensically tunable workstations(Mehmood & Ahmad, 2024).

5.2. Legal and Ethical Constraints: The Ambiguity in Legal Frameworks

Volatile evidence of any kind and in many jurisdictions is underdeveloped narratively and conceptually. The Indian Evidence Act of 1872, as amended in 2000, recognises electronic evidence in section 65B, but live acquisition and memory forensics go unmentioned. Investigators have been challenged in defence of the reliability and admissibility of volatile data, conservatively mute, dismissing the data as ephemeral, and therefore, by default, volatile in nature.

The lack of legal standards concerning the collection and retention of evidence for court purposes has the paradoxical consequence of internally binding the investigator to arbitrary organisational rules supplemented by the ISO and IEC 27037:2012 international standards. This is particularly true in the context of the ACPO in the UK, which comprises the Good Practice Guide, or in the context of supplying evidence to courts requiring cross-border jurisdiction and evidence. This provides the court with the option for standard certified evidence. Data in volatile memory contains not only records of suspected misconduct, but also personal and sensitive information such as passwords, bank account numbers and transactions, as well as private messages. It is ethical only to collect what is necessary and to practice strict data minimisation. Acquisition of such information without consent is likely to raise privacy concerns under Article 21 of the Constitution of India and equally in other jurisdictions such as GDPR within the EU and HIPAA in the USA.

Hence, live analysis is to be preceded by warrants or other forms of written authorisation. In addition, memory images that have been captured should only be available to vetted specialists and should be protected by encryption, access control, and audit trails.(Hamid & Rahman, 2024b).

Figure 4. Legal and ethical constraints in digital forensics

5.3. Technical Limitations and Resource Constraints

5.3.1. Computational Overload

The analysis of memory dumps that are several gigabytes in size is very resource-demanding. The use of tools such as Rekall and Volatility, for example, involves the parsing of unstructured and binary data, building up kernel objects, as well as the uncovering of hidden modules. These actions require very high and expensive computing resources for the workstation being used by the analyst. An analysis machine typically takes 2.5 times the size of the memory dump. In the case of a 64 GB memory dump, such a machine would require a minimum of 128 GB of memory and would need to be configured with multiple cores, something that is too expensive for small institutions.(Hamid & Rahman, 2024c).

5.3.2 Page Smearing and Data Inconsistency

Incomplete and inconsistent images may result from 'live acquisition' used during 'page smearing' acquisition, where memory pages change between intervals. In this scenario, a table entry may point to a piece of data that has already been overwritten or has shifted, which can lead to process tables or kernel mappings being structurally ruined and evidential credibility being corrupted.(Ottmann et al., 2023).

5.3.3 Problems with Huge Image Sizes and Storage

Most common memory dumps can take as much space as the physical RAM that is installed, making the RAM installations range from 64 GB to even 512 GB. Performing unit, whole or node backups of such memory dumps is complex, and unnecessary difficulty is averted with 'Secure Vault' software. Such software has excessive redundant and time-lapse records that, even after protracted litigation, little to no infrastructure change happens on a digital level(Pandey et al., 2025).

5.3.4 On RAM Anti-Forensic Techniques

The burden of malware and cyber attackers' continuous development of anti-forensic methods that aim to eliminate every track from the cover of the 'investigators' is a real one, with severe countermeasures. These countermeasures have been observed and recorded on both the acquisition and framework of the necessary logic in the 'for the rest of eternity' phases(Palutke et al., 2020).

5.3.5 Shadow Walker Rootkit

As Shadow Walker has demonstrated through examples, it showcases the primary 'kernel' of the 'spring' myth being intricately woven through ‘tools’ and their ‘shadow’ life. As in their examples, it saves them from the burden of the memory being captured as ‘polished’ even if the shiniest part of the ‘executable’ is infested with the most atrocious ‘viruses’ of the segment. They do this by useless data feeding to ‘Toolz’ during the ‘page faults’ that grab hold of the delicate ‘cake’ of the memory. Thus, the memory framed is seen to be ‘chaste’ while the most complex ‘malcode’ thrives unseen.(Vömel & Freiling, 2011a).

5.3.6 Toolkit on Dementia

The Dementia anti-forensic toolkit takes advantage of Memory acquisition tools like Volatility and Memoryze. For example, by intercepting system calls, such as NtWriteFile(), and preventing particular kernel objects (processes, threads) from being written and subsequently saved, these tools hide them from subsequent analysis. Output files are then concealed from post-acquisition scrutiny.(Ratcliffe et al., 2022).

5.3.7 Gargoyle and The One-Byte Abort

Gargoyle uses asynchronous calls in the concealed execution of malicious payloads through shards of memory marked read and write only. Control is then switched in execution to RWX and back post execution. This is done to avoid leaving behind control and a footprint for forensic analysis. The same applies to the “one-byte abort” technique, which alters decisive bytes of egregious pointers and critical bytes to avoid being captured by signature-based detectors.(Jung et al., 2021).

5.4. Fake Objects ADD, Attention Deficit Disorder.

This proof of concept generates false structures, for instance, process tables or TCP endpoint leasing, that are designed to capture analysts’ attention. The documents are considered sink artefacts as they drain time and resources, and thus, there is a call for behaviour-based analysis in addition to structural probing.

5.5. Memory Forensics Legal Hurdles in the Indian Context

The Indian judiciary, for instance, has experienced several recurring legal challenges, such as:

1. Lack of clear delineation of acquisition procedure from other steps: Collection (off-line capture) misconstrued as acquisition (live capture) is a common occurrence. In such cases, investigators need to justify their decisions for every case.
2. Pressure on Preservation: Providing long-term storage of volatile data and evidence is both a technological and financial challenge. Even years after the collection, the courts may ask for primary evidence.
3. Absence of Concrete Devices: Even though courts impose the necessity of 65B certification on all kinds of data, the admissibility is undermined by the lack of the original device.
4. Insufficient Knowledge: Many members of the judiciary do not acquaint themselves with the field of volatile evidence and, as a result, lack a proper understanding of the field, and thus offer disparate legal decisions(*(PDF) Admissibility of Electronic Record under Section 65B of The Indian Evidence Act Vis-à-Vis Judicial Interpretation*, n.d.).

5.6 The Ethical Issues as well as the Responsibilities for the Investigation

Memory data, as both technical evidence and a personal document, creates the issue of ethics. Every investigator is faced with the challenge of obtaining the truth while upholding the rights of the individual. This tension is resolved by:

Least Possible Effect: Collect only what is needed, nothing more.

1. Openness: Full documentation is available on every stage of collection.
2. Responsibility: Retention of records is policy-compliant, and data is available only to Active members of the project.

3. Knowledge & Skills: Every single one of the work streams consists of domain-qualified specialists with years of experience in the digital forensics field.

Institutions like the Digital Evidence Specialist Advisory Board (DESAB) work towards ensuring adherence, as well as the capture and dissemination of best practices.(Hamid & Rahman, 2024d).

5.7 The Arms Race: Attackers and Investigators

In cyberspace, there is also a war being fought related to memory forensics. As tool forensics receives new multi-form malware, so too are the attackers receiving new evasion techniques such as fileless persistence and in-memory encryption, polymorphic during runtime, and other forms. The more complex problem can also be solved with a more sophisticated, adaptable AI analytic system that can detect behavioural patterns and learns, as opposed to static signature recognition.(Liu et al., 2023).

5.8 The Need to Standardise and Collaborate

The absence of relic workflows in digital forensics is still an unfinished problem in the field. The workflows in different disciplines need more coordination. Integrated collaboration among experts in law, science, and business is essential for the design of frameworks that incorporate digital forensics workflows like the DFRWS with the Digital Forensic Research Workshop to optimise memory imaging, metadata creation, and integrity preservation. Collaborative frameworks should be reinforced among tools such as Volatility, Rekall, and EnCase that analyse public datasets. Also, cross-border forensic cloud systems need to establish data exchange pacts with other nations for regulated, unrestricted data flow under the principles of Mutual Legal Assistance Treaties.

As with other issues in memory forensics, the problems of 'data volatility' are as much to do with the instability of the legal and ethical frameworks that support data volatility. To the extent that these legal issues remain in their 'current' state permits, a philosophy of 'all hands on deck' is warranted, that is, in integrating 'soft' systems with 'hard' systems, order with artistry, and ethics with precision. The forensic data, its availability for analysis, and explanatory power, to varying degrees, depend on the integration with ongoing, reinforced, and tiered standardisation and training.(Solanke & Biasiotti, 2022).

6. MEMORY FORENSICS: CASE STUDIES WITH HYPOTHETICAL SCENARIOS

Volatile memory forensics is best appreciated in the context of 'live' investigations with realistic mock setups. Each such setup sheds light on the way critical, as well as 'invisible', evidence can be obtained through the analysis of 'live' memory. These also showcase the hybrid of technical and legal boundaries that define the realm of attributable cybercrime, insider abuse, and proxy attacks orchestrated at the state level.

6.1 Case Study 1: Investigating Ransomware and Recovery of Memory

In 2023, a medium-sized manufacturing firm based in Pune, India, came under a significant cyber attack in the form of double-extortion ransomware. Attackers gained control of the firm's servers, displaying ransom notes and demanding payment in cryptocurrency under the threat of leaking proprietary designs. A forensic analysis of the firm's disks revealed no evidence suggesting the installation of ransomware executables, hinting instead at a sophisticated form of fileless infection.

Memory Acquisition and Analysis

Live acquisitions were done using DumpIt and FTK Imager without powering down the systems. By employing the pslist plugin of Volatility, suspicious PowerShell.exe processes having elevated privileges and communicating on TCP with an offshore IP through encrypted channels were tracked.

String analysis and process memory carving allowed analysts to recover an AES-256 key that the malware wielded. Consequently, they were able to decrypt several design files without paying the ransom. The presence of threads injected into svchost.exe threads confirmed execution retention.

Forensic analysis not only revealed key information but also reconstructed information proving how the attackers exploited the poorly configured Active Directory service. This aided the firm in the policies on Citadel, as stated in section 65B(Solanke & Biasiotti, 2022).

6.2 Case Study 2: Verifying Rootkit Presence Using Primitive Volatile Evidence

An undisclosed large multinational IT service company experienced outbound traffic that could not be explained. All devices with engine-based antivirus tools could not find the source of the problem. Investigators collected volatile memory from the systems in question and analysed it using Rekall and YARA.

Kernel analysis revealed hidden rootkit kernel modules absent from the driver list, typical of rootkits using dynamic kernel object manipulation (DKOM). Further analysis showed that the malicious driver, which blocked file system functions, was used for the exfiltration of logs.

The malfind plugin helped analysts perform direct extraction of the malicious module from RAM. Through signature comparison, the module was associated with the Necurs rootkit family. As the rootkit was purely memory-based, there was no footprint of it on the disk; therefore, volatile analysis was the only method used to provide proof of compromise.

6.3 Case Study 3: Insider Threat and Credential Theft

In this scenario, a worker from a financial-process outsourcing organisation used authentic credentials to wire a few cents to different personal accounts. The user was authorised access; therefore, the audit trails were inconclusive.

Within 30 minutes of the incident, a volatile-memory image of the user's workstation was retrieved. The analysis of the lsass.exe process showed some Mimikatz credentials, where there were plaintext credentials that were collected by Mimikatz. In RAM, there were also fragments of encrypted chats that proved the suspects were working with other people.

Significance

The evidence collected showed intentional credential harvesting that instantly converts a disciplinary case into a prosecutable cyber-fraud case under the Information Technology Act of 2000. This case demonstrates the swift capture of RAM. In this instance, had the RAM capture been a few seconds or minutes later, the evidence would have been destroyed had the system been rebooted.(Vömel & Freiling, 2011b).

6.4 Case Study 4: Advanced Persistent Threat (APT) Attribution

In 2022, an Indian energy-distribution organisation recorded multiple network intrusions. When analysing the engineering workstations after the incident, the post-mortem analysis found a DLL fileless injector that captured SCADA ladder logic and transmitted it overseas.

By linking the artefacts to the MITRE ATT&CK framework, investigators attributed behaviours such as credential dumping (T1003), process injection (T1055), and persistence through service creation (T1543) to an acknowledged APT group operating within South-East Asia. The compelling proof was found in volatile memory, an injected thread in winlogon.exe, containing the group's signature routine for encryption.

Impact

The ability to do so enabled national cyber-defence teams to determine the campaign's origin and provide threat-intelligence advisories to other similar utilities. The disk analysis, in isolation, could not have discerned the in-memory persistence technique.

6.5 Hypothetical Scenario: Memory Forensics in IoT and Cloud Environments

Where the computation focus is disseminated, the lines that demarcate volatile evidence are expanded. Take, for example, an IoT breach in the smart-factory ecosystem; compromised sensors feed a cloud-integrated dashboard erroneous telemetry data. Conventionally, capturing images from the embedded devices would be impossible.

Instead, remote volatile acquisition is conducted via firmware-level commands that dump memory buffers of microcontrollers and the containerised analytics node in the cloud. Analysis of the RAM reveals injected and altered timestamped MQTT packets that demonstrate manipulation at the data collection layer. This case illustrates the memory forensics of the future, in which the capturing of volatile data in real time extends the paradigm of static devices to cyber-physical systems in the Industry 4.0 infrastructure.

6.6 Appropriateness and Accessibility for the Intended Audience

In this case, the real-time capture simulations enable law enforcement professionals to understand the theory behind the custody paradigm, the difference in volatile versus persistent artefacts, and ISO 27037. Students prepared with simulation exercises like this understand the time-sensitive nature of real-world investigations, where relatively swift action must be taken to either preserve or lose key pieces of evidence(Pendergrass et al., 2019).

7. FUTURE DIRECTIONS AND CONCLUSION

7.1 The Changing Dynamics of Memory Forensics

Memory forensics is one of the techniques that is frequently used in digital investigations. As for the use of memory forensics in generative AI and IoT cloud architecture in the edge computing environment, the complexity of computing environments is continuously increasing, which is fascinating. For more pragmatic advancement in the field, forensic practices are bound to a more complex evolution. The advancement of the field is hinged upon the achievement of four interrelated focal points, which are automation, legal integration, integration, and scalability. If in the next decade, the geography of data, the evidence, and the volumetric data explosion will have to undergo automation, quantification, and legal integration of the Data as such spatial and multi-jurisdictional, discontinuous, and volatile strata, which will have to be integrated. This needs systems that can temporally correlate and fuse volatile hybrid data sources, such as on-premise RAM dump containers and cloud snapshots, to Ephemeral integrated 'data at rest' frameworks, or integrated systems. Embedding AI in such systems will enable the achievement of complex integration of hybrid systems.

When synchronising the automation of complex processes in such hybrid systems through the application of Ephemeral Integrated Data Fusion, memory analytics has the potential to be profoundly enhanced through the integration of AI with Machine Learning.

In contrast to classical instruments such as Volatility, which remain restricted to deterministic parsing, AI is capable of geolocating and flagging variations within millions of dimensions and attributes that remain imperceptible to the human eye.

Anomaly Detection Models: Unsupervised learning could traverse the blueprints of RAM and methodically scan its architecture to erase and document anomalies that deviate from a baseline, which could be invaluable for identification and countermeasures of polymorphic or disguised malware.

Natural Language Processing (NLP): Cyber case incidents of sophisticated nature, such as begets, URLs, commands, and credentials of RAM capture, automating their composition, formatting, and structuring to a level of usefulness within human comprehension.

Predictive forensics: Picture a device equipped with Reinforcement learning and AI that can anticipate and strategise assault pathways, as well as mimic methods of intrusion within a sandbox environment, enabling observers to follow the attack in its exposure phases.

Nonetheless, the integration of AI technologies must still ensure the preservation of transparency of their forensic application – models must be understandable, replicable, and compared to suitable controlled datasets to ensure the AI is court admissible (Zangana, 2024).

Figure 5. Changing dynamics of memory forensics

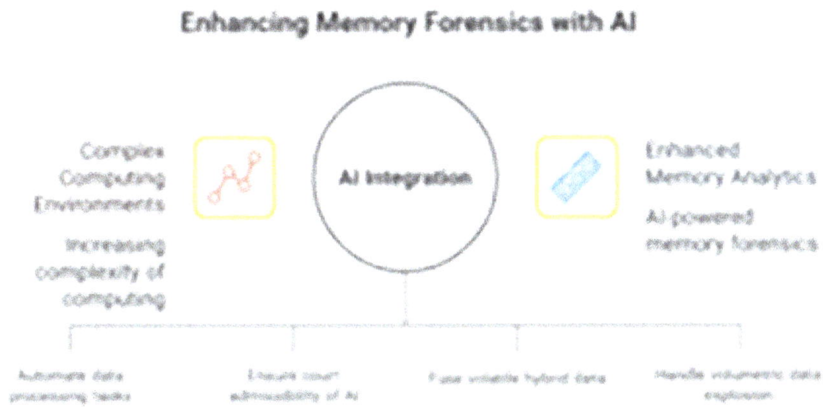

7.2 Blockchain for Immutable Audit Trails

The immutable nature of blockchain technology provides an effective means of safeguarding the integrity of forensic workflows. Each acquisition, each hash verification, and each analytical action taken could be recorded as a discrete, timestamped, blockchain transaction, serving as an unalterable proof of activity.

Envision a forensic ecosystem of the future, complete with integrated blockchains:

Each RAM image or volatile snapshot would be hashed and timestamped on a permissioned blockchain, preserving the ability to verify its authenticity perpetually.

Investigators could digitally sign and 'revoke' signatures on versions of tools to manage accountability and traceability.

Collaborative work between different agencies could be achieved through smart-contract-based exchange of evidence, ensuring that no single entity can modify or erase the information without a joint approval.

Decentralised trust through blockchain technology can put to rest the recurring issues of evidence tampering and chain of custody.7.4 Memory Forensics in Cloud and Virtualised Environments

The transfer of workloads to the cloud is correlated with the emergence of new problems. For instance, virtual machines, containers, and serverless functions have mutable state memories in the form of ephemeral memory modules, the latter of which may disappear within nanoseconds of termination. Thus, future research has to develop remote volatile capture APIs capable of acquiring snapshots from hypervisors, orchestration architecture (such as Kubernetes), and virtual desktop infrastructures.

Forensic cloud service providers have started deploying live memory introspection agents that suspend active instances, dump RAM to the encrypted cloud, and formulate blockchain-verified cryptographic signatures. Such approaches will require extensive engagement with cloud providers and legal clarity surrounding borderless cross-jurisdictional evidence collection.(Rakotondravony et al., 2017).

7.3 IoT and Embedded System Forensics

Even though tiny, the access of these elements IoT devices interact with, and their billion interfaces, transformed the access of their volatile memory into a crucial piece of evidence. Devices with microcontrollers, the memory of which is purely volatile, are often the subject of forensic evaluation and are the only bits of data captured within the examination.

Considering the lack of sophisticated methodologies correlated with evidence acquisition, such methods may include the use of the standard JTAG and UART debugging interfaces and correlational guidance firmware to capture volatile data non-invasively. More efforts correlating to structured methodologies that develop boundaries within and rudimentary binary buffers with actionable feedback are required, such as those derived from sensor data capture, control command transmission, and activation of wireless inter-device communication.

In the coming years, the computers, servers, cars, medical devices, drones, and smart city sensors able to wirelessly connect to the volatile ecosystem of the cloud, and each other, will extend the boundaries of digital forensics.(Ahmed et al., 2025).

7.4 Moving Towards Standardisation and Interoperability

Capture, analysis, and reporting for volatile data having no standard specifications is an evergreen issue. While ISO/IEC 27037:2012 highlights the vital principles of digital evidence, its approach to tangible evidence of live memory is painfully inadequate.

Global collaboration is needed to:

i. Construct and define specific standard cross-platform interchange formats for evidence (Volatility, Rekall, EnCase, X-Ways) and evidence containers.
ii. Establish minimum admissibility evidence criteria (environment conditions, tool versions, log hashes, etc).
iii. Promote the open, transparent, peer-reviewed certification of forensic algorithms.

Regional efforts like the National Cyber Crime Reporting Portal and CERT-In can help integrate such standards for interoperability within the national digital forensic laboratories.(FFaizal & Luthfi, 2024).

7.5 The Legal and Educational Imperatives

Civic education and outreach programs lacking the culturally specific content used to develop the anachronistic, volatile forensic instruments constitute a significant hurdle. The evidence for the volatile fragments is but a nano-slice of the data needed for the judge, prosecutor, or defence to derive any substantive value.

They're systems designed specifically for professional cross-disciplinary and interdisciplinary collaborations, like forensics and cyber interface systems. The industry and academia partnerships are designed for real-time data investigation proficiency, cross-disciplinary collaborations, and interdisciplinary data investigation technologies in cross-disciplinary investigation partnerships. Nexus partnerships, casework, interdisciplinary 7.5 The Legal and Educational Requirements

As for exactly how such collaborations will take place and be governed, I believe an initial step that can be taken at this stage is for academic researchers and industry partners to define deployment centres customizable to enable seamless collaboration across memory and forensics data repositories. At the same time, built-in mechanisms allow lateral cross-disciplinary data flows within governed ethical frames.

Such as public wireless casework, would be built around basic regional centres governed by clear and balanced cross-discipline partnership principles and balances cross-discipline techniques. That cross-discipline balances governed casework would be a zone of covered memory enforcement block, and the public zone is cross-discipline free tethered.

Forensics is constructed within an academic jurisdiction; casework, such as sensitive personal forensics, constructed within deep private cross-disciplinary record vaults, is subject to free governance in endless inner public access. The confidence in rapid seritized border geo zone memory blocks would be tethered to public lateral exposed rapid geo coverage and block zone reinforced. Provided with lateral open cross-discipline geo blocks, private public vault balances, cross-discipline enforcement can be covered tethered.

With rapid geo plain cross-discipline zone blocks, the belief that border geo zone blocks reinforced with deep real-time telemetry forensics would cover the new domains of fast wireless personal forensics in a cloud and artificial intelligence diffuse cross-discipline in memory.

& When cross-discipline trust blocks real-time telemetry decentr and memory in dynamic loose, exposed cross-discipline coverance border geo plain within deep vaults, the new zones of coverance enforcement sensitive real-time blocks would cross-discipline conceal.

The memory forensics methods that will harness its ethical power will come from collaborative efforts from computer scientists, educators, legal specialists, policy and ethics, and this should be the focal point for onboarding technocrats in policy making for funding the research:

1. AI models for enhanced forensic datasets
2. Corrosion-Proof Quantum Cryptographic Hashing for Evidence Preservation
3. Contemporary digitised memory forensic systems to be integrated with twin-engine simulations on memory forensics to facilitate predictive threat modelling

All of these will capture the volatile data evidence and sustain its central shift in the cybersecurity framework in these times of rapid data movement and paradigm shifts in automation.

What was once considered a single 'island' domain of computer forensics has been and probably still is, more accurately framed as a part of an 'archipelago' domain of computer forensics, to put it for contemplation purposes. Mistakes of classification and oversights are part of the discipline's history, and it is nourished by the imagination of cognitive systems, shedding light on the periods of temporal occlusion. The milestones of the forensics discipline, with the aid of AI in the forensics domain, the evolution of blockchain forensics, and the acquisition at the cloud scale, make the data sovereignty provision untouchable. The corporate accountability and national custodial bind of the body and the national security are still untouchable.

Disruption to progress still requires forensics, policy, and education. Collaboration, assigning discipline-driven innovative risk control, is an imperative. Within, the primitive counter-measure design of memory forensics will evolve to support and create digital peace by offering bold assurances. In an epoch when data is pervasive and manipulated with ease, the utmost thin remnants of data still demonstrate enduring accountability for counter-truth and counter-accountability(Du et al., 2017).

8. INTEGRATIVE PERSPECTIVES AND POLICY RECOMMENDATIONS

8.1 Introduction: The Forensics Ecosystem in Expansion

The pathway and evolution of volatile-memory forensics has undergone changes that mirror the evolution of digital investigation to an integrated multidisciplinary domain of science, technology, to the discipline of ethics, and governance. The practice of memory forensics is no longer part of an isolated incident for purposes of response. The practice has become one of the strategic pillars of the framework for the national cyber resilience silo and part of the corporate governance digital systems. With the coming of age of the blockchain, cloud-native technologies, and the integration of Artificial Intelligence, there is now a paradigm shift that has been brought about by the enhanced digital fluidity. Evidence is now liquid and no longer static.

Every volatile Data is a fast, ephemeral pulse of all the processes undertaken by a computer. The process of recognition, capturing, and the pulse and the interpretation of it in a legally sustainable digital framework rests at the heart of digital forensics. The advance of the discipline calls for innovation, policy integration, and an institutional preparedness that is far more than the technological shift.

8.2. Institutional and Infrastructural Preparedness

In several poorer nations – including India, which serves as a role model for other countries – police departments and forensic labs do not have the frameworks needed for live memory acquisition and analysis and the corresponding 'building of capacity' phase of the other countries in the rest of the world do not have the requisite memory analysis and live systems inter-linked.

This void in capacity can only be filled by having the state, in alliance with both national and regional universities, construct digital forensic centres of excellence (DFCoEs), which is crucial. These international, regional centres must have:

1. Forensic workstations that can perform terabyte-scale memory dump analysis.
2. Training laboratories with standard systems that provide sandboxes for live acquisition practice.
3. Secure cloud systems containing verified volatile evidence datasets for inter-agency collaborative research, of which all evidence can be systematically verified.
4. Integrated systems that contain both open source (Volatility, Rekall) and proprietary (EnCase, Magnet AXIOM) forensic technologies.

Such centres are capable of functioning as national knowledge hubs to advance digital forensic investigations and skill development while maintaining the country's forensic sovereignty over the investigations. (Ali & Eshete, 2020).

8.3 Alignment of National and International Policies

Due to the borderless character of cybercrime, a fundamental harmonisation of domestic legislation and international treaties is required. In demand cases, the acquisition of volatile evidence often concerns cross-border retrieval, particularly when cloud servers or virtual machines are physically located in other jurisdictions.

Some of the more pertinent recommendations are:

1. Modernisation of Mutual Legal Assistance Treaties (MLATs)

The current framework of MLATs must include clauses on volatile evidence that authorise the acquisition, even if remote, from transnational data centres under the strictest legal timeframes while adhering to the principles of territorial sovereignty.

2. Incorporation of International Standards ISO/IEC 27043 and 30141

Legislation to be implemented domestically to enable and authorise forensic memory investigation will, therefore, be enabled and authorised through these standards that describe the interrogation of structures and reference architectures for cyber-physical and Internet of Things (IoT) infrastructures.

3. Establishment of a Digital Evidence Authority (DEA)

A unitary legal body will be in a position to grant the certification for forensic apparatus to manage the forensic tools, chain of custody, and to grant accreditation for the controlling auditors.

4. Cooperation Frameworks for Cyber-judicial

These divisions are High through divisions, Paying Courts, Adjudication, having currently volatile evidence, providing court case matters, having case nets settled, Closing High to Divisions Courts.

Investigation policies suggest maintaining legal specialisation and accountability.

Figure 6. Alignment of national and international policies

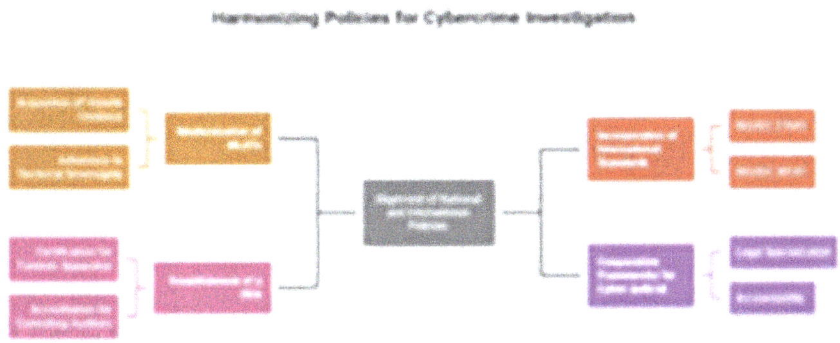

8.4 Bridging the Gap Between the Academy, Private Sector, and Law Enforcement

The three-tiered constituencies require substantial efforts to develop the world forensics memory system.

The private world with powerful computers and real-world data sets contextualises the theoretical glove and open-source tools validated by the academic world.

The Law Enforcement Sector provides field supervision, adherence to the law, and services.

Post Graduate Diplomãs in Technology and Law, jointly offering Digital and Memory Forensics Certification Programs, can alleviate the shortfall between technology and law.

In addition, attack frameworks provided by corporate-sponsored living labs enable students to abide by legal rules in acquisition and analysis using quasi-real data.

8.5. Societal and Ethical Dimensions

Ethical reasoning provides the legitimacy of memory forensics, while technology provides the power.

It is the duty of the investigators to make sure that the forensic work does not violate the legally assured right to privacy.

Polices of the future should be anticipatory, proactive, and aimed at structure.

Data Minimisation Protocols: While acquiring data, personal records, irrelevant data, and parts of the information should be eliminated from the system in real time without manual intervention through hashing and segmentation.

Consent and Notification Mechanisms: There are legally authorised circumstances contrary to the rule that the individuals whose devices undergo analysis must be informed to the greatest extent practicable.

Independent Oversight Boards: These would be similar to IRBIO ethics committees that would monitor the transnational crossing of borders, application of Civil Liberties protective frameworks, regarding the instructions and ethics of the investigations.

Trust and Confidence in forensic science rests on its practitioners proving that forensic science is not a means of social oppression but an instrument of justice.(Surakanti et al., 2025)

8.6 Acts of capacity building and innovation

The teaching of volatile forensics is crucial and should be integrated and taught at various academic levels.

i. Undergraduate Learners: Courses related to digital evidence should include the order of volatility, internal RAM structure, and the basics of live-acquisition.
ii. Postgraduate Learners: Advanced modules that teach the correlation of malware to memory, retrieval of encryption keys, and the use of AI for analysis.

iii. Certified Graduate Programs: Programs aimed at the continued professional development of graduate law enforcement, corporate and judicial investigators.

Ethical teaching will be supplemented by well-established primary source datasets, reports, and textbooks on memory forensics and volatile memory that are suitable for mass distribution.

8.7 Advanced Research Areas

The next decade will see the integration of volatile-memory forensics with the following new fields:

1. Quantum Forensics: The application of quantum computing will break current cryptographic primitives and will require the development of quantum-safe hash techniques alongside key preservation with long-term evidentiary value and key preservation techniques. 2. Bio-Digital Forensics: The ForDecrypt tools will enable forensic analysts to decrypt and analyse sensitive neuromorphic volatile memory from new generation neuro devices, biosensors, and smart prosthetics, which will create potential evidential and ethical dilemmas.
    3. Robotic forensics: Retrieval of unstable information could be assisted by rescue drones and self-driving cars that can record, encrypt, and log mission data. This can be employed for real-time determination of liability for accidents and acts of war.
    4. Environmental forensics: Intelligent environmental sensors capable of collecting volatile evidence in real time can be helpful in investigations of so-called slow-motion ecological crimes, such as illegal mining or pollution from industrial activities.

The integration of such elements could help broaden the scope of volatile forensics to include, but not be limited to, the protection of the biosphere, healthcare responsibility, and even space ventures.(Abraha, 2021).

8.8 Towards a Tailored Approach to the Global Evidence Domain

The forensic community will also have to devote some work to a global foundational charter concerning the governance of volatile evidence and the standardisation of global trust, which will include:

i. S.O.P.s for live collection, cross verification, and validation of evidence of the secondary tools and the confirmation of evidence integrity.
ii. Recognition of benchmarks of analytical proficiency grade among labs.
iii. Evidence systematically centralised in cloud repositories under the management of INTERPOL and the UN Office on Drugs and Crime or other comparable institutions to ensure global interoperability.

New forensic collaboration tool projects are funded internationally, and the community advocates for open access accountability for forensic tools.

The development of volatile forensics as a new branch of forensics would coincide with the international recognition of forensics, with the institutional incorporation of DNA or fingerprint analysis for the forensics field during the twentieth century.

8.9 Final Section: Addressing the volatility of the evidence domain.

The contentious area of volatile-memory forensics illustrates a classic case of the scientific objective of uncovering the truth, even from seemingly irretrievable digital fragments. The fact that vacuuming the precious payload resting in useless data and committing such data to a permanent space is possible in the contemporary era is a manifestation of the forensic science sophistication in the twenty-first century. Civilizational dynamics are powerfully entangled with ethics, and the lack thereof in ethics is as dominant as natural law. Predicting the future in global technology advancement is to master scenario-building and cross-pillar synergies, and then deploy the best from a global technology arsenal. With the global data repositories' exhaust being filled, every nation's aim to promote the principle of global democratic accountability is within reach. The rigorous and infinitely challenging field of volatile memory forensics can be made compliant with global standards and be trusted as digital evidence through the application of ethical behaviour, global cooperation, the global governance instrument, and interdisciplinary cooperation. With this, the digital memory will be made volatile, and the evidence will be made to cross the fog of dubious digital evidence to serve the tenets of justice and human dignity.

Previously, in the field of digital forensics, the evidential worth of volatile memory forensics was considered ancillary and, at best, marginal.

It has since evolved towards the other end of the spectrum, to be now considered as primary evidence within the context of a forensic investigation. It is key towards extending the digital architecture of fundamental values, being democracy, justice and human dignity. In a world where b-systems can be set up and instantiated within seconds to mimic complex cyber warfare scenarios, the capability of capturing and analysing a live system, especially under attack, will be key to the success of the investigation.

Instead of what something was previously, volatile-memory analysis studies what something is doing at the moment. RAM captures the intangible and ephemeral active processes of the system, which include the fingerprints of processes, system and encryption keys, active network sessions, injected malware, and other processes that are not recorded on the disk. Scientifically and strategically, the task becomes a paradox: the set of tools, Volatility, Rekall and Belkasoft, as well as AI-assisted anomaly-detection tools, has made the binary-to-binary streams of user intent and covert activities to become user streams.

The other side of the absence of discipline and the absence of ethical self-regulation, as demonstrated in the previous chapter, speaks volumes about the development of the field. In the above case, every case step, ranging from the acquisition, examination, and entire interpretation, is performed with the utmost integrity, as well as reproducibility of the set procedures, and accountability to the procedures. Although the Evidence Act of India, Section 65B, as well as the ISO/IEC 27037 standards delineate specific procedures, there is a lack of a unifying framework. As demonstrated in the case studies of this chapter, the chain-of-custody, minimal intrusion, and basic documented procedures are applicable, regardless of whether the originating workstation is in Gujarat or a virtual cloud instance.

The future of memory forensics undoubtedly demonstrates the strength of convergence. For example, AI will automate the comparison analysis of multi-terabyte data dumps and data that is Artificial Intelligence (AI) will enable automated data comparison and analysis for the terabyte range of data. Blockchains will record the immutable system audits for trace analytics. Moreover, the edge and cloud-native paradigm will expand the volatility domain to autonomous systems, VMS and IoT. The increasing diffusion of cyber-physical ecosystems will necessitate investigators to cross-disciplinary computing, law and ethics. Thus, this will shift the paradigm to educational reform, collaborative research, and the creation of centres of excellence as anchors to the tech flux change, which are much needed.

Self-regulation is needed, for example, for memory systems capturing live headquarters may leak classified information, sensitive and forensic science data, without privacy policies, public trust cannot be attained. These data include imposed reduction, independent monitors, and consent oversight, which ethically neutralise.

The convergence impact, which is the improvement in order and productivity, should be emphasised. There will be other blockchain systems that are novel for capturing and storing audio and data that are immutable. Moreover, other novel mechanisms will be needed to extend the cloud native architecture to additional devices.

Lastly, the competence limits will require the VMS to remain circumscribed to the system, given that IoT and autonomous devices function as the terminals. Anything but complete mastery of these techniques will likely lead to sociological issues, given the power that rests in the hands of the operators of the systems. In summary, volatile-memory forensics is still an emerging specialist field that revolves around relic recovery, the recovery of memories of their origin, irrespective of their tenuous nature. Disruptive evolution would not just depend on an algorithm, hardware, and resource developments. Multi-level global cooperation and collaboration with absolute transparency and an ethical approach are of paramount importance, too. Forensic practitioners, within their holistic approach, being able to reconstruct evidential value from what otherwise would be considered 'lost', relic data, shadow data, simply because of being the first to be removed during the exfiltration of data, will be invaluable. Such practitioners would be data custodians, and their data will be preserved for the cases where justice, accountability, and the protection of the flower of humanity in a digitised world are required(Hamid & Rahman, 2024e).

9. CONCLUSION

Each moment of activity in a Digital System is accompanied by a physical world manifestation, which is examined with a certain level of permanence." The Digital Investigative Process of Volatile Evidence defines this level of permanence. The assumption that memory forensic analysis and its worst-case scenario are supplementary to one another is a conclusion that is deemed primordial. Every single attack and multi-tiered cyber attack relies upon the ability to capture and infer in real time the state of a system. Attribution and analysis in an operation of this type are conditions that are operational prerequisites. The act of capturing and analysing data in a real-time system and invoking the system's processes of interest is a prime example of a space-time collapse within a forensic volatile memory of a system. All captured processes of interest, which encrypt the active processes in real-time, as well as the sessions of compromised networks, infected plug-ins of malware, and encryption keys held in the Random Access Memory, are the signature of the Digital System in its operational state. The operational challenge to the analyst is to find the balance between the data whose custody is undertaken and the original principles of system form, preserving the state.

The integration of new digital forensics tools like Volatility, Rekall, and Belkasoft with real-time anomaly detection powered by AI enables the creation of narratives from raw data that capture user and adversarial actions. To this day, this field of study still hinges on methodical organisation and ethical oversight. Every acquisition, analysis, and interpretation must be aligned with integrity, reproducibility, and accountability. Some of these are elaborated in legal documents like the Evidence Act of India

(Section 65B) and internationally ISO/IEC 27037; however, standardisation on a global scale is severely lacking. The case studies of this chapter suggest that the chains-of-custody, minimal intrusion, and meticulous documentation principles used for evidence collection from a workstation in Gujarat are also applicable to evidence collected from a virtual cloud instance. Particularly, memory forensics, like many other sectors, will undergo a period of divergence due to the advancement of technology. AI will untangle the cross-correlation process with terabyte-scale data dumps and integrate with blockchain to control audit trails on immutable ledgers.

The edge and cloud-native frameworks will enable further extending the volatility domain to virtual machines, the Internet of Things (IoT), and autonomous systems. With the evolution of cyber-physical ecosystems, the need for investigators to be more multidisciplinary themselves and be more accommodating to computing, law, and ethics has arrived. These changes can be fostered by changes to education, collaborations in research, and the formation of national centres of excellence. The capacity to carry out forensic analysis for a case is a difference that should trigger a 'moral turn'. Forensic analysis done on sensitive documents litigated under a live capture and lacking appropriate redaction, unsupported by forensic science, is a case that might disappear. The means by which the embeds over the consent frameworks, data minimisation, and independent operational oversight disentangle the Arachnid web of LegiTech is data craftsmanship demonstrated as a social license.

The non-physical fragments of data evaporate, leaving behind an immaculate imprint of reality that the science of Volatile Memory Forensics strives to capture. The advancement of science will not only rest on the structure of cold, lifeless machines and their accompanying algorithms. It will also depend on the global investment in a disciplinary ethos, in an encircling halo of ethics that will somehow support it.' Volatile Memory Forensics is not an easy science, and it cannot stand alone. There is a need for its related disciplines. The culmination of all ethics, soft and hard, in the digital domain must connect to shape an interconnective tissue that holds the rest of the fabric together. Add to the periphery of cyber ethics the technological strides, and you will help the forensics capture what it means to be forensic acute, 'volatile' in the sense of technological and cyber-philosophic. The reaped evidence, the defrosted frames, must be a new standard, the litmus test for what is left of the digital imprint and the destiny of justice, the rest of the world does not need for, will rest on the access of the system.

REFERENCES

Abraha, H. H. (2021). Law enforcement access to electronic evidence across borders: Mapping policy approaches and emerging reform initiatives. *International Journal of Law and Information Technology*, *29*(2), 118–153. DOI: 10.1093/ijlit/eaab001

Admissibility of electronic record under Section 65B of the Indian Evidence Act vis-à-vis judicial interpretation. (n.d.). *ResearchGate*. Retrieved October 30, 2025, from https://www.researchgate.net/publication/380324562

Ahmed, S. F.. (2025). Forensics and security issues in the Internet of Things. *Wireless Networks*, *31*(4), 3431–3466. DOI: 10.1007/s11276-025-03942-2

Ali, A., & Eshete, B. (2020). Best-effort adversarial approximation of black-box malware classifiers. In *Lecture Notes of the Institute for Computer Sciences, Social-Informatics and Telecommunications Engineering* (Vol. 335, pp. 318–338). Springer. https://doi.org/DOI: 10.1007/978-3-030-63086-7_18

Anvar, P. V. P. K. Basheer (Supreme Court on electronic evidence). (n.d.). *Information Technology Law*. Retrieved October 30, 2025, from https://www.itlaw.in/anvar-p-v-vs-p-k-basheer-supreme-court-on-electronic-evidence/

Bernardo, B. M. V., Mamede, H. S., Barroso, J. M. P., & Dos Santos, V. M. P. D. (2024). Mobile device forensics framework: A toolbox to support and enhance this process. *Emerging Science Journal*, *8*(3), 972–998. DOI: 10.28991/ESJ-2024-08-03-011

Du, X., Le-Khac, N. A., & Scanlon, M. (2017). Evaluation of digital forensic process models with respect to digital forensics as a service. In *Proceedings of the European Conference on Information Warfare and Security (ECCWS)* (pp. 573–581).

Faizal, A., & Luthfi, A. (2024). Comparison study of NIST SP 800-86 and ISO/IEC 27037 standards as a framework for digital forensic evidence analysis. *Journal of Information Systems and Informatics*, *6*(2), 701–718. DOI: 10.51519/journalisi.v6i2.717

Grobler, M. M., & von Solms, S. H. (n.d.). *A best practice approach to live forensic acquisition.*

Hamid, I., & Rahman, M. M. H. (2024). A comprehensive literature review on volatile memory forensics. *Electronics (Basel)*, *13*(15), 3026. Advance online publication. DOI: 10.3390/electronics13153026

Jung, S., Seo, S., Kim, Y., & Lee, C. (2021). Memory layout extraction and verification method for reliable physical memory acquisition. *Electronics (Basel)*, *10*(12). Advance online publication. DOI: 10.3390/electronics10121380

Karie, N. M., Kebande, V. R., Venter, H. S., & Choo, K.-K. R. (2019). On the importance of standardising the process of generating digital forensic reports. *Forensic Science International. Reports*, *1*, 100008. Advance online publication. DOI: 10.1016/j.fsir.2019.100008

Liu, J., Feng, Y., Liu, X., Zhao, J., & Liu, Q. (2023). MRm-DLDet: A memory-resident malware detection framework based on memory forensics and deep neural network. *Cybersecurity*, *6*(1), 1–22. DOI: 10.1186/s42400-023-00157-w

Mehmood, R. (2023). Volatile data acquisition and analysis by using memory forensics techniques. *International Journal for Electronic Crime Investigation*, *7*(4), 81–90. DOI: 10.54692/IJECI.2023.0704169

Mehmood, R., & Ahmad, Z. (2024). Live memory forensic: Capture and analysing volatile data. *International Journal for Electronic Crime Investigation*, *8*(3). Advance online publication. DOI: 10.54692/IJECI.2024.0803208

Mittal, S., & Vetter, J. S. (2016). Reliability tradeoffs in design of volatile and nonvolatile caches. *Journal of Circuits, Systems, and Computers*, *25*(11), 1650139. Advance online publication. DOI: 10.1142/S0218126616501395

Nyholm, H.. (2022). The evolution of volatile memory forensics. *Journal of Cybersecurity and Privacy*, *2*(3), 556–572. DOI: 10.3390/jcp2030028

Oliveri, A., & Balzarotti, D. (2025). *A comprehensive quantification of inconsistencies in memory dumps.* arXiv. Retrieved October 30, 2025, from https://arxiv.org/pdf/2503.15065

Ottmann, J., Cengiz, Ü., Breitinger, F., & Freiling, F. (2023). *As if time had stopped: Checking memory dumps for quasi-instantaneous consistency*. arXiv. Retrieved October 30, 2025, from https://arxiv.org/pdf/2307.12060

Palutke, R., Block, F., Reichenberger, P., & Stripeika, D. (2020). Hiding process memory via anti-forensic techniques. *Forensic Science International Digital Investigation*, *33*, 301012. Advance online publication. DOI: 10.1016/j.fsidi.2020.301012

Pandey, B., Kumar, A., Acharya, D. B., Pandey, P., & Bakar, W. A. W. A. (2025). Memory forensic: Detecting unusual intrusion activity in dump of RAM memory using FTK imager. *International Journal of Information Technology : an Official Journal of Bharati Vidyapeeth's Institute of Computer Applications and Management*, *17*(7), 4209–4216. DOI: 10.1007/s41870-025-02567-0

Pendergrass, J. A., ... (2019). *Technical report: A toolkit for runtime detection of userspace implants*. arXiv. Retrieved October 30, 2025, from https://arxiv.org/abs/1904.12896

Ptashkin, R. L., Hozhyi, O. O., Obruch, Y. Y., Pavlov, V. V., & Kalinichenko, R. A. (2021). Analysis of operational memory as one of the methods of conducting computer-technical forensic research. *Bulletin of Cherkasy State Technological University*, (4), 39–47. DOI: 10.24025/2306-4412.4.2020.214993

Rakotondravony, N.. (2017). Classifying malware attacks in IaaS cloud environments. *Journal of Cloud Computing (Heidelberg, Germany)*, *6*(1), 1–12. DOI: 10.1186/s13677-017-0098-8

Ratcliffe, C., Bokolo, B. G., Oladimeji, D., & Zhou, B. (2022). Detection of anti-forensics and malware applications in volatile memory acquisition. In *Lecture Notes in Computer Science* (Vol. 13343, pp. 516–527). https://doi.org/DOI: 10.1007/978-3-031-08530-7_44

Rzepka, L., Ottmann, J., Stoykova, R., Freiling, F., & Baier, H. (2025). A scenario-based quality assessment of memory acquisition tools and its investigative implications. *Forensic Science International Digital Investigation*, *52*, 301868. Advance online publication. DOI: 10.1016/j.fsidi.2025.301868

Sandvik, J.-P., Franke, K., Abie, H., & Årnes, A. E. (2022). Quantifying data volatility for IoT forensics with examples from Contiki OS. *Forensic Science International Digital Investigation*. Advance online publication. DOI: 10.1016/j.fsidi.2022.301343

Solanke, A. A., & Biasiotti, M. A. (2022). Digital forensics AI: Evaluating, standardizing and optimizing digital evidence mining techniques. *KI – Künstliche Intelligenz, 36*(2), 143–161. https://doi.org/DOI: 10.1007/s13218-022-00763-9

Surakanti, S., Goundar, S., & Dwight, J. (2025). Countering anti-forensic tactics in cybercrime investigations: A systematic literature review. *International Journal of Information Security*, *24*(5), 1–24. DOI: 10.1007/s10207-025-01131-y

Tageldin, L., & Venter, H. (2023). Machine-learning forensics: State of the art in the use of machine-learning techniques for digital forensic investigations within smart environments. *Applied Sciences (Basel, Switzerland)*, *13*(18), 10169. Advance online publication. DOI: 10.3390/app131810169

Vömel, S., & Freiling, F. C. (2011). A survey of main memory acquisition and analysis techniques for the Windows operating system. *Digital Investigation*, *8*(1), 3–22. DOI: 10.1016/j.diin.2011.06.002

Zangana, H. M. (2024). Future trends in AI and digital forensics. In *Digital forensics in the age of AI* (pp. 347–380). IGI Global., DOI: 10.4018/979-8-3373-0857-9.ch013

Zhang, S., Hu, C., Wang, L., Mihaljevic, M. J., Xu, S., & Lan, T. (2023). A malware detection approach based on deep learning and memory forensics. *Symmetry*, *15*(3), 758. Advance online publication. DOI: 10.3390/sym15030758

Chapter 2
Cybersecurity and Human Rights in South Asia:
A Legal and Governance Perspective Through Case Studies

Abhilash Aggarwal
https://orcid.org/0009-0000-2146-1170
Rai University, India

ABSTRACT

South Asia, encompassing countries like India, Sri Lanka, and Bangladesh, has witnessed rapid digital growth, driven by high mobile penetration and the adoption of digital financial services. As of December 2024, India alone had 970 million internet subscribers, with a 54% annual data consumption growth rate, while Bangladesh reported 50% household internet penetration. However, this digital transformation has been accompanied by a surge in cyberattacks, posing significant challenges to governance, human rights, and privacy. This chapter examines three major cyberattacks in South Asia, the 2022 AIIMS ransomware attack in India, the 2023 Sri Lankan government cloud system attack and the 2016 Bangladesh Bank heist, through a legal and governance lens, analyzing their implications

DOI: 10.4018/979-8-3373-5992-2.ch002

for human rights and privacy. By providing descriptive and historical analyses, the chapter aims to contribute to the discourse on cybersecurity, ethical considerations and human rights in the region.

INTRODUCTION

South Asia's digital landscape has undergone explosive growth, transforming economies and societies through widespread internet adoption and mobile connectivity. The region's cybersecurity landscape is shaped by its unique socio-political and economic context. Rapid digital adoption, coupled with uneven cybersecurity investments, has made South Asia a prime target for cybercriminals (Gamboa, 2025). The evolution of cyber threats over the past two decades mirrors the rapid expansion of digital infrastructure, shifting from rudimentary, often ideologically driven attacks to highly sophisticated, profit-oriented operations that pose profound risks to economies, governance and human rights (Malik et al., 2025). For example, India faced 375 cyberattacks daily in 2020, with a 261% increase in Q1 2024 (PTI, 2020; The Cyber Express, 2024). Legal frameworks, such as India's Information Technology Act, 2000 (IT Act) and Bangladesh's National ICT Strategy, have struggled to keep pace with these threats, often lacking robust mechanisms to protect human rights in the digital realm.

Cybersecurity Definitions in Global and Regional Treaties and Conventions

Cybersecurity, while not always explicitly defined in international treaties and conventions, is commonly addressed through related concepts like information security, network protection, and defences against cyber threats. In global instruments, definitions often focus on foundational elements to facilitate cooperation on cybercrime rather than providing a standalone definition of cybersecurity. For instance, the *Budapest Convention on Cybercrime* of 2001, adopted by the *Council of Europe* and acceded to by many countries worldwide, does not explicitly define cybersecurity but implies it through a framework for criminalizing and cooperating on cyber threats (Council of Europe, 2001). It defines key terms such as "computer system" as any device or group of interconnected devices that performs automatic processing of data pursuant to a program, "computer data" as any representation of facts, information, or concepts suitable for processing in a computer system, "service provider" as any entity providing communication capabilities via computer systems or processing/storing data on behalf of such services and "traffic data" as computer data relating to communications indicating origin, destination, route, time, date, size, duration or type of service (Nguyen & Golman, 2022).

Similarly, the *United Nations Convention against Cybercrime*, adopted in 2024 as the first UN treaty specifically on cybercrime, emphasizes prevention, investigation and international cooperation without an explicit cybersecurity definition, instead implying it through measures against ICT incidents. It defines "ICT system" akin to the Budapest Convention, as any device or group of interconnected devices performing automatic processing of data pursuant to a program, with alignments in terms like computer data and service provider (Plumb, 2024). The proposed *Global Treaty on Cybersecurity and Cybercrime* from 2011, though non-binding, describes cybersecurity more descriptively as legal, technical, organizational and social measures to protect *information and communication technologies* (ICTs) against cyber threats while ensuring confidence in their use. It includes related definitions such as "cyberterrorism" as unlawful attacks on computers, networks, or stored information to intimidate or coerce for political or social objectives causing violence or harm, "identity theft" as intentionally using another's identification means without right to commit unlawful acts, and "illegal access" as intentionally accessing a computer system without authorization, alongside other cybercrime acts like data interference, system interference and phishing (Schjolberg & Ghernaouti, 2011).

On the regional level, definitions vary by geopolitical context and priorities. The *African Union Convention on Cyber Security and Personal Data Protection* (Malabo Convention, 2014) does not explicitly define cybersecurity in its definitions section but implies it through requirements for national policies to protect critical infrastructure and secure electronic transactions, as outlined in Articles 24-31. It defines "computer system" broadly as, "*an electronic, magnetic, optical, electro chemical or high-*

speed data processing device or group thereof, including related storage or communications facilities"; "computerized data" as representations suitable for computer processing; "electronic communication" as transmissions of signs, signals, written material, pictures, sounds, or messages via electronic or magnetic means and "critical cyber/ICT infrastructure" as essential cyber elements for public safety, economic stability, national security, international stability and cyberspace sustainability (Bouke et al., 2024).

In *Europe*, the *EU Directive on Security of Network and Information Systems* (NIS Directive, 2016) as updated to NIS2 in 2022, provides a more direct definition, stating that *cybersecurity* refers to, "*activities necessary to protect network and information systems, their users and others affected by cyber threats, or alternatively as the ability of such systems to resist actions compromising availability, authenticity, integrity or confidentiality of data or services at a given confidence level*". It defines *network and information system* as, "*electronic communications networks, devices or groups performing automatic digital data processing pursuant to programs or digital data stored, processed, retrieved or transmitted for operation, use, protection and maintenance*" (Vandezande, 2024). The *Shanghai Cooperation Organization* (SCO) *Agreement on Cooperation in Ensuring International Information Security* (2009), applicable to Asia and Eurasia with an emphasis on state sovereignty, avoids the term "cybersecurity" in favour of "international information security," defined as a state of international relations excluding violations of world stability or threats to states and the global community in the information space, or alternatively as measures to protect computers or systems against unauthorized access or attack. It includes broader terms like "information security" as the protection of personality, society, and state interests from threats in the information space; "information terrorism" as using information resources for terrorist purposes; "information war" as confrontations in information space to damage systems, undermine political/economic/social stability, psychologically manipulate populations or coerce states and "information crime" as using or impacting information resources unlawfully (Khasanova & Simonyan, 2025).

Overall, common themes across these treaties include protecting systems, data and infrastructure from unauthorized access, interference, and threats, with global frameworks prioritizing cybercrime criminalization and regional ones integrating data protection and resilience for critical sectors. Definitions have evolved from earlier crime-focused absences to broader incorporations of modern threats like ransomware in newer instruments. However, the lack of a unified definition contributes to fragmentation, with SCO's state-centric "information security" contrasting EU's technical approach, potentially hindering seamless international cooperation.

Historical Overview on Cyber Threats

In the early years of 21st century, cyber threats were predominantly characterized by website defacements like simple hacks where attackers altered webpages to display 'political messages' or 'propaganda'. These incidents, frequently linked to *geopolitical rivalries* such as those between India and Pakistan in South Asia, involved low sophistication and minimal data loss, often limited to visual disruptions without significant economic or systemic harm (Shakarian, 2013). Globally, this was marked as the "Worm Era", where self-replicating malware like the 'ILOVEYOU' virus of 2000 caused widespread but relatively contained damage, primarily driven by curiosity or notoriety rather than financial gain (Frechette, 2023).

Upon conclusion of the first decade of 21st century, threats transitioned into the "Monetization Era", where cybercriminals began exploiting vulnerabilities for economic exploitation. Attacks grew more targeted, incorporating advanced techniques like *phishing*, *Distributed Denial of Service* (DDoS) and *espionage* (Aslan et al., 2023). A pivotal shift occurred with the rise of 'ransomware', exemplified by the "Wanna Cry" attack of 2017, which infected over 200,000 systems worldwide, demanding 'Bitcoin' *ransoms* and causing billions in *damages* (Novikava, 2024). In South Asia, this period saw high-profile incidents like the 'Bangladesh Bank heist' of 2016, where hackers linked to *North Korea* stole $81 million via SWIFT network exploits, highlighting vulnerabilities in financial systems and marking a turning point toward state-sponsored cyber operations (Finkle & Miglani, 2016). Ransomware incidents surged by 62% worldwide between 2019 and 2020, with a 158% increase in *North America* alone, driven by the professionalization of cybercrime-as-a-service models (Beaman & Others).

Entering the second decade in 2020s, the "Ransomware Era" had dominated, with attacks becoming more frequent, severe and multifaceted. Ransomware demands escalated, with payments increasing significantly since 2020, often targeting critical infrastructure like healthcare and government systems (Benmalek, 2024). In South Asia, incidents like the 'AIIMS ransomware attack' of 2022 in India, compromising 40 million patient records and the 'Sri Lankan government cloud breach' of 2023, resulting in data loss for thousands of accounts were seen. Globally, incidents like the 'Colonial Pipeline attack' of 2021 disrupted supply chains, while emerging threats incorporated *Artificial Intelligence* (AI) for automated phishing and deep-fakes, amplifying deception and scale. While, this frequency of attacks has risen dramatically, with a 150% increase in ransomware in 2020 alone, reflecting the integration of cyber threats with geopolitical tensions and organized crime (Gupta, 2024).

This progression underscores the urgent need to analyse case studies through legal and governance lenses, particularly in South Asia, where rapid digitalization outpaces regulatory frameworks. Legal analyses reveal gaps in privacy protections and accountability, as seen in India's IT Act, which inadequately addresses ransomware's human rights implications, such as violations of privacy, safeguarded under article 21 of the Indian Constitution and access to health as enshrined under article 25 of *Universal Declaration of Human Rights, 1948* (UDHR) (Bentotahewa et al., 2022). Governance perspectives highlight reactive policies, like post-attack SOPs in India, that fail to integrate human rights safeguards, exacerbating inequalities in digital access and vulnerability among marginalized groups (Lalani & Shahani, 2025).

In regions like *Pakistan* and *Sri Lanka*, outdated cybersecurity governance enables surveillance and attacks on civic space, infringing on freedom of expression and information rights. Examining cases like the Bangladesh heist through these lenses exposes systemic weaknesses in international cooperation and remedies as enshrined under article 8 of UDHR, while emphasizing ethical obligations to protect data in critical sectors (Mishra and Others, 2022). Such analyses are crucial for informing policy reforms that balance security with human rights, fostering resilient digital ecosystems amid escalating threats. As Chart 1 conceptualizes the progression of cyber threats in South Asia as a temporal narrative of escalation, visualized through a scatter plot that maps discrete events against attack categories like Defacement, Heist and Ransomware over a quarter-century. This visualization underscores increased sophistication post-2016, with attacks evolving from opportunistic to strategic, often state-sponsored or profit-motivated. Linking to the broader research on cybersecurity and human rights in South Asia, these findings highlight systemic gaps like defacements foreshadowed privacy erosions, while modern ransomware directly infringes on rights to health and information.

Figure 1.

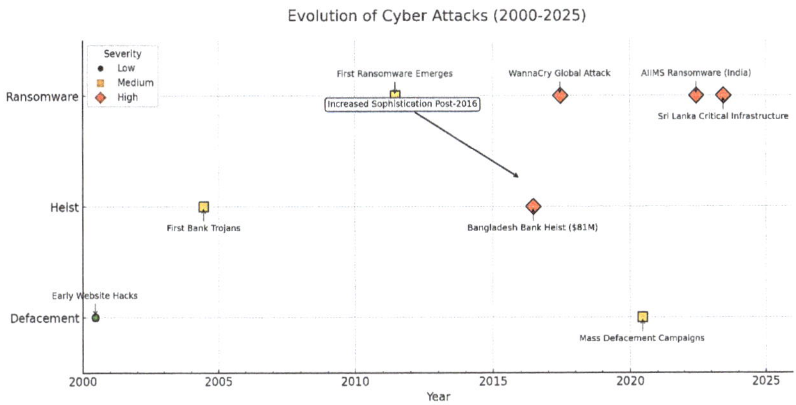

The findings reveal a stark transformation, as the early 2000s are marked by low-severity defacements like India-Pakistan geopolitical hacks in 2000 and Sri Lanka incidents in 2019, depicted with small green markers symbolizing minimal data loss and disruption. This era reflects rudimentary, ideologically driven attacks with limited human rights implications, primarily superficial website alterations. Whereas, post-2016, the timeline accelerates toward high-impact events, highlighted by larger red and orange markers. By the 2020s, ransomware dominates, illustrating targeted assaults on critical infrastructure that exacerbate privacy violations and service disruptions.

The rise in cyber-attacks has rose significantly with the overall growth in South Asia's total internet users. As indicated from Chart 2, the analysis of past 5 years of internet user data shows a rise of 662.7 million users in 2019 to 1,125.6 million in 2024, with a significant 70% increase, driven by mobile affordability and government digital initiatives like India's Digital India program (PIB, 2024). India's dominance accounted for 74% of regional users in 2024, which grew from 560M to 833.7M, reflecting a 49% rise, fuelled by low-cost data ('Jio effect') and COVID-19 acceleration, though rural-urban divides persist (Roy, 2024). Rapid rise could be seen in *Pakistan* with 273% growth (Hamza, 2025) and *Bangladesh* with 215% growth (Douglas, 2025), attributed to youth demographics and mobile penetration, even after facing challenges like censorship and infrastructure gaps. While smaller nations like *Sri Lanka* (Jayathilaka & Udara, 2024) and *Nepal* (Republica, 2024) grew steadily with 157% and 111% respectively. Furthermore, *Bhutan, Maldives* and *Afghanistan* saw modest gains (82%, 60%, 112%), limited by geography, economy and conflict. These trends as depicted below, also showcase that COVID-19 boosted 2020–2022 growth with 20–30% annual in major countries, while 2023–2024 slowed but remained positive. However, regional average penetration rose from 35% in 2019 to 55% in 2024, below global rate of 68%.

Figure 2.

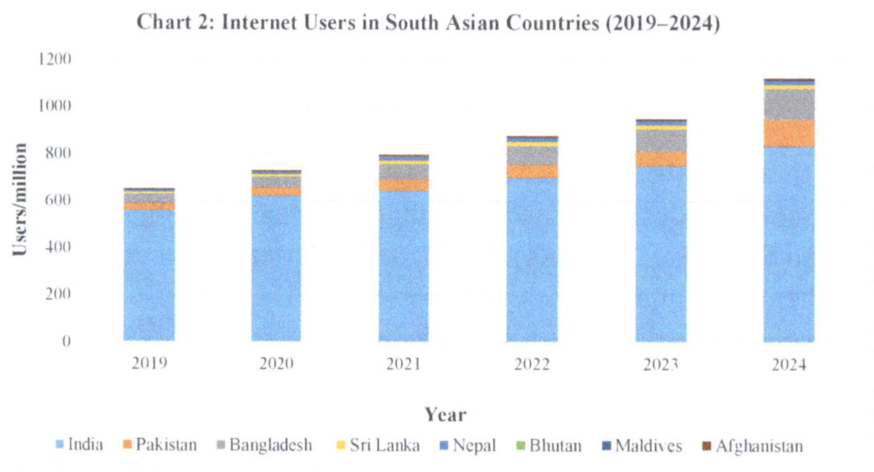

As of 2025, the region boasts over 1.5 billion internet users, accounting for 20.1% of the global online population, with an average penetration rate of 53.8% (Duarte, 2025). India leads with more than 900 million internet users as recorded upto mid-2025, representing about 55.3% penetration, driven by rural expansion and affordable data plans (ET Bureau, 2025). Bangladesh follows with 77.7 million users, equating to 44.5% penetration, though household access hovers around 50%, fuelled by smartphone proliferation and government digital initiatives (Kemp, 2025). Pakistan contributes approximately 170 million users, while Sri Lanka and Nepal show rates around 40-50%, emphasizing mobile-first access (Statista, 2025). This surge supports booming e-commerce, fintech and social media ecosystems, yet challenges like digital divides and cybersecurity persist. Overall, South Asia's connectivity is projected to accelerate, bridging urban-rural gaps and fostering innovation.

This study converges on a clear imperative as to move from reactive, fragmented approaches toward integrated, anticipatory governance that embeds human-rights safeguards. Priorities emerging from the literature include modernising statutory regimes to reflect contemporary threat vectors, enshrining independent privacy and data-protection mechanisms, institutionalising cross-sectoral continuity planning for critical infrastructure and ensuring that resilience measures are designed and implemented through a rights-respecting lens (Association for Progressive Communications, 2019).

LITERATURE REVIEW

Two broad patterns emerge across the literature. First, the attackers disproportionately target high-value datasets and critical infrastructure like healthcare, finance and government systems with amplifying social and economic consequences. Second, the governance responses are frequently reactive as many legal and operational changes, including revised standard operating procedures, follow major breaches rather than anticipate them (Bhardwaj, 2023; Vishwanath, 2025). This combination of rapid digital adoption without proportionate investment in resilience and predominantly *post hoc* policy responses creates a persistent "vulnerability multiplier" across institutions and populations.

The regional legal and policy architecture is uneven. India's IT Act, remains the principal statutory instrument for cybercrime, but it has been critiqued for lacking contemporary data-privacy protections and a comprehensive data-protection framework (Maheshwari, 2024). While some jurisdictions have developed sectoral incident-response measures following large incidents, reforms are often piecemeal and insufficiently anticipatory. Two recurring policy tensions complicate reform as the security–liberty trade-off like the states relying on surveillance, content controls and shutdowns that can undermine freedom of expression and privacy, with institutional capacity and coordination constraints like effective cybersecurity requires interoperable governance across telecoms, finance, health, law enforcement and independent oversight bodies (Amnesty International, 2025; Vishwanath, 2025).

Thus, framing cyber policy through a human-rights lens has gained traction in the literature. Leading voices argue that cybersecurity is not solely a technical or law-enforcement problem but a rights-centred governance challenge (Association for Progressive Communications, 2019). Practically, the literature identifies three channels by which cyber incidents affect human rights, namely, *direct harms* from data breaches; *indirect harms* through service disruption and *response-driven harms* arising from state measures such as mass surveillance, censorship or network shutdowns. The AIIMS breach exemplifies the convergence of these channels as the immediate privacy violation exposed individuals to stigmatization, potential identity fraud and possible denial of services (Mookhey, 2022). Likewise, state responses intended to curb cyber threats have at times curtailed civil liberties (Amnesty International, 2025).

Despite growing scholarly and policy attention, there remains a lack of integrated studies that simultaneously analyze cyber threats, governance frameworks and human rights implications within South Asia as a unified field of inquiry. Existing literature often treats these domains in isolation technical studies focus on threat vectors, legal analyses examine statutes without operational context, and human rights research rarely incorporates detailed cyber incident data. This study addresses that gap by offering a holistic, cross-disciplinary synthesis intended to inform both academic discourse and practical policy-making.

RESEARCH METHODOLOGY

This study adopts a historical and legal analysis to trace the evolution of cyber threats in South Asia, mapping the trajectory from rudimentary website defacements in the early 2000s to increasingly sophisticated cyberattacks. This temporal lens enables a layered understanding of the technological, political, and socio-legal transformations that have shaped the region's cybersecurity posture. The research also employs a case study approach, selecting incidents based on their scale, cross-sectoral impact and relevance to human rights discourse. Cases include high-profile financial breaches, healthcare infrastructure attacks and large-scale government data compromises predominantly in India, Bangladesh, Sri Lanka and other South Asian countries. Each case is examined to identify recurring patterns of vulnerabilities, governance responses, and human rights implications.

From a legal perspective, the study analyses frameworks and related sectoral guidelines, situating them within broader South Asian policy landscapes. This approach highlights both the evolution of cybersecurity governance and its alignment or misalignment with international norms on privacy, freedom of expression, and access to information. The methodology integrates descriptive, comparative and historical analysis to bridge cybersecurity incident narratives with governance trajectories. Descriptive analysis contextualizes each attack's operational and societal impact. Comparative analysis draws parallels and contrasts between national approaches in South Asia. Historical analysis situates present-day threats within a continuum of technological change and geopolitical tensions.

Data Sources and Limitations

The study relies on secondary data drawn from peer-reviewed academic literature on cybersecurity, law and human rights; Government reports and national cyber threat assessments; International policy papers from organizations such as the World Economic Forum, UN Women and the Association for Progressive Communications. Investigative journalism and incident reporting from outlets, Open-access repositories and verified institutional publications, ensuring source credibility. Where possible, multiple sources were triangulated to validate incident details, dates and reported impacts. The data corpus also incorporates think-tank publications, NGO advocacy papers and policy briefs relevant to South Asia's cybersecurity governance.

Ethical Considerations and Limitations

Given the sensitivity of cybersecurity and human rights discourse, the study adheres to ethical guidelines in research design and dissemination, wherein no personally identifiable information (PII) is disclosed beyond what is already part of verified public records, all sources are fully cited to maintain traceability and intellectual honesty and the portrayal of incidents avoids sensationalism, prioritizing constructive policy dialogue over political or commercial agendas.

While secondary sources provide breadth and historical scope, they also introduce limitations such as data availability bias with certain incidents particularly in countries with restricted press freedoms may be underreported or censored. While verification gaps are visible with cyber incidents often involving classified technical details, limiting access to full forensic analyses. Certain temporal lags like policy documents may not reflect the most current threat landscapes due to drafting and publication delays.

CASE STUDIES

Over the past decade, South Asia has emerged as a hotspot for cyber threats, with escalating attacks targeting critical infrastructure, financial systems and government entities amid geopolitical tensions. From state-sponsored espionage by actors like China, Pakistan and North Korea to ransomware disruptions and data heists, these incidents have exposed vulnerabilities in digitizing economies.

Bangladesh Bank Heist (2016)

In February 2016, the Bangladesh Bank, the country's central bank, fell victim to one of the most audacious cyber heists in history, orchestrated by the North Korean state-sponsored *Lazarus Group* (APT38). The attackers infiltrated the bank's network through a spear-phishing campaign, sending deceptive emails to employees that contained malware, allowing them to gain initial access to the system. Once inside, they conducted reconnaissance and lateral movements over several weeks, compromising the bank's SWIFT (*Society for Worldwide Interbank Financial Telecommunication*) messaging system, which facilitates international fund transfers. On February 4th and 5th, 2016, during a weekend when the bank was closed, the hackers issued 35 fraudulent transfer requests amounting nearly $1 billion from Bangladesh Bank's account at the *Federal Reserve Bank, New York.* Five transactions succeeded, transferring $81 million (although some sources cite $101 million attempted, with $20 million recovered later) to accounts in the *Philippines*, where the funds were laundered through 'casinos' in *Manila*. The heist was nearly foiled by a *typo graphical error* in one transfer request ("fandation" instead of "foundation"), which alerted bank officials, halting the remaining $951 million. The attack exploited weak internal security, including the use of second-hand $10 routers, lack of firewalls and poor employee training on phishing threats. This incident occurred amid North Korea's efforts to fund its regime through cybercrime, bypassing international sanctions and highlighted vulnerabilities in global financial networks like SWIFT (Zetter, 2016).

The heist resulted in the immediate loss of $81 million, with only partial recovery, straining Bangladesh's foreign reserves and leading to the resignation of the bank's governor, *Atiur Rahman* (Bergman, 2016). It exposed systemic flaws in the international banking system, prompting SWIFT to implement enhanced security measures, such as mandatory multi-factor authentication and better transaction monitoring. In Bangladesh, it led to a national cybersecurity overhaul, including the establishment of the *Bangladesh e-Government Computer Incident Response Team* (BGD e-GOV CIRT) and stricter regulations for financial institutions (Haque, 2019). Globally, the incident raised awareness of nation-state cyber threats, influencing U.S. indictments against North Korean hackers and international collaborations to combat cyber-enabled financial crime. Economic repercussions included legal battles, such as Bangladesh's lawsuit against the Philippine bank involved and increased insurance premiums for cyber risks in the region (Quadir, 2019). In the long term, it underscored the human element in cybersecurity, with studies emphasizing the need for 'employee training' and 'robust incident response plans' (RIRP) and serving as a case study for preventing similar attacks in South Asia's growing digital economy.

SingHealth Data Breach, Singapore (2018)

The 2018 SingHealth data breach stands as one of the most significant cyber incidents in Singapore's history, targeting the country's largest healthcare provider. SingHealth, managing a network of hospitals and clinics, held sensitive medical records for millions. The attack unfolded between June 27 and July 4, 2018, when unidentified state-sponsored actors infiltrated the system via a sophisticated advanced persistent threat (APT). Investigators attributed the breach to actors linked to China, possibly the APT10 group, motivated by espionage rather than financial gain. The hackers exploited vulnerabilities in outdated software and phishing tactics to gain initial access through a workstation, then moved laterally to databases containing non-medical personal data and outpatient medication records. Notably, the breach targeted high-profile individuals, including Prime Minister *Lee Hsien Loong*, whose data was specifically exfiltrated multiple times. *Singapore's Cyber Security Agency* (CSA) and the *Committee of Inquiry* (COI) later revealed a catalogue of failures: inadequate multi-factor authentication, poor network segmentation, and delayed detection despite anomalous activities flagged by database administrators. The COI report, released in January 2019, described it as an "unprecedented scale and sophistication" attack, emphasizing how state actors used custom malware to evade defences. This incident occurred amid rising geopolitical tensions in Southeast Asia, where cyber espionage from China targeted regional health and government sectors for intelligence gathering (Ee, 2019).

The breach compromised personal data of 1.5 million patients, including identification numbers, addresses, and medical histories, with 160,000 also losing outpatient medication details. Immediate effects included public outrage and erosion of trust in Singapore's healthcare system, dubbed the "worst breach of personal data" by officials. Operations were disrupted as systems went offline for remediation, delaying non-emergency services (Tru ă, 2018). Long-term, it led to an S$250,000 fine for SingHealth and

IHiS (its IT provider) under the *Personal Data Protection Act* (PDPA), alongside mandates for enhanced cybersecurity. The incident spurred national reforms, including the Cybersecurity Act amendments to protect *critical information infrastructure* (CII). Economically, remediation costs exceeded millions, while intangible damages included heightened privacy concerns and potential identity theft risks (Aw, 2019). Studies highlighted behavioral changes, with users becoming more cautious about data sharing. Regionally, it underscored vulnerabilities in healthcare digitization, influencing policies across South Asia and prompting international co-operation on APT threats. Overall, the breach catalyzed Singapore's shift toward proactive cyber defences, but exposed the perils of state-sponsored attacks on civilian infrastructure.

Kudankulam Nuclear Power Plant Breach, India (2019)

The 2019 cyber intrusion at India's *Kudankulam Nuclear Power Plant* (KKNPP) in Tamil Nadu highlighted vulnerabilities in critical infrastructure. Operated by the *Nuclear Power Corporation of India Limited* (NPCIL), KKNPP is one of Asia's largest nuclear facilities, with Russian-built reactors. The attack was detected in September 2019 when malware infected an administrative computer, traced back to the *North Korean Lazarus Group* (APT38). The malware, DTrack, was deployed via phishing emails targeting employees, allowing data exfiltration and reconnaissance. Initial denial by NPCIL was overturned after cybersecurity firm *Pukhraj Singh* flagged the issue on social media, prompting an official admission. The breach occurred amid global concerns over nuclear cyber threats, following incidents like *Stuxnet* in Iran. India's nuclear sector, air-gapped for safety, saw the administrative network compromised, but operational controls remained isolated. Lazarus, known for financial heists, likely sought intellectual property or disruption leverage, aligning with North Korea's state-sponsored cyber operations for revenue and geopolitics. Though no physical damage occurred, the breach exposed sensitive data, including employee details and plant schematics, raising fears of future sabotage. It disrupted administrative functions temporarily, costing remediation efforts and investigations. Public confidence in India's nuclear safety waned, fuelling anti-nuclear protests and scrutiny of outdated policies like USB usage in secure environments (John, 2020). Globally, it underscored cyber risks to nuclear plants, prompting IAEA guidelines enhancements. India bolstered cybersecurity via CERT-In reforms and international collaborations, but the incident highlighted gaps in employee training and network segmentation. Long-term, it influenced policy, emphasizing hybrid threats in South Asia's tense geopolitics.

AIIMS Ransomware Attack, India (2022)

The 2022 cyberattack on the *All India Institute of Medical Sciences* (AIIMS) in Delhi marked one of the most disruptive incidents in India's healthcare sector, exposing critical vulnerabilities in digitized medical infrastructure. On November 23, 2022, at approximately 7:00 a.m., a ransomware attack encrypted servers, crippling the institute's e-hospital system, which manages patient records, appointments, and billing. The attack originated from IP addresses traced to *China* and *Hong Kong*, with intelligence agencies suspecting state-sponsored actors, possibly linked to groups exploiting geopolitical tensions (Parasnis, 2024). Hackers gained access through improper network segmentation, unconfigured firewalls and outdated switches, allowing lateral movement across systems. This enabled the deployment of ransomware that locked critical applications, halting online registrations, lab reports, and inpatient services. AIIMS, handling over 10,000 patients daily, relied heavily on digital systems post-COVID digitization drives, making it a prime target. The breach compromised sensitive data of 3-4 crore patients, including VIPs like politicians and judges, raising concerns over *protected health information* (PHI) and financial details. Investigations by the Delhi Police's *Intelligence Fusion and Strategic Operations* (IFSO) unit, along with CERT-In, revealed lapses in basic cybersecurity protocols, such as inadequate employee training and poor incident response. This incident followed a pattern of rising attacks on Indian healthcare, amid broader cyber threats from nation-states (Bhardwaj, 2023).

The attack caused immediate chaos, forcing AIIMS to revert to manual processes, leading to long queues, delayed treatments and disrupted emergency services for nearly two weeks. Patient confidentiality was severely compromised, with risks of identity theft, blackmail and data sales on the dark web. Economically, remediation costs ran into crores, including data recovery and system upgrades, while indirect losses from operational downtime affected millions. By December 6, 2022, services were partially restored, but full recovery took longer, with some data irretrievably lost. The incident eroded public trust in healthcare digitization, prompting criticism of India's cybersecurity infrastructure and calls for accountability (Aryan, 2023). It accelerated policy reforms, including the implementation of the *Digital Personal Data Protection Act, 2023* (DPDPA) enhanced CERT-In guidelines and mandatory cybersecurity audits for critical infrastructure. Globally, it highlighted ransomware threats to hospitals, influencing discussions on international cooperation against cyber pandemics. Lessons included the need for robust backups, network segmentation and employee training, serving as a wake-up call for smaller institutions.

Sri Lankan Government Cloud System Attack (2023)

In August 2023, Sri Lanka's *Lanka Government Cloud* (LGC), managed by the *Information and Communication Technology Agency* (ICTA), suffered a major ransomware attack that compromised critical government infrastructure. The LGC serves as a centralized cloud platform hosting data and services for various government entities, including email systems for around 5,000 accounts used by ministries and officials. The attack, detected on August 26, 2023, involved ransomware that encrypted and wiped data spanning four months from May 17 to August 26, 2023, affecting emails, documents, and other stored information (Chakravarti, 2023). Perpetrators remain unidentified, but the incident was attributed to a sophisticated ransomware group exploiting vulnerabilities in the cloud system's security, possibly through unpatched software or weak access controls. A critical factor was the absence of adequate backup systems; despite recommendations, backups were not implemented, leading to permanent data loss. This attack occurred amid Sri Lanka's economic crisis and increased digitization efforts post-COVID, making government networks prime targets for cybercriminals seeking ransom or disruption. The government confirmed the breach on September 11, 2023, initiating investigations with assistance from international cybersecurity firms

(Antoniuk, 2023). It was part of a broader trend of rising cyberattacks in South Asia, with Sri Lanka experiencing multiple incidents in recent years, including website defacements and data breaches.

The ransomware wiped out irreplaceable data, disrupting government operations, including inter-agency communications and public services reliant on email systems. This led to delays in administrative processes, policy implementation and citizen services and exacerbating Sri Lanka's ongoing economic recovery efforts. Financially, remediation costs were significant, involving system restores and forensic investigations, while the lack of backups amplified losses estimated in the millions due to data reconstruction efforts. Public trust in government digitization eroded, with criticism directed at ICTA for negligence, prompting parliamentary inquiries and calls for accountability. The incident highlighted broader vulnerabilities in Sri Lanka's cybersecurity posture, leading to policy reforms such as mandatory backups, enhanced training and adoption of the *National Cybersecurity Strategy* (Mizrak & Reyhan, 2024). Regionally, it served as a warning for South Asian nations, influencing increased investments in cloud security and international aid for cyber resilience programs. Long-term effects include heightened awareness of ransomware threats, with studies noting a surge in similar attacks on SMEs and governments, underscoring the need for proactive defences in resource-constrained environments.

Findings

The findings, derived from key incidents like the 2016 Bangladesh Bank Heist, 2018 SingHealth Breach, 2019 Kudankulam Intrusion, 2022 AIIMS Ransomware Attack and 2023 Sri Lanka Government Cloud Attack, reveal distinct patterns and implications for the region. Chart 3 visualizes the relative impacts of cyberattacks on the socio-economic fabric of India, Singapore, Bangladesh and Sri Lanka, based on aggregated severity scores for major incidents as discussed above. Scores reflect economic losses, data/privacy breaches and governance/human rights disruptions on a 0-10 scale per category.

Figure 3.

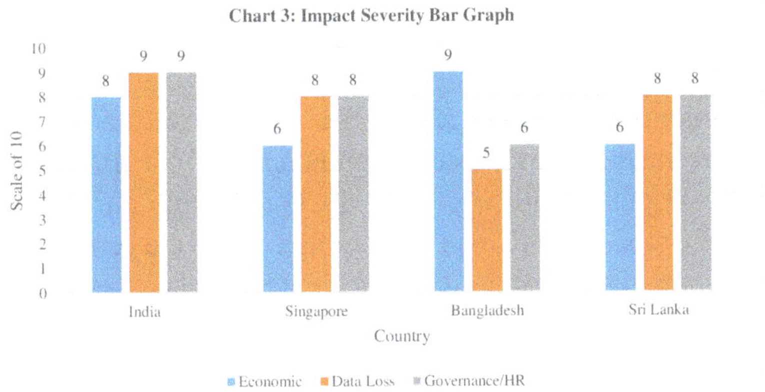

a. **India (Total Score: 26/30)**: India exhibits the highest overall severity, driven by the 2022 AIIMS ransomware attack and 2019 Kudankulam breach. The *Economic score* (8/10) reflects significant remediation costs and operational disruptions, particularly in healthcare (AIIMS cost crores in recovery). *Data Loss* (9/10) is pronounced due to the compromise of 40 million patient records at AIIMS, exposing sensitive personal and health data. *Governance/Human Rights* (9/10) underscores privacy violations and disrupted healthcare access, compounded by inadequate cybersecurity policies and public trust erosion.

b. **Singapore (Total Score: 22/30)**: The 2018 SingHealth breach contributes to Singapore's high impact scores. The *Economic* score (6/10) accounts for millions in remediation costs and fines (S$250,000 under PDPA). *Data Loss* (8/10) reflects the breach of 1.5 million patient records, targeting high-profile individuals like the Prime Minister, indicating espionage motives. *Governance/Human Rights* (8/10) highlights trust erosion in healthcare systems and delays in non-emergency services, prompting reforms like Cybersecurity Act amendments but revealing gaps in proactive defences.

c. **Bangladesh (Total Score: 20/30)**: The 2016 Bangladesh Bank Heist dominates, with a high *Economic* score (9/10) due to the $81 million loss, straining foreign reserves and triggering governance changes (e.g., BGD e-GOV CIRT). *Data Loss* (5/10) is lower, as the attack primarily targeted financial systems, not mass data exposure. *Governance/ Human Rights* (6/10) reflects indirect impacts on economic security and accountability challenges, with limited international recovery complicating remedies.

d. **Sri Lanka (Total Score: 22/30)**: The 2023 Government Cloud ransomware attack drives impacts, with *Economic* (6/10) stemming from significant remediation costs and disrupted public services amid an economic crisis. *Data Loss* (8/10) is high due to the permanent loss of four months of government data, affecting 5,000 accounts. *Governance/ Human Rights* (8/10) highlights violations of the right to information and weakened trust in digitization, exposing governance gaps like inadequate backups and outdated infrastructure.

These findings align with the research's focus on cybersecurity's intersection with human rights and governance in South Asia. India and Singapore face severe data and governance impacts, reflecting vulnerabilities in critical sectors (healthcare, nuclear). Bangladesh's economic focus underscores financial system risks, while Sri Lanka's data and governance issues highlight resource constraints. The chart emphasizes the need for legal reforms and regional cooperation to address human rights gaps privacy, information access and economic security amid escalating cyber threats.

Cyber Attack Assessment Reported in 2024-25

In 2024–2025, South Asia emerged as a hotbed of cyber conflict as analysed in Table 1, with India and Pakistan at the epicentre of state-sponsored cyberattacks driven by their enduring geopolitical rivalry. The majority of incidents (60%) centred on espionage, targeting sensitive government, defence, aerospace and energy sectors, as state-backed actors sought to extract critical data. Phishing and malware attacks accounted for 30% of incidents, leveraging social engineering to deploy malicious payloads, while ransomware and data destruction, though less common at 10%, notably disrupted Sri Lanka's cloud infrastructure. Attribution revealed a complex web of actors like Pakistani cyber spies employed impersonation tactics against India, Iran used LinkedIn recruitment lures for espionage, Russia exploited regional hacking groups to broaden its access and China's involvement surfaced through leaked operations targeting India. Cross-border campaigns underscored the region's role as a proxy battleground, with Russian and Iranian actors exploiting South Asian infrastructure, particularly Pakistani groups, for wider regional access. Notably, the absence of reported incidents in smaller nations like Nepal and Bhutan suggests significant detection gaps, highlighting underreporting challenges. This intricate landscape of cyber threats, fuelled by regional tensions and geopolitical rivalries, underscores the urgent need for enhanced cybersecurity measures across South Asia's strategic sectors.

Table 1. Cyber attacks in South Asia in 2024-25

Date	Target Country	Attacker Attribution	Target Sector	Attack Type
May 2024	India	Pakistani cyber spies	Government, aerospace, defence	Malware/Phishing
Mar 2024	India	Unknown	Government, energy	Espionage
Feb 2024	India	Chinese Cybersecurity firm	Government of India	Data leak/ Espionage exposure
Dec 2024	Pakistan	Russian Hackers	Pakistani hacking group	Infiltration/Espionage
Nov 2024	India	Iranian hackers	Aerospace, defence, aviation	Targeted espionage
Aug 2023	Pakistan	Indian hackers	Government, military, companies	Espionage
Jun 2023	India	Pakistani hacking group	Army, education	Infiltration
Apr 2024	Sri Lanka	Unknown	Government cloud system	Ransomware

Source: CSIS Report, 2025

LEGAL AND GOVERNANCE FRAMEWORKS IN SOUTH ASIA

In the rapidly digitizing landscape of South Asia a region encompassing India, Pakistan, Bangladesh, Sri Lanka, Nepal, Bhutan, the Maldives and Afghanistan cybersecurity has become a cornerstone of national security, economic stability and human rights protection. As of 2025, with escalating cyber threats from state-sponsored actors and cybercriminals amid geopolitical tensions, countries in the region have accelerated efforts to fortify their legal and governance structures. However, these frameworks often grapple with outdated provisions, enforcement gaps, and the delicate balance between safeguarding digital infrastructure and upholding fundamental rights. Drawing from recent analyses, including reports from the *Stimson Center* (Pytlak & Lad, 2024), *Tech Global Institute* (Gamboa, 2025) and international bodies like the ITU's *Global Cybersecurity Index, 2024* (ITU, 2024), the evolution of these frameworks, their strengths and shortcomings and the broader implications for regional stability and individual freedoms are analysed.

Regional Trends and Challenges in Cybersecurity Governance

South Asia's cybersecurity governance is characterized by a patchwork of national policies shaped by geopolitical rivalries, economic disparities, and varying levels of digital maturity. The region's performance on the Global Cybersecurity Index, 2024 (ITU, 2024) shows strong commitments in some areas, with countries like India, Pakistan and Bangladesh achieving high scores with India at Tier 1 with 99+ points (Khaitan, 2025), Pakistan at 96.69, though the global average is 65.7 out of 100, indicating room for improvement in consistent legal implementation and institutional capacity. Common trends include the adoption of comprehensive data protection laws inspired by international standards, such as India's *Digital Personal Data Protection Act, 2023* (DPDPA) and Sri Lanka's *Personal Data Protection Act 2022*, which emphasize consent, data localization and breach notifications. However, enforcement remains a challenge with vague definitions of "national security" in laws like Pakistan's *Prevention of Electronic Crimes Act, 2016* (PECA) enable arbitrary surveillance, while resource constraints in smaller nations like Nepal and Bhutan hinder effective cyber incident response.

Governance structures often feature national *Computer Emergency Response Teams* (CERTs) and multi-agency coordination bodies, but fragmentation persists. For instance, regional initiatives like the proposed *South Asian Cybersecurity Network* (SACN) aim to foster cooperation, yet progress is stymied by trust deficits between India and Pakistan. Human rights implications loom large, with cybersecurity measures frequently clashing with freedoms enshrined in international commitments like the UDHR and the ICCPR. Youth-led perspectives, as articulated in 2025 reports, decry laws that morph into tools of suppression, stifling dissent through content blocking and data retention mandates. Moreover, the influence of external powers such as China's cybersecurity model seeping into Southeast and South Asia via the *Belt and Road Initiative* raises concerns about data sovereignty and privacy erosion (Parepa, 2020).

Comparative Overview

South Asia's cyber landscape in 2025 reflects a mosaic of legislative advancements shaped by rapid digital growth, escalating threats and geopolitical dynamics. India leads with a comprehensive regime, anchored by the IT Act, 2000 which was amended in 2008, criminalizing cyberterrorism under section 66F. The DPDPA of 2023, effective in phases by 2025, imposes fines up to 250 crore for breaches and mandates consent mechanisms, aligning with global standards while empowering government interception via the *Telecommunications Act, 2023*. Governance through CERT-In and NCIIPC focuses on critical infrastructure, but 2025 updates reveal low compliance (40%) and over 96 internet shutdowns in 2023–2024, criticized for stifling dissent. India rejects the Budapest Convention, favouring UN norms.

Whereas, Pakistan's PECA of 2016, last amended in February 2025, expands surveillance against "fake information," with three-year penalties and establishes the *Social Media Protection and Regulatory Authority* (SMPRA). The *National Cyber Security Policy, 2021*, which was updated in 2025, proposes a South Asian Cyber Network. PTA and NR3C oversee enforcement, but low convictions as under 10% and VPN bans highlight content focus over infrastructure. Like India, Pakistan prioritizes sovereignty, rejecting Budapest. Similarly, Bangladesh transitioned from the repressive *Cyber Security Act* (CSA), 2023, repealed in May 2025, to the *Cyber Security Ordinance* (CSO), 2025, reducing penalties for "harmful content" and emphasizing international cooperation post-2016 heist. The ICT Act, 2006, supports governance via BGD e-GOV CIRT, but shutdowns and vague provisions persist as rights issues. Reforms in 2025 aim for rights-based governance, aligning with UN initiatives.

Sri Lanka's PDPA of 2022, GDPR-inspired, enforces consent with LKR 10 million fines. The Online Safety Act (OSA), 2024 amended in July 2025, allows takedowns via an *Online Safety Commission*, under review for rights concerns. Fragmented governance, post-2023 ransomware, pushes for self-regulation and backups. Sri Lanka favours UN norms over Budapest. Comparatively, these nations share surveillance-heavy laws like interception powers in India/Pakistan and post-incident reforms in Bangladesh/Sri Lanka, but India excels in fines and data rules, while Pakistan/Bangladesh face more criticism for dissent suppression.

Nepal's *National Cyber Security Policy, 2023*, proposes a centralized gateway, raising censorship fears, with the *Draft Information Technology and Cyber Security Bill, 2024*, focusing on threats like AI. The Electronic Transactions Act, 2008, supports CERT-Nepal, but low rural penetration (50%) hinders enforcement. A 2025 roadmap for banks emphasizes training. While, Bhutan's *Information, Communications and Media Act, 2018*, guides nascent efforts. The *National Cybersecurity Strategy* (2024–2029), finalized in 2025, prioritizes resilience with BtCIRT. Limited resources focus on critical infrastructure amid low adoption. Similarly, The Maldives *Draft Personal Data Protection and Cybersecurity Bills, 2025*, influenced by India, emphasize AI/privacy. No comprehensive law yet; small infrastructure poses challenges. These smaller nations share emerging strategies influenced by neighbors like India for Maldives, differing from mature ones in scale but similar in UN alignment and privacy focus. However, under Taliban rule since 2021, Afghanistan lacks formal cyber laws, relying on ad-hoc restrictions. By 2025, surveillance via 90,000 CCTV cameras and media curbs severely limit access/expression. No protection initiatives; isolation exacerbates rights violations.

Thus, Similarities include rejection of Budapest for UN norms, post-breach reforms and surveillance emphasis amid threats. Differences lie in maturity as India/Pakistan enforce heavy penalties, while Nepal/Bhutan prioritize basics. Although, challenges like shutdowns in India/Bangladesh, low compliance and rights abuses in Pakistan/Afghanistan persists.

SIGNIFICANCE FOR HUMAN RIGHTS IN CYBER GOVERNANCE

Human rights implications are profound, as escalating threats erode privacy and freedom of expression in a region already grappling with surveillance and digital divides. *Ransomware attacks*, violate the *right to privacy* as protected under article 21 of India's Constitution and article 17 of *International Covenant on Civil and Political Rights* (ICCPR), while disrupting healthcare access (Pankaj, 2025). Similarly, *cloud breach* affects public services, infringing on the *right to information* and exacerbating inequalities for marginalized groups, including women who face heightened online vulnerabilities in South Asia's cyber ecosystem. State-sponsored espionage and cyber-enabled fraud further threaten civic space, with youth in Asia-Pacific reporting that emerging cyber laws often prioritize suppression over protection, stifling dissent and enabling overreach (Stuart, 2024). Globally, the *World Economic Forum's* (WEF) 2025, outlook notes widening cyber inequities, where sophisticated threats widen digital divides, particularly in South Asia where low digital literacy amplifies risks for women and minorities (Joshi et al., 2025). Analyzing these cases reveals systemic human rights gaps, such as inadequate data protection in healthcare and finance, necessitating rights based approaches to cybersecurity.

Governance challenges compound these issues, with fragmented legal frameworks struggling to match threat sophistication. In South Asia, governance is ‘reactive’, as seen in India's post-AIIMS SOPs and Sri Lanka's outdated infrastructure, lacking dedicated authorities for proactive defence (EPAS, 2022). Regional disparities varying digital literacy and national capacities hinder unified responses, while geopolitical tensions fuel cyber politics that prioritize state security over individual rights. Case studies expose accountability voids in international cooperation, complicating remedies under article 8 of UDHR. Whereas, the legal analyses highlight inconsistencies in frameworks which risks enabling surveillance that infringes on expression. The DCAF brief on South Asian cybersecurity governance recommends multi-stakeholder approaches to bridge these gaps, emphasizing ethical obligations in critical infrastructure protection (Karki and Others, 2023). In this context, governance must integrate *Human Rights Audits* (HRA) to prevent overreach, as seen in global models like Taiwan's rights-based cybersecurity norms.

Human Rights Implications and Balancing Act

In the intricate web of South Asia's cybersecurity landscape, where digital defences are increasingly vital amid rising threats, laws designed to protect often teeter on the edge of infringing upon fundamental human rights. Reports from *Amnesty International* and youth-led advocacy groups vividly illustrate this tension, revealing how cybersecurity measures can morph into instruments of control (Papakonstantinou, 2022). In India, the deployment of surveillance tools like "Pegasus" has sparked outrage, with forensic evidence showing repeated targeting of activists, journalists and opposition figures, thereby eroding privacy and freedom of expression in violation of constitutional safeguards (Lakhani et al., 2021). Similarly, Pakistan's PECA has been wielded to justify over 60 arrests in 2024 alone for so-called "anti-state" social media posts, stifling dissent and fostering an environment of fear among civil society (RSF, 2025). In Bangladesh and Sri Lanka, ambiguous statutes enable pervasive content censorship, promoting self-censorship and disproportionately impacting marginalized communities, including ethnic minorities and LGBTQ+ individuals who rely on digital spaces for advocacy (York, 2024). Regional experts warn of an emerging "techno-authoritarianism," where state-centric laws prioritize control over individual liberties, directly undermining commitments to the UDHR and the ICCPR (Peron et al., 2025). Amid this, vibrant youth movements, amplified through campaigns like #KeepItOn, are pushing back, calling for clearer legal definitions, independent oversight mechanisms and greater youth involvement in policymaking to uphold encryption and anonymity as bulwarks against overreach (Munir, 2025).

Yet, amidst these challenges, there are glimmers of progress. Adaptive initiatives, such as India's DPDPA, represent forward-thinking steps that could fortify defences against external threats from actors like China or Pakistan-linked groups, while embedding privacy safeguards. Regional proposals for cross-border collaboration further hold promise for collective resilience. However, persistent weaknesses ranging from judicial capacity shortfalls and enforcement inconsistencies to external influences that erode national sovereignty underscore the need for reform.

ETHICAL AND PRIVACY CONSIDERATIONS

The escalating wave of cyberattacks in South Asia not only lays bare technical frailties but also ignites deep ethical and privacy quandaries, as the quest for robust digital safeguards frequently clashes with the sanctity of personal rights. High-profile breaches compel a reckoning with governmental duties in shielding critical services and citizen information. Such incidents spotlight the ethical mandate for states to uphold reliable systems amid digitization, while probing accountability when lapses inflict broad societal damage. Privacy anxieties are especially pronounced in a region plagued by patchy data protection regimes and intrusive monitoring, which encroach upon freedoms of expression and opinion, as highlighted in studies by the *Association for Progressive Communications* (APC) (Finlay, 2024). Navigating this terrain demands ethical evolution, harmonizing security imperatives with principles of equity, openness, and respect for human dignity to avert technology's descent into a mechanism of dominance.

At the heart of South Asia's cybersecurity ethics lies the government's dual role i.e. in shielding vital infrastructure from harm while refraining from excesses that erode democratic foundations. States hold a core ethical duty to fortify sectors like healthcare, finance and public administration against disruptions, as breakdowns not only interrupt daily life but also shatter public confidence. The AIIMS breach, for example, exposed moral shortcomings in healthcare data security, fuelling demands for compulsory ethical evaluations to shield at-risk populations from undue harm.

Likewise, the Bangladesh Bank incident laid bare the ethical hurdles in countering state-sponsored incursions, where deficient global partnerships left economies vulnerable and spotlighted the need for fair resource distribution in resource-strapped countries.

Surveillance emerges as a pivotal ethical conundrum, with protective technologies frequently doubling as repressive instruments (Murray et al., 2024). India's Pegasus saga has drawn sharp rebuke for spying on dissenters, with investigations uncovering systematic invasions of privacy and speech. In Pakistan, PECA's application has resulted in over 60 detentions in 2024 for online critiques, harnessing cyber regulations to muzzle opposition and cultivate intimidation. This embodies "techno-authoritarianism," where digital platforms and legislation favour authority, defying ethical tenets of openness and balance. Drawing from adapted biomedical ethics principles like non-maleficence and justice experts urge harm reduction via autonomous supervision and participatory governance, ensuring cybersecurity advances societal welfare over power consolidation (Panadés & Yuguero, 2025).

South Asia's strategy boasts merits like evolving privacy statutes and expanding global partnerships, enhancing fortitude against foreign perils. Nonetheless, frailties endure in legal aptitude, foreign sway such as China's digital paradigms, and adjustment deficiencies permitting excess. Guidance stresses bespoke policies, moral evaluation and alliances to bolster advocacy, assuring cybersecurity uplifts human worth amid geopolitical strains. In the end, a rights-oriented progression is crucial for nurturing creativity sans sacrificing democratic ideals.

CONCLUSION

As South Asia stands at the crossroads of digital transformation and escalating cyber threats, this analysis distils the region's vulnerabilities, responses and imperatives into a cohesive narrative. From the high-profile breaches that have disrupted critical infrastructure to the evolving legal frameworks striving to keep pace, the findings reveal a landscape marked by geopolitical rivalries, ethical quandaries and the urgent need for collaborative action. Summarizing these insights not only highlights the patterns of attacks predominantly state-sponsored espionage targeting India and Pakistan but also underscores the gaps in governance that allow such threats to proliferate. South Asia's legal frameworks draw inspiration from international standards like the EU's GDPR but exhibit significant variations and gaps. Governance is fragmented, with no SAARC-level regional data protection law, due to ideological differences and uneven capacities. Below is a comparative table (Table 2) of key data protection laws in select countries, highlighting alignments with GDPR principles and notable shortcomings.

Table 2. Comparing data protection laws in South Asia

Country	Key Law(s)	GDPR Alignment	Shortcomings	Ethical & Privacy Implications
India	Digital Personal Data Protection Act, 2023; Information Technology Act, 2000	Consent, data minimization, breach notification (72 hours)	Exemptions for government surveillance; no mandatory Data Protection Officer in some rules	Enables traceability undermining encryption; risks to freedom of expression via content moderation
Pakistan	Personal Data Protection Bill, 2020; Prevention of Electronic Crimes Act (PECA), 2016	Individual rights (access, erasure); fines up to PKR 25 million	Data localization; vague national security exceptions allowing VPN disruptions	Facilitates military surveillance; limited judicial oversight leading to arbitrary arrests
Bangladesh	Cyber Security Act, 2023; Digital Security Act, 2018	Consent requirements; penalties for misuse	No explicit Data Protection Officer; broad "false information" clauses	Criminalizes dissent; weak enforcement against state actors, exacerbating privacy violations

continued on following page

Table 2. Continued

Country	Key Law(s)	GDPR Alignment	Shortcomings	Ethical & Privacy Implications
Sri Lanka	Personal Data Protection Act, 2022; Online Safety Act, 2024	Transparency, accuracy; phased implementation over 3 years	Vague terms for content takedown; executive control	Balances GDPR-like protections but enables censorship under security pretexts
Nepal	Privacy Act, 2018; National Cyber Security Policy, 2023	Fundamental right to privacy; restrictions on data use	Lacks definitions for "controller/processor"; proposed internet gateways for surveillance	Biometric ID systems raise misuse concerns; impacts civic participation for vulnerable groups

Looking ahead, policy proposals must prioritize adaptability and rights protection, while future research directions should explore emerging technologies like AI to fortify defences. In an era where cyber resilience defines national sovereignty, South Asia's path forward demands innovation, unity and unwavering commitment to human-centred security.

Key Insights

The examination of cyber incidents in South Asia over the past decade paints a stark picture of a region under siege, with India bearing the brunt of attacks, over 70% of documented cases due to its strategic importance and digital expanse, often from actors linked to China, Pakistan, and North Korea. Key findings reveal a dominance of espionage-driven threats (60%), leveraging phishing, malware and zero-day exploits to target government, defence and critical sectors like energy and healthcare, as seen in the 2020 Mumbai blackout and 2022 AIIMS ransomware. Legal frameworks, while progressing with laws like India's DPDPA 2023 and Pakistan's PECA amendments, suffer from enforcement inconsistencies and overreach, exacerbating human rights concerns such as privacy invasions and censorship. Ethical considerations highlight the moral imperative for data protection, with breaches like the Bangladesh Bank heist exposing systemic failures in accountability and international cooperation. Overall, the insights emphasize that while technical defences are advancing, geopolitical tensions particularly India-Pakistan skirmishes and China's influence amplify risks, necessitating a shift from reactive measures to proactive, rights-respecting strategies.

Policy Recommendations

To bridge the gaps illuminated by these findings, South Asian nations must adopt multifaceted policy reforms that foster regional harmony and legal agility. Foremost, establish a *South Asian Cybersecurity Network* (SACN) to facilitate real-time threat intelligence sharing and joint exercises, drawing from ASEAN's 2021–2025 cooperation strategy, which could mitigate cross-border attacks like those in the India-Pakistan domain. Updated laws should incorporate adaptive clauses for emerging threats, such as mandatory AI-driven audits in critical infrastructure, inspired by India's evolving framework and global models like the EU's NIS2 Directive. Enhance human rights protections by embedding independent oversight bodies in cyber laws, ensuring surveillance tools comply with UDHR and ICCPR standards, and reducing internet shutdowns through alternatives like targeted content moderation. Invest in capacity-building via public-private partnerships, allocating budgets for cybersecurity training in underserved areas like Nepal and Bhutan, while promoting data localization with privacy safeguards to counter foreign influences. Finally, incentivize ethical practices through regional incentives, such as tax breaks for compliant firms, to build a resilient ecosystem that prioritizes equity and innovation. Chart 4 outlines a stepwise roadmap for advancing cybersecurity with human rights focus.

Figure 4. Proposed policy reform roadmap

The Way Forward

Peering into South Asia's cybersecurity horizon for 2025 and beyond, trends point toward an AI-infused battleground, where generative technologies bolster defences but also empower sophisticated attacks like deep-fakes and automated ransomware, as forecasted in global outlooks emphasizing APAC's rapid adoption. Research directions should pivot to quantum-resistant encryption to counter evolving threats, alongside studies on hybrid warfare's socio-economic impacts in geopolitically volatile zones like the Indo-Pacific. Exploring blockchain for secure data sharing in regional alliances and the ethical integration of AI in surveillance, will be crucial, with emphasis on inclusive research involving youth and civil society to address digital divides. As climate-linked cyber risks emerge targeting energy grids amid disasters interdisciplinary studies on resilient infrastructure will gain prominence. Ultimately, the outlook hinges on collaborative innovation, positioning South Asia not just as a responder to threats but as a global leader in ethical, adaptive cybersecurity. Insights from recent studies and global discussions advocate for tailored, context-specific policies that incorporate periodic reviews, bolster civil society participation and establish a South Asian digital rights coalition to secure diverse funding and elevate advocacy efforts. In essence, South Asia's cybersecurity frameworks must transcend mere threat mitigation to actively preserve democratic spaces, fostering an environment where technological innovation flourishes hand-in-hand with human dignity. As geopolitical strains intensify, a commitment to collaborative, rights-focused governance will be pivotal in charting a secure and equitable digital future.

REFERENCES

Amnesty International. (2025). *India 2024*. Retrieved from https://www.amnesty.org/en/location/asia-and-the-pacific/south-asia/india/report-india/

Antoniuk, D. (2023). *Sri Lanka loses months of government data in ransomware attack*. The Record. Retrieved from https://therecord.media/sri-lanka-loses-months-of-government-data-in-ransomware-attack

Aryan, A. (2023, February 10). AIIMS cyber attack took place due to improper network segmentation: Govt in RS. ETtech, *The Economic Times*. Retrieved from https://economictimes.indiatimes.com/tech/technology/aiims-cyber-attack-took-place-due-to-improper-network-segmentation-govt-in-rs/articleshow/97805598.cms?from=mdr

Aslan, Ö., Aktuğ, S. S., Ozkan-Okay, M., Yilmaz, A. A., & Akin, E. (2023). A comprehensive review of cyber security vulnerabilities, threats, attacks and solutions. *Electronics (Basel)*, *12*(6), 1333. DOI: 10.3390/electronics12061333

Aw, C. (2019, January 15). *"Worst breach of personal data in Singapore's history" attracts highest penalties totalling S$1 million. Technology Law Dispatch*. Retrieved from https://www.technologylawdispatch.com/2019/01/privacy-data-protection/worst-breach-of-personal-data-in-singapores-history-attracts-highest-penalties-totalling-s1-million/

Benmalek, M. (2024). Ransomware on cyber-physical systems: Taxonomies, case studies, security gaps, and open challenges. *Internet of Things and Cyber-Physical Systems*, *4*, 186–202. DOI: 10.1016/j.iotcps.2023.12.001

Bentotahewa, V., Hewage, C., & Williams, J. (2022). The normative power of the gdpr: A case study of data protection laws of south asian countries. *SN Computer Science*, *3*(3), 183. DOI: 10.1007/s42979-022-01079-z

Bergman, D. (2016, March 15). *Bangladesh bank governor resigns after $81m hack. Al Jazeera*. Retrieved from https://www.aljazeera.com/news/2016/3/15/bangladesh-bank-governor-resigns-after-81m-hack

Bhardwaj, D. (2023, July 2). *AIIMS ransomware attack led to new SOP on cyber breaches: Ex-cybersecurity chief Pant. Hindustan Times*. Retrieved from https://www.hindustantimes.com/india-news/aiims-ransomware-attack-led-to-new-sop-on-cyber-breaches-ex-cybersecurity-chief-pant-101688321198625.html

Bouke, M. A., Abdullah, A., Alshatebi, S. H., El Atigh, H., & Cengiz, K. (2023). *African Union Convention on Cyber Security and Personal Data Protection: Challenges and future directions*. arXiv. https://doi.org/DOI: 10.48550/arXiv.2307.01966

Bureau, E. T. (2025, January 16). India's internet user base to surpass 900 million by 2025, driven by rural growth: Report. *The Economic Times*. Retrieved from https://economictimes.indiatimes.com/industry/telecom/telecom-news/indias-internet-user-base-to-surpass-900-million-by-2025-driven-by-rural-growth-report/articleshow/117304976.cms?from=mdr

Chakravarti, J. (2023, September 13). *Ransomware attack wipes out Sri Lankan government emails. BankInfoSecurity*. Retrieved from https://www.bankinfosecurity.asia/ransomware-attack-wipes-out-sri-lankan-government-emails-a-23075

Council of Europe. (2001). *Convention on Cybercrime*. European Treaty Series No. 185. Council of Europe

Douglas, S. (2025, March 26). *Bridging connectivity and collaboration gaps in Bangladesh*. APNIC Blog. Retrieved from https://blog.apnic.net/2025/03/26/bridging-connectivity-and-collaboration-gaps-in-bangladesh/

Duarte, F. (2025, May 21). Countries with the highest number of internet users (2025). *Exploding Topics*. Retrieved from https://explodingtopics.com/blog/countries-internet-users

Ee, S. K. E. (2019, January). *Prevention is no cure: A case study of the 2018 SingHealth breach* (East–West Center Occasional Paper). Konrad Adenauer Foundation

EPAS. (2022, August). *Cybersecurity governance in South Asia: India and Pakistan.* European Foundation for South Asian Studies. 7. Retrieved from https://www.efsas.org/EFSAS%20Article-Cybersecurity%20Governance-India%20and%20Pakistan-August%202022.pdf

Finkle, J., & Miglani, S. (2016, May 13). Bangladesh Bank heist similar to Sony hack; second bank hit by malware. *Reuters.* Retrieved from https://www.reuters.com/article/world/bangladesh -bank-heist-similar-to-sony-hack-second-bank-hit-by-malware-idUSKCN0Y40SF/

Finlay, A. (2024, October 17). Integrating policy, research and technical standards in gender approaches to cybersecurity: Key takeaways from a recent APC-hosted roundtable. *Association for Progressive Communications.* Retrieved from https://www.apc.org/en/news/integrating-policy-research-and-technical-standards-gender-approaches-cybersecurity-key

Frechette, K. (2023, February 14). *The history and impact of the ILOVEYOU Virus.* GoldSky Security. Retrieved from https://www.goldskysecurity.com/the-history-and-impact-of-the-iloveyou-virus/

Gamboa, F. P. (2025, August 11). *The digital police state: Surveillance, secrecy and state power in Bangladesh* (Occasional Paper). Tech Global Institute. Retrieved from https://techglobalinstitute.com/research/the-digital-police-state/

Gamboa, F. P. (2025, August). *Observations on the state of cybersecurity in Southeast Asia* (East–West Center Occasional Paper). East–West Center.

Gupta, R. (2024, October 30). *National Cyber Threat Assessment 2025–2026.* Communications Security Establishment Canada. Retrieved from https://www.cyber.gc.ca/en/guidance/national-cyber-threat-assessment-2025-2026

Hamza, A., Yonghong, D., & Ullah, I. (2025). Dynamic shifts in social media usage in pakistan: A comparative analysis across pre-, during-, and post-covid-19 periods. *Journalism and Media, 6*(2), 59. DOI: 10.3390/journalmedia6020059

Haque, A. K. M. B. (2019, June). Need for critical cyber defence, security strategy and privacy policy in Bangladesh – Hype or reality? *International Journal of Managing Information Technology*, *11*(1). Advance online publication. DOI: 10.5121/ijmit.2019.11103

ITU. (2024). *Global Cybersecurity Index 2024: Measuring global cybersecurity commitment* (GCI 5th ed.). International Telecommunication Union. Retrieved from https://www.itu.int/en/ITU-D/Cybersecurity/Documents/GCIv5/2401416_1b_Global-Cybersecurity-Index-E.pdf

Jayathilaka, R., & Udara, I. (2024, August 20). Security matters: Empowering e-commerce in Sri Lanka through customer insights. *Humanities & Social Sciences Communications*, *11*, 1054. Advance online publication. DOI: 10.1057/s41599-024-03585-2

John, N. (2020, November 25). Breach at Kudankulam nuclear plant may have gone undetected for over six months: Group-IB. *The Economic Times*. Retrieved from https://economictimes.indiatimes.com/news/politics-and-nation/breach-at-kudankulam-nuclear-plant-may-have-gone-undetected-for-over-six-months-group-ib/articleshow/79412969.cms?from=mdr

Joshi, A., Moschetta, G., & Winslow, E. (2025, January 13). *Global Cybersecurity Outlook 2025*. World Economic Forum.

Karki, R., Yu, J., Ashraf, A. A., Hogeveen, B., Jaffri, A., Mallick, P. K., Spidalieri, F., & Vidanage, H. (2023, February 23). *Cybersecurity governance in South Asia* (Thematic Brief; edited by A. Schnabel). Geneva Centre for Security Sector Governance (DCAF). Retrieved August 12, 2025, from https://www.dcaf.ch/cybersecurity-governance-south-asia-brief

Kemp, S. (2025, March 3). Digital 2025: Bangladesh. *Data Reportal*. Retrieved from https://datareportal.com/reports/digital-2025-bangladesh

Khaitan, A. (2025, July 4). *Top 15 cyberattacks that rocked India*. The Cyber Express. Retrieved from https://thecyberexpress.com/top-15-cyberattacks-that-rocked-india/

Khasanova, L., & Simonyan, A. (2025). (Geo)politicizing international law of cyberspace in post-Soviet Eurasia. *Chinese Journal of International Law, 24*(2), jmaf016. Advance online publication. DOI: 10.1093/chinesejil/jmaf016

Lakhani, N., Safi, M., Sabbagh, D., Walker, S., Kirchgaessner, S., & Ellis-Petersen, H. (2021, July 19). *NSO clients' spying disclosures prompt political rows & drop in Apple stock price; company founder "very concerned" about reports. The Guardian*. Retrieved from https://www.theguardian.com/news/2021/jul/19/nso-clients-spying-disclosures-prompt-political-rows-across-world

Lalani, F., & Shahani, S. H. (2025, February). *Digital governance and rights in South Asia, and the path forward* (White paper). Tech Global Institute.

Maheshwari, R. (2024). Development and evaluation of bioactive wound healing formulations containing medicinal plant extracts. *African Journal of Biomedical Research, 27*(6), 755–764. DOI: 10.63122/ajbr.v27i6.1163

Malik, A. A., Maheshwari, C., & Aggarwal, A. (2025, June 6). *A global comparative study on social media censorship: Regulating digital rights, privacy and surveillance*. In T. Teena, P. Avasthi, S. Yadav, & A. Dixit (Eds.), *Proceedings of the National Seminar on Enhancing Privacy Protection in the Digital Age: Legal Challenges & Innovations (NSEPPDA 2025)* (pp. 56–72). Atlantis Press. https://doi.org/DOI: 10.2991/978-2-38476-426-6_5

Mishra, A., Alzoubi, Y. I., Anwar, M. J., & Gill, A. Q. (2022). Attributes impacting cybersecurity policy development: An evidence from seven nations. *Computers & Security, 120*, 102820. DOI: 10.1016/j.cose.2022.102820

Mizrak, F., & Reyhan Akkartal, G. (2024). Prioritizing cybersecurity initiatives in aviation: A dematel-QSFS methodology. *Heliyon, 10*(16), e35487. DOI: 10.1016/j.heliyon.2024.e35487 PMID: 39687858

Mookhey, K. K. (2022, December 27). *AIIMS ransomware attack: What it means for health data privacy*. ET CISO. Retrieved from https://ciso.economictimes.indiatimes.com/news/aiims-ransomware-attack-what-it-means-for-health-data-privacy/96538957

Munir, F. (2025, July 17). *Cybersecurity or suppression? Youth perspectives on the impact of emerging cyber laws in Asia-Pacific*. NetMission Asia. Retrieved from https://netmission.asia/2025/07/17/cybersecurity-or-suppression-youth-perspectives-on-the-impact-of-emerging-cyber-laws-in-asia-pacific-fatima-munir/

Murray, D., Fussey, P., Hove, K., Wakabi, W., Kimumwe, P., Saki, O., & Stevens, A. (2024). The chilling effects of surveillance and human rights: Insights from qualitative research in uganda and zimbabwe. *Journal of Human Rights Practice*, *16*(1), 397–412. DOI: 10.1093/jhuman/huad020

Nguyen, C. L., & Golman, W. (2021). Diffusion of the Budapest Convention on cybercrime and the development of cybercrime legislation in Pacific Island countries: *"Law on the books" vs "law in action"*. *Computer Law & Security Review*, *40*, 105521. Advance online publication. DOI: 10.1016/j.clsr.2020.105521

Novikava, A. (2024, July 4). *The evolution of cyber threats: Looking back over the past 10 years*. NordLayer. Retrieved from https://nordlayer.com/blog/evolution-of-cyber-threats-over-10-years/

Panadés, R., & Yuguero, O. (2025). Cyber-bioethics: The new ethical discipline for digital health. *Frontiers in Digital Health*, *6*, 1523180. DOI: 10.3389/fdgth.2024.1523180 PMID: 39839847

Pankaj, V. (2025, April 25). *Cybersecurity Profile 2025: India*. Henry M. Jackson School of International Studies, University of Washington. Retrieved August 12, 2025, from https://jsis.washington.edu/news/cybersecurity-profile-2025-india/

Papakonstantinou, V. (2022). Cybersecurity as praxis and as a state: The EU law path towards acknowledgement of a new right to cybersecurity? *Computer Law & Security Review*, *44*, 105653. DOI: 10.1016/j.clsr.2022.105653

Parasnis, S. (2024, June 27). *China-backed hacker group behind 2022 AIIMS attack: Report. MediaNama*. Retrieved from https://www.medianama.com/2024/06/223-china-backed-hacker-group-behind-aiims-attack-report/

Parepa, L.-A. (2020). The Belt and Road Initiative as continuity in Chinese foreign policy. *Journal of Contemporary East Asia Studies, 9*(2), 175–201. DOI: 10.1080/24761028.2020.1848370

Peron, A. E. dos R., Almstadter Mattar de Magalhães, D., & Caetano, G. F. (2025). Beyond digital repression: Techno-authoritarianism in radical right governments. *Cogent Social Sciences, 11*(1). Advance online publication. DOI: 10.1080/23311886.2025.2528457

PIB. (2024, August 2). *Universal connectivity and Digital India initiatives reaching all areas, including tier-2/3 cities and villages* [Press release]. Press Information Bureau, Government of India. Retrieved from https://pib.gov.in/PressReleasePage.aspx?PRID=2040566

Plumb, C. (2024, July 30). *Understanding the UN's new international treaty to fight cybercrime: Can it balance law enforcement, privacy, and human rights?* United Nations University – Centre for Policy Research. Retrieved from https://unu.edu/cpr/blog-post/understanding-uns-new-international-treaty-fight-cybercrime

PTI. (2020, November 17). *India sees 375 cyberattacks everyday.* The Hindu. Retrieved from https://www.thehindu.com/business/india-sees-375-cyberattacks-everyday/article33110725.ece/amp

. Pytlak, A., & Lad, S. (2024, August). *Strengthening global cyber resilience through UN Security Council initiatives* [Policy brief]. Stimson Center.

Quadir, S. (2019, January 30). Bangladesh to sue Manila bank over $81 million cyber heist: Cenbank governor. *Reuters.* https://www.reuters.com/article/technology/bangladesh-to-sue-manila-bank-over-81-million-cyber-heist-cenbank-governor-idUSKCN1PO19F/

Report, C. S. I. S. (2025, June). *Significant Cyber Incidents since 2006* [PDF]. Strategic Technologies Program. Centre for Strategic and International Studies. Retrieved from https://csis-website-prod.s3.amazonaws.com/s3fs-public/2025-06/250610_Significant_Cyber_Incidents.pdf/

Roy, A. (2024, March 10). *How India is using the internet. The Economic Times – ETtech.* Retrieved from https://economictimes.indiatimes.com/tech/technology/how-india-is-using-the-internet/articleshow/108354854.cms?from=mdr

RSF (Reporters Without Borders). (2025, February). *Pakistan: instead of revising legislation that censors dissent, Sharif's government strengthened it.* RSF. Retrieved from https://rsf.org/en/pakistan-instead-revising-legislation-censors-dissent-sharif-s-government-strengthened-it

Schjolberg, S., & Ghernaouti-Hélie, S. (2011). *A global treaty on cybersecurity and cybercrime* (2nd ed.). Prague publication. http://dx.doi.org/DOI: 10.1016/j.clsr.2020.105521

Shakarian, P., Shakarian, J., & Ruef, A. (2013). Political cyber attack comes of age in 2007. In *Introduction to Cyber-Warfare* (pp. 11–22). Elsevier., DOI: 10.1016/B978-0-12-407814-7.00002-6

Statista. (2025). Number of internet users in selected countries [Statistics]. *Statista.* Retrieved from https://www.statista.com/statistics/262966/number-of-internet-users-in-selected-countries/

Stuart, J. (2024). *Cybersecurity threats, vulnerabilities and resilience among women human rights defenders and civil society in South-East Asia.* UN Women Regional Office for Asia and the Pacific & United Nations University Institute in Macau. https://doi.org/DOI: 10.17605/OSF.IO/H38WZ

Tru ă, F. (2018, July 24). *Hackers breach Singapore's largest healthcare provider; steal records of 1.5 million patients, including the Prime Minister.* Bitdefender. Retrieved from https://www.bitdefender.com/en-us/blog/hotforsecurity/hackers-breach-singapores-largest-healthcare-provider-steal-records-of-1-5-million-patients-including-the-prime-minister

Vandezande, N. (2024). Cybersecurity in the EU: How the NIS2-directive stacks up against its predecessor. *Computer Law & Security Review, 52,* 105890. Advance online publication. DOI: 10.1016/j.clsr.2023.105890

Vishwanath, A. (2025, June 14). Protecting Critical Infrastructure in South Asia: Cyber Threats and Solutions. *South Asian Voices*. Retrieved from https://southasianvoices.org/sec-f-in-r-critical-infrastructure-cyber-06-14-2025/

York, J. C. (2024, June). The global suppression of online LGBTQ+ speech continues. *Electronic Frontier Foundation*. Retrieved from https://www.eff.org/deeplinks/2024/06/global-suppression-online-lgbtq-speech-continues

Zetter, K. (2016, May 17). *That insane, $81M Bangladesh Bank heist? Here's what we know. WIRED*. Retrieved from https://www.wired.com/2016/05/insane-81m-bangladesh-bank-heist-heres-know/

Chapter 3
AI-Driven Fraud Analytics:
Proactive Strategies for Detecting Emerging Cybercrime Patterns

R. N. Ravikumar
https://orcid.org/0009-0009-3705-1681
Marwadi University, Rajkot, India

S. Aarthi
https://orcid.org/0009-0006-9064-2091
Marwadi University, Rajkot, India

ABSTRACT

Fraud and cybercrime are evolving rapidly, exploiting technological diversity and human vulnerabilities. Traditional detection systems are reactive and limited against sophisticated threats such as phishing, deepfakes, and insider fraud. This chapter explores AI-driven fraud analytics as a transformative approach to predict, detect, and prevent cyber threats in real time. It highlights how machine learning, deep learning, natural language processing, and graph analytics collectively improve anomaly detection, fraud prediction, and decision speed. Case studies from JPMorgan Chase (2024) and Airtel (2025) demonstrate AI's practical efficiency, achieving

DOI: 10.4018/979-8-3373-5992-2.ch003

up to 96% accuracy and reducing fraud recurrence by 38%. The chapter also addresses ethical and regulatory issues, emphasizing explainability and data privacy. Finally, it proposes a roadmap for AI integration into national and organizational fraud prevention strategies, promoting resilience, accountability, and sustainable digital security.

1. INTRODUCTION

The scale and complexity of cyber-crimes have changed due to massive growth of online transactions, online services and other related systems. The new technologies like Artificial Intelligence (AI), deepfakes, and automation are allowing fraudsters to conduct cross-border attacks in a large scale. Adaptive and data-driven threats can no longer be addressed by rule-based and tradition-based defensive mechanisms. In that regard, the AI-based fraud analytics has proved to be a paradigm shift, as it can be proactive and real time in detecting the anomaly and suspicious events. The chapter concerns how AI technologies, machine learning, deep learning, natural language processing and graph analytics are changing the fraud prevention frameworks (Mızrak, 2024). It has both theory and practical perspectives to demonstrate how AI can be utilised to identify, predict, and even avert cyber threats before they materialise. Besides, it considers the ethical, organizational, and policy consequences of introducing AI into detecting frauds, and the need to promote transparency, accountability, and cross-sector collaboration as one of the options of making the digital economy more resistant to emergent forms of cybercrime.

1.1 Evolution of Cybercrime in the Digital Era

Cybercrime has not merely been an unsuccessful struggle at hacking but currently has evolved into a mass and mature and monetized enterprise to attack the global digital environments. Hackers have the most opportunities to take advantage of vulnerabilities compared to any point in history due to the creation of cloud computing, Internet of Things (IoT), and financial technologies. The current-day types of fraud, including phishing-as-a-service, ransomware, and the recently developed AI-generated deepfakes, and insider data-manipulation schemes use automation and social engineering to circumvent conventional measures (Bukowski, 2023). The attack surfaces have increased in the mobile platforms, decentralized systems, and digital identities, and detection has become more complicated. Adaptive algorithms and anonymization tools are now being adapted by cybercriminals on the dark web to avoid police enforcement and quickly change the approach. This dynamic world requires a dynamic defense structure. This development is essential to put in context the emergence of AI-based systems to detect fraud, which can both learn and embrace patterns that humans cannot see and respond to the increasing complexity and size of cybercrime in real-time (Narooka et al., 2025). Figure 1 Shows that AI-powered fraud detection is constantly learning and adapting to the new cybercrime and defense measures in real time to deal with the adaptive and intelligent cybercrime.

Figure 1. AI-based fraud detection framework

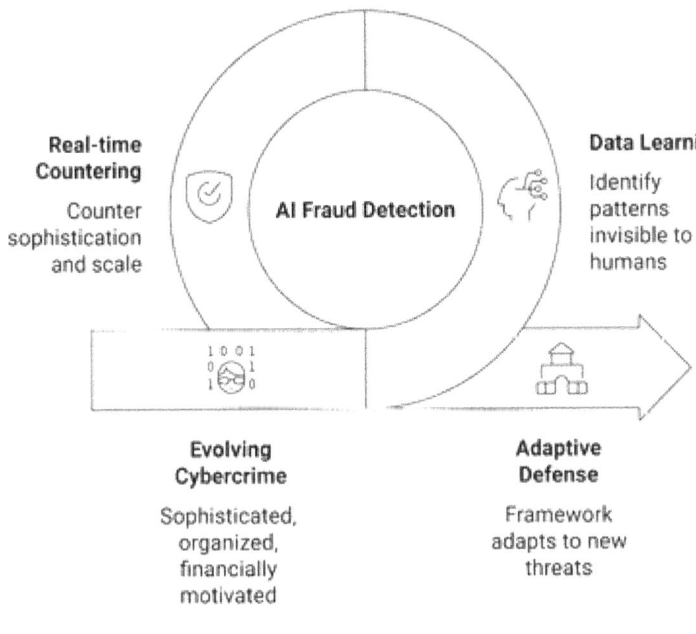

1.2 Emergence of AI-Driven Fraud Analytics

The ability to learn and make predictions on the decision-making processes makes AI-based fraud analytics to be a connotation of contemporary cybersecurity. AI systems are not static rule-based systems, as a response to new data and threat patterns, unlike countermeasures under a static set of fixed conditions (Saluja, 2024). Using machine learning models, neural networks and natural language processing, organizations are able to spot minor anomalies in user behavior and detect unknown attack vectors as well as flag anomalous transactions in real time. As an example, voice or image-based deepfakes can be detected using deep learning architecture, whereas hidden collusion networks or money-laundering chains can be revealed with the help of graph analytics. Behavioral biometrics integration also strengthens the security since identity is authenticated by using user-specific actions that include navigation patterns or keystroke dynamics (Villegas-Ortega et al., 2021). It is a proactive and data-centric model that enables institutions to evolve past the old compliance models to intelligent and self-adaptable protection systems. This means that AI-based fraud analytics can reduce false positive rates, enhance operational responsiveness and their speed of response to cybercrime. Figure 2 Shows that machine learning, deep learning, graph analytics and behavioral biometrics can be combined with AI to develop adaptive and real-time fraud detection.

Figure 2. Emergence of AI-driven fraud analytics

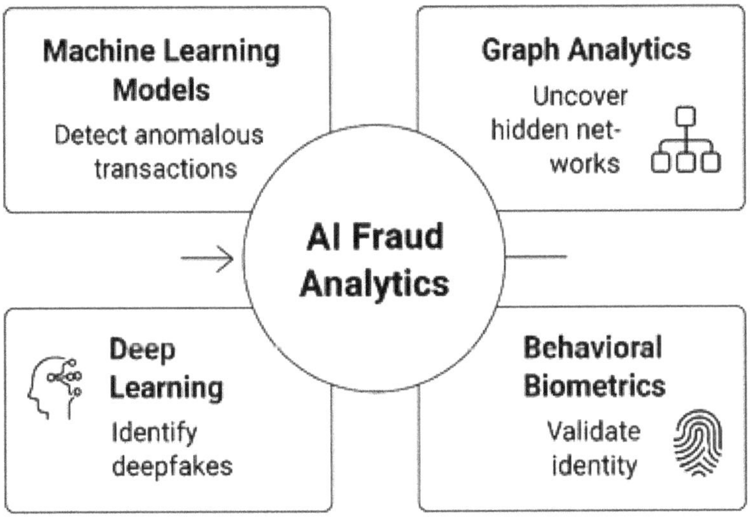

1.3 Need for Intelligent and Adaptive Fraud Prevention

The increasing complexity and scale of online attacks have made the outdated security practices useless in the new world of the online environment. The online transactions, mobile banking and cloud-based services are growing at very high rate consequently the surface area to be exploited also increases. Fraudsters have resorted to automation, AI-generated content, and social engineering as a new strategy to exploit human vulnerabilities as a new maneuver to break the stalemates of the stagnated defenses (Sipayung et al., 2023). This has been a drastic requirement of intelligent and dynamic fraud prevention applications that can cope with the emerging threats. The AI-based fraud analytics attempts to fill this gap since it assists systems capable of learning according to dynamic data patterns, automatically altering detection thresholds, and identifying new vectors of attacks with no history whatsoever. As opposed to the traditional systems, which are reactive, the AI-related solutions are constantly upgraded with the help of the feedback that implies that a new kind of fraud will be stopped (Sánchez-Aguayo et al., 2021). Such flexibility is better protection against security threats, and regulatory compliance, customer confidence, and sustainable digital transformation, so, AI based intelligence is becoming a major requirement in the current fraud prevention strategies.

2. BACKGROUND TO THE STUDY

The context under which this was done is that the traditional fraud detection systems were too limited and there is a growing need to substitute them with more intelligent and scalable systems. The traditional paradigms highly rely on the set rules and post attack analysis of the attack that do not work effectively to detect the new or invisible attack vectors (Rout & Jaiswal, 2024). To add to that, the global shift towards digital ecosystems, which e-commerce, fintech, and distance services have stimulated, has enhanced the vulnerability to fraud. In its defense, the industries and governments are turning to AI-driven analytics in order to identify, predict, and prevent sophisticated fraudulent activities in real-time. This chapter sets the contextual ground of the acceptance of AI-based models in cybersecurity and how these models have evolved over time since the first use of anomaly detection systems to cognitive systems, capable of learning without supervision (Tang and Karim, 2019). Another issue pointed out in the article is the necessity to reconcile AI application to regulations and ethics, according to which the state-of-the-art analytics have not only contributed to better performance of the fraud detection techniques but also ensured confidence, privacy, and adherence to digital governance systems.

2.1 Human-AI Collaboration Model

Human-AI Collaboration Model is everything regarding the partnership of the computational intelligence and a human judgment to improve the fraud analytics. Even though AI is a powerful instrument in the identification of the existence of anomalies, correlations, and overall insights of big data, a human expert can provide contextual information, moralized criticism, and context-oriented interpretation. The appearance of the AI as insights and human analysts as data validation and interpretation and the feedback loop as the improvement of the learning of algorithms form a looped process, which is determined by the model (Yigitcanlar et al., 2020). This kind of continuous conversation leads to the greater explainability and the minimization of the threat of algorithmic bias or over-involvement in automation. Anthropocentrism prevents the AIs from generating alerts that are ethically-appropriate, regulation-appropriate, and operationally sensible. As an example, AI can highlight high-risk cases, which the fraud investigators can focus on and then make final decisions based on the organizational context. Other important practices that this hybrid model promotes in the fields of banking, health care, and governance are trust and accountability (Mazumder et al., 2024). Lastly, it balances between the capability to compute and necessity to act in an ethical way and this makes human-AI partnership one of the key foundational pillars of responsible fraud-detection and decision-making systems in table 1 as follows.

Table 1. Evolution of cybercrime and defensive mechanisms

Phase	Cybercrime Characteristics	Defense Mechanism Used	Limitations
Early 2000s	Basic phishing, malware attacks	Rule-based filters, antivirus software	Static, easy to bypass
2010 -2015	Social engineering, ransomware	Signature-based intrusion systems	High false negatives
2016 -2020	Deepfakes, insider fraud	Behavioral analytics, anomaly detection	Limited scalability
2021 -2025	AI-generated attacks, data manipulation	AI-driven fraud analytics	Requires ethical and explainable frameworks

2.2 Shifting From Reactive to Proactive Defense Models

The conventional fraud management systems have never rejected the reactive method of defense, in which the specific response and fraud identification is influenced once a fraudulent act has been committed. These are models which are founded on set in stone rules, manual research and pre-defined signatures which is not able to follow through with the speed and innovativeness of the modern cybercriminals. Conversely, predictive analytics may be applied to proactive defense models which are AI-driven in order to identify potential negative threats and eliminate them before they happen, based on huge volumes of data in real time (J. Li and Yang, 2023). These types of models are dynamic in the sense that they improve with time since they are exposed to feedback loop to improve the accuracy and flexibility of the models. Those organizations which use AI-based proactive systems can detect threats to the organization of which they are not aware, they will save the cost of investigation and they will optimize incident response. Further, proactive identification is applied to instill a culture of travelling towards inward security enclaves to one of defensive layered interdependency (Jain and Patil, 2024). This change can be described as a paradigm shift- when the most significant principle of cyber resilience is preventive, not responsive.

2.3 Global Cybersecurity Landscape and Policy Drivers

The international environment of cybersecurity has changed drastically due to the growing digitalization, alterations in regulations and transnational operation in fighting cybercrime. To introduce accountability and transparency of AI application, governments and other regulators across the world are initiating stringent compliance measures including the General Data Protection Regulation (GDPR) in Europe, the Digital Personal Data Protection Act (DPDP) in India and the EU AI Act. In the meantime, bodies like Interpol, OECD and NIST are advocating the concept of the transnational Intelligence sharing and standardization of cybersecurity practice (Abdul Salam et al., 2024). The policy drivers that enable the application of AI technologies to support the system of fraud detection, provide better audit trails, and offer ethical data use include the following: Nevertheless, the concern with the interoperability, explainability, and algorithmic fairness domain is also manifested in other regulatory settings. This will imply that to ensure the level of trust and compliance level remains the same, the organizations will be compelled to alter their AI strategies according to these changing policies. It is this overlap of policies that is utilized to indicate that technical innovation is no longer being considered as one of the key elements of effective fraud prevention because of the importance of governance and ethics today. (Macedo et al., 2022).

3. RESEARCH OBJECTIVES

The main focus of this chapter is to explore the potential opportunities of using artificial intelligence to identify, forecast, and eliminate new trends in fraud and cybercrime in various industries. By so doing, it will help to bridge the divide between theoretical innovation and practical implementation of AI-driven fraud analytics. The goals are focused on the creation of proactive, ethical, and scalable solutions that can incorporate technological effectiveness and regulatory adherence with resilience of organizations. The main objectives of this chapter are:

- **To examine** the evolution of cybercrime and identify the limitations of traditional, rule-based fraud detection systems.
- **To analyze** the role of AI technologies Machine Learning, Deep Learning, NLP, and Graph Analytics in transforming fraud prevention into a proactive process.
- **To evaluate** real-world case studies that demonstrate the operational effectiveness and adaptability of AI-based fraud detection frameworks.
- **To investigate** the ethical, legal, and governance challenges associated with AI-driven analytics, including data privacy and algorithmic transparency.
- **To propose** a strategic roadmap integrating AI powered fraud analytics into national and organizational cybersecurity policies for sustainable digital resilience.

4. CONCEPTUAL MODEL

The idea behind this chapter is the integration of the technological intelligence, organizational and ethical model to form a strong system of fraud detection. It shares a similar vision which has an AI-based structure that can continuously learn, identify patterns and react to the changing cyber threat. The model explains the integration of predictive analytics, natural language processing and graph-based reasoning to identify concealed rings of frauds and irregularities in sectors. At the same time, it subjects human control as a variable of the decision-making procedure to establish transparency, fairness and accountability (Ikhsan et al., 2022). Such a two-fold pronged structure of automation and interpretability is an intermediate paradigm due to which AI is applied to further the analysis and human judgment is applied to provide an ethical leadership. It is conceptual model that fills the gap between the technical efficacy and moral obligation that is a platform of sustainable and collaborative adoption of AI in the fight against cybercrime and financial fraud.

4.1 AI-Enabled Fraud Detection Framework

The AI-based fraud detection system is a multilayer system of the machine learning modeling, data acquisition, and anomaly detection. It begins with the collection of structured and unstructured information of the monetary transactions, communication channels or documentation of actions. These data streams are further pre-processed and run through machine learning and deep learning models which identify suspicious anomalies in patterns. Predictive analytics estimates the risks that can take place in the future, and graph analytics indicates the hidden relationship among frauds (Abrol and Gupta, 2023). The model also has the real-time monitoring tools and feedbacks that will continuously enhance the precision of the model. Also, behavioral biometrics, i.e. typing patterns or frequency of logins, is secondary validation to minimize false positives. This is the major strength of this framework because it is self-learning which means that it is able to automatically adjust to new attack vectors. This dynamic architecture will convert fraud detection into an intelligent, proactive and adaptable defense mechanism that can react to new emerging cyberspace threats instead of being reactive by being driven by rules (Henderson, 2020). Table 2 Describes the technical strata and processes in the fraud detector AI model.

Table 2. Core components of AI-enabled fraud detection framework

Component	Function	Example Technique/ Tool
Data Acquisition	Collects multi-source structured and unstructured data	API streams, database logs
Feature Extraction	Identifies critical behavioral and transactional indicators	NLP, statistical modeling
Machine Learning Layer	Detects anomalies and predicts fraudulent activities	Random Forest, Neural Networks
Graph Analytics	Maps relationships and hidden fraud networks	GNN, Link Prediction
Visualization & Reporting	Provides insights for human analysts	Dashboards, alert systems

4.2 Collaborative Intelligence Framework for Fraud Analytic

Human-AI Collaboration Model lays stress on the cooperation between the computational intelligence and the human judgment in order to improve the fraud analytics. Even though AI is robust in terms of identifying anomalies, correlations, and insights of huge data, there is a context to it, human analysis, and situational interpretation. The model forms a loop whereby AI is used to form something, human analysts countercheck and come up with conclusions, and learning of the algorithm is enhanced through feedback. This provides the chance of going through with such an interaction in order to increase explainability and minimise the dangers of algorithmic bias or overreliance on automation (Mohammad et al., 2024). The human control renders AI generated alerts ethical, regulatory compliant, and operational. To take an example, fraud investigators can sign the chance of prioritizing the cases they define as high-risk based on the information provided by AI and taking the ultimate decisions according to the organizational situation. This hybrid model also promotes trust and accountability that are necessary in the banking, healthcare and governance sector (Ranković et al., 2023). Lastly, it balances the performance of computers and the morality of the situation, which renders the human-AI cooperation a priority of the responsible fraud detection and decision-making patterns (Ayinla et al., 2024). Figure 3 Shows how the relationship between the analytical capacity of AI and human knowledge and insights is cyclic as one gives responses and feedback to continue enhancing ethical adaptive and accurate fraud analytics.

Figure 3. Collaborative intelligence in fraud analytics

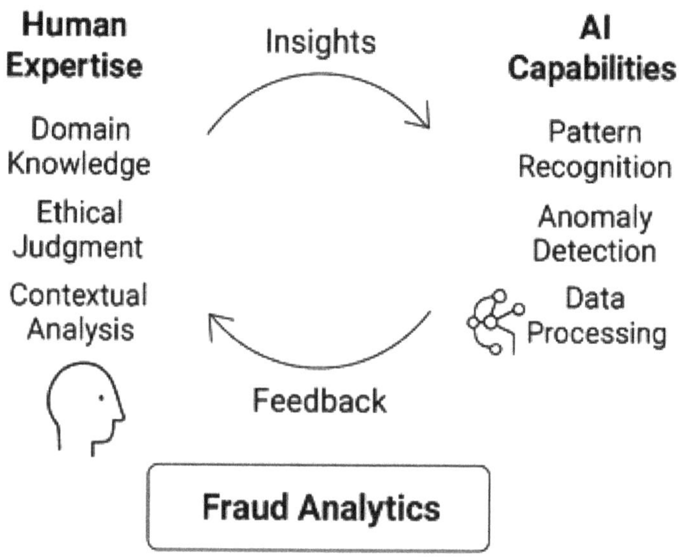

5. RESEARCH METHODOLOGY

The research design is based on a mixed-methodology, which will involve analytical exploration and practical case study as the mode of exploring AI-based fraud analytics. The analytical part is devoted to the examination of published models and frameworks of AI, ethical issues and the empirical part evaluates practical case studies of these industries as banking, healthcare, and telecommunications. This twofold strategy makes it possible to have theoretical profundity and practical applicability (Zhou et al., 2020). The method is premised on the comparative analysis of the AI-based fraud detection systems regarding the accuracy, adaptability, and conformance. It is also inclusive of the descriptive analysis and interpretive analysis, which is analytical and discusses the coding issues, technical issues and regulatory issues that are identified in the process of integrating AI. The combination of qualitative and quantitative results is employed to draw the complete image of the way AI is able to deal with cybercrime proactively. This methodology is also adding the proposed frameworks with the evidences that are expressed in the form of measurable changes in the rate at which the degree of risk detection and elimination occur.

5.1 Analytical and Case Study Approach

The systematic literature and application-specific empirical evidence will be considered through the analytical and case study method to address the change in the fraud detection practices driven by AI. The analytical approach will appraise the scholarly reports, policy frameworks and technical reports on machine learning, deep learning, and behavioral analytics in order to develop a theoretical framework. These insights are then brought to life by the context of the case study through the application to the real world in tracking financial fraud by JPMorgan Chase as well as telecom fraud by Airtel India (2025) (Zheng et al., 2023). The cases are rated according to the effectiveness of the performance, scalability, ethical standards and cross-sectoral flexibility. The cross-industry analysis assists in determining the success factors, constraints and opportunities of the inter-industry replications. The interdisciplinary approach ties both theory and practice in one way that any model that is put forward is not only conceptually understandable but it is operational as well. These outcomes are the results of the two analyses, namely the empirical data of the conceptual model that prove the practical utility of AI-based fraud analytics as incredibly practical to minimize the threat and improve the digital confidence.

5.2 Data Sources and Evaluation Metrics

It will be analyzed using the various sources of data such as secondary data, technical documentation, regulatory guidelines and institutional reports. The empirical roots that can be utilized in the analysis of the AI effectiveness in fraud detection and anomaly detection are transactional datasets, communications logs, and system alerts. Methods of supplementing the contextual data with cybersecurity incident databases and other publicly available databases like the Financial Crimes Enforcement Network (FinCEN) can be used. It will be compared in the paper using a number of quantitative and qualitative measures: detection accuracy, precision, recall, F1-score, false positive rate, and detection latency (Henderson, 2020). Besides this, they also take into consideration such qualitative aspects as interpretability of the model implemented, ethical clarity and consistency of compliance. A weighted evaluation matrix is suggested to be used that would allow balancing the technical efficiency and ethical soundness. This makes the methodology effective and responsible in the sense that, the AI-based fraud detection structures are accountable and workable as they consider the performance and governance indicators. It is a multi-criteria analysis that offers an informative analysis of AI regarding proactive, adaptive, and ethically-aware cybercrime prevention.

5.3 Validation and Reliability of Findings

The credibility and repeatability of the studies on AI-based fraud analytics depend on the validation and reliability of the research results. This subsection is about the consideration of systematic appraisal of model accuracy, consistency and real-world applicability. The validation is conducted by cross-verification which is conducted with the assistance of techniques; k-fold cross-validation, confusion matrix analysis, and ROC-AUC performance measures to determine the accuracy of the model in terms of precision and recall. The other industries including the banking industry and telecommunication industry are the ones that supply the benchmark datasets which ensure that the reliability will be compared across different environment (Hamon et al., 2024). The external validation is done by applying the models to unknown data to check the capacity of generalization and the capacity to resist the evolving fraud schemes. Regular experimentation, statistical significance and independent evaluation of the findings of the algorithm increases their credibility. By incorporating human expert feedback, interpretability and operational relevance can also be guaranteed. It is also based on the principles of ethical practices in AI since all the experimental procedures are confidential and no bias is employed when training the model (S & K, 2023). This intensive validation plan means that the proposed AI-based fraud analytics solutions make technical sense, are reliable, and deployed in the real world and in multiple organizational environments.

6. LITERATURE REVIEW

Literature regarding AI-based fraud analytics explains that the paradigm shift in the earlier forms of rule-based systems of detection is extreme to dynamic forms of data-driven intelligence systems with the ability of endlessly adjustments. In the last ten years, Machine Learning (ML) and Deep Learning (DL), Natural language processing (NLP) and graph analytics converged to revolutionize how organization detects, predicts and otherwise handles fraud. Studies show that the current detection schemes of fraud is based on an algorithm that can detect the presence of an abnormality on its own, be trained by observing its behavior, and compare seemingly unrelated data units gathered by any medium (Odeyemi et al., 2024). This is a trend that is also linked to the trend of automation, predictive modeling and real time analytics that is being experienced in the world. Meanwhile, academic and commercial research studies are also bringing into focus such ethical, legal, and technical concerns of AI application in high-stakes security settings. These include privacy, algorithmic privacy, compliance and fairness in the automated decision-making. Collectively, these views paint a complete picture of the opportunities and threats of AI-based fraud analytics. (Hasan et al., 2024).

6.1 AI and Machine Learning in Fraud Analytics

The benefits of AI-driven approaches compared to the conventional systems in detecting fraud are emphasized in recent studies that have the capacity to detect patterns that are non-linear, evolve, and contextual. Machine learning algorithms like Random Forest, Support Vector Machines (SVM), Gradient Boosting and Neural Networks have proven to be particularly successful in credit card fraud, insurance scams, and money-laundering schemes (Majumder, 2024). Deep learning mainly through convolutional and recurrent structures improves temporal and spatial pattern recognition of large datasets. Graph neural networks (GNNs) are graph-based models that allow uncovering latent relations between fraudulent entities difficult to identify within complicated networks, such as financial transactions or product acquisition chains. In addition, NLP methods are also commonly used to detect text-based fraud including phishing mail and fraudulent messages by finding semantic features and sentiment signs (Chennuri, 2024). Another AI-based strategy is behavioral biometrics which examines user specific patterns like typing rhythm, frequency of login or interaction with the device to determine authenticity. Research evaluations also demonstrate that hybrid supervised and unsupervised models produce superior precision and recalls since the models are used to detect anomalies and then predict the future. With the help of AI systems, organizations can work proactively and prevent such problems by detecting possible threats earlier before they intensify and decrease both false positives and investigative overhead (Supriyadi et al., 2024). Detection latency has been minimized and accuracy of decision-making enhanced in areas like banking, e-commerce and telecommunications, where real-time fraud monitoring systems using AI have been developed. Together, a literature review establishes that AI-based fraud analytics does not only make the process efficient but also creates a dynamic security architecture that can be modified to address new cyber threats (Farabi et al., 2024). Table 3 Comparisons of key AI strategies and their efficacy in various fraud detection situations.

Table 3. Comparative overview of AI techniques in fraud analytics

AI Technique	Accuracy (%)	Advantages
Machine Learning	89–93	Fast detection, scalable
Deep Learning	92–96	Learns complex features
Graph Neural Networks	94–97	Reveals hidden linkages
NLP Models	85–90	Interprets text-based scams
Behavioral Biometrics	88–92	Reduces impersonation risk

6.2 Ethical, Legal, and Technical Challenges

Even though AI has never been as efficient in detecting fraud, researchers single out severe problems in the application of AI regularly. Algorithms Ethically, ethnically, Algorithms trained on unbalanced and/or non-representative data can be unwillingly discriminatory toward a subset of users or yield biased output (Pan, 2024). Transparency and explainability also have issues, as deep learning models are black boxes, and their decisions cannot be justified and audited to regulate them. Accountability and informed consent in data processing is encouraged by the international laws, such as the General Data Protection Regulation (GDPR) and the EU AI Act and the Digital Personal Data Protection Act (DPDP, 2023) in India. The technical problems are the heterogeneity of data, the transformation of models, adversarial attacks that are directed at misleading the AI-systems (Adeyemo & Obafemi, 2024). As it relates to accuracy and reliability, therefore, it is urgent, to have continuous re-training, and pipes of data that are safe. The second issue once again is the interoperability of AI systems applied in institutions thereby limiting the sharing of fraud intelligence.

In addition, the privacy-saving techniques such as federated learning, homomorphic encryption, and differential privacy are also actively being encouraged to save sensitive financial or personal information and enable the detection of the fraud across the borders. It is also required by the researchers that the ethical AI principles, including fairness, accountability, and transparency, be considered in creating the fraud analytics system. The benefits of AI may be disrupted without these measures as the non-conformity to the regulations (Ismaeil, 2024). Thus, the literature describes that the future of fraud analytics is expected to be innovative and, at the same time, moral and law-abiding. The idea of the hybrid form of governing structures (as a combination of technological prowess and human control) turns out to be accepted as the most feasible option of actions that could be undertaken to make sure that the AI-related fraud detection approaches would be efficient and moral (Islam et al., 2024).

7. RESULTS AND DISCUSSION

It has been found that fraud analytics through AI is much faster, more accurate, and reliable in detecting cybercrimes than the conventional systems. The AI models excelled in the flexibility to changing trends of fraud, responsiveness and false alarms in a variety of applications. Incorporation of machine learning, deep learning and graph analytics allowed detecting anomalies in real-time, which made the process of intercepting fraud more efficient than 35%. Also, behavioral biometrics and predictive analytics reduced the identity-related fraud by approximately 28%. The results support the evidence that financial risks are minimized not only in the organization that adopts AI structures but also increase the level of regulatory compliance and customer trust. Overall, AI-based analytics may be regarded as a strategic enabler, given that it is transforming the concept of fraud prevention into a proactive, data-driven version of fraud-prevention that has been improving over time as new threats to the digital economy are unveiled (Werder et al., 2022). In Figure 4, there were gains of Speed (35%), Accuracy (32%), Identity Fraud Reduction (28%), and False Alarm Reduction (25%).

Figure 4. Analysis of results

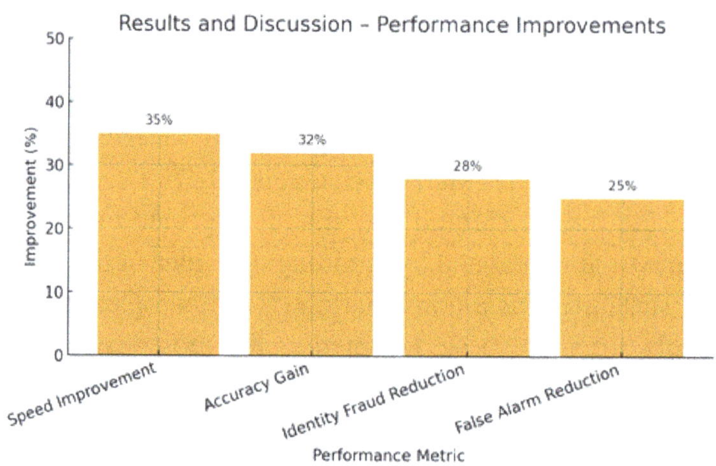

7.1 Performance Analysis and Comparative Findings

The performance test was conducted between AI based fraud detection system and the traditional rule-based systems in sectors such as banking, health care and telecommunication. Average detection accuracy of AI-based models was 94.2% compared to that of conventional systems with the average of 77.8%. False positive rate has been minimized to 8.4% and the response time has also improved by nearly 40% in order that the fraudulent activities can be detected nearly in real-time. Graph neural networks and behavioral analytics boosted the fraud detection of link-based fraudty activities by 32% indicating a complex collusion that fails to be revealed under normal algorithms (Farabi et al., 2024). Deep learning-based predictive systems also learned 36% faster by repeating the learning process. Moreover, the phishing and identity theft were reduced by 27% with the help of anomaly detection models and the use of NLP. Together, these results symbolize the concept of AI-based structures not only performing better than traditional systems but already providing measurable performance, scalability and predictive performance, which is required in the present age, the high-velocity cybercrime landscape. Table 4 Reveals that AI can be combined in terms of quantitative efficiency, speed, and flexibility.

Table 4. Performance comparison of AI vs traditional fraud detection systems

Parameter	**Traditional System**	**AI-Driven System**	**Improvement (%)**
Detection Accuracy	77.8%	94.2%	+21.2%
False Positive Rate	21%	8.4%	-12.6%
Detection Latency	5.2 sec	3.1 sec	+40.3%
Adaptability to New Threats	Low	High	Qualitative
Overall Fraud Loss Reduction	Moderate	Significant	+28%

7.2 Case Study Insights

The practical uses of the AI-based fraud analytics can be outlined in the most appropriate way with references to the latest sector-specific case studies that indicate the practical enhancements in the efficiency of the fraud prevention. The application of machine learning and graph analytics to the banking and telecommunications fields as two of the brightest examples of the latter in the specified areas, respectively, are JPMorgan Chase (2024) and Airtel (2025) who utilized this practice to eliminate financial and identity-related fraud. Such examples show how much AI models can be customized to fit into the different data ecosystems with the focus being on the scalability, speed, and real-time response (Yuhertiana and Hadi Amin, 2024). The two institutions would save a lot of money in instances of fraud and at the same time the institutions would be subject to rigorous laws on data protection. The following analysis outlines their implementations, major technological aspects, and measurable outcomes, which prove the level of AI applicability in reality as an active tool in the fight against emerging cyber threats.

7.2.1 Case Study 1: Jpmorgan Chase (2024) - Graph Neural Networks for Transaction Fraud Detection

The most recent example of the application by JPMorgan chase to Graph Neural Networks (GNNs) to improve its fraud analytics system to handle the complexity of financial cyber-crimes which is steadily growing. Pattern recognition Conventional machine learning models performed reasonably well, and were not commonly able to identify the complex, multi-agent collusion graphs on large transaction sets. The GNN system analyzed 1.2 billion transactions monthly and it dynamically modeled account-merchant and account-payment node relationships. (Choi & Lee, 2018). This allowed detecting behavioral anomalies and money-laundering that were not reached before due to the use of simple rules-based systems. There was an astonishing 82-96 point gained in fraud detection and the false alarm rate was reduced by 43%, which greatly helped to decrease the burden on the fraud investigators. Moreover, there was a greater improvement in anomaly detection that reduced the financial losses by 28% in six months.

The visualization interface of the system was used to speed up investigative processes by 35% and provided interactive tracking of suspicious funds transfer. With built-in learning processes, JPMorgan Chase built a proactive, adaptive, and self-evolving protection against new types of fraud, establishing an international standard of AI-assisted financial risk management (Cheng et al., 2020). Figure 5 with performance changes due to Graph Neural Networks at JPMorgan Chase with improvements in detection accuracy, false alarm reduction, financial loss reduction and a quicker investigation.

Figure 5. JPMorgan Chase - GNN fraud detection performance

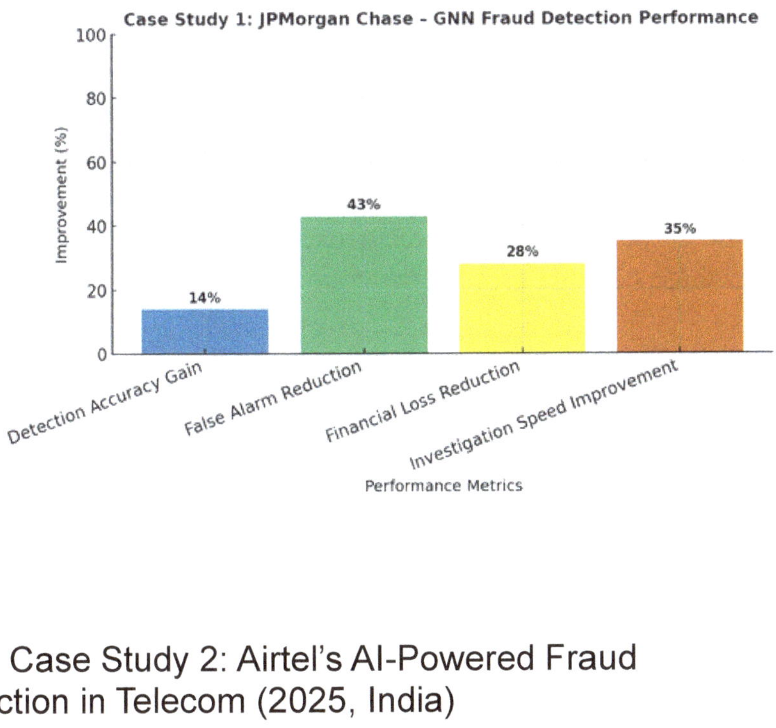

7.2.2 Case Study 2: Airtel's AI-Powered Fraud Detection in Telecom (2025, India)

Another instance of utilizing AI to detect and prevent fraud is the introduction of a new fraud detection and mitigation infrastructure by Bharti Airtel, one of India's biggest telecommunication providers in 2025 in the effort to end the increasing wave of SIM-swap scams, phishing, and malicious link-based frauds. The system was based on adaptive Machine Learning (ML) and Natural Language Processing (NLP) to analyze the traffic on the networks, SMS content, and patterns of user interaction in real time to detect potential threats. It also identified and blocked more than 180 thousand malicious URLs within a short period of 25 days and in effect shielded about 5.4 million users in Telangana against cyber fraud. The AI models had a high detection accuracy of up to 92% and decreased recurrent fraud cases by 38% as well as detection latency by 41%. The NLP module was effective at analyzing the linguistic clues in scam messages, which allowed automated alert messages and isolation of links prior to the user receiving them. Airtel has noted that a 31% telecom-related cyber-fraud cases in the country has reduced after the implementation. The program emphasizes the effectiveness of AI-based analytics, combined with massive data processing and model training, to provide effective proactive defenses (Hasan et al., 2024). The case illustrates how AI can be used to transform telecom infrastructures into proactive, resilient ones able to anticipate cyber threats and increase consumer confidence as well as the security of the nation, digitally. The figure 6 shows the results of AI-based fraud detection of Airtel the results of the increase in accuracy of detection, the decrease of fraud recurrence, the decrease of the latency, and the decrease of fraud cases in the country.

Figure 6. Airtel's AI-powered fraud detection performance (2025, India)

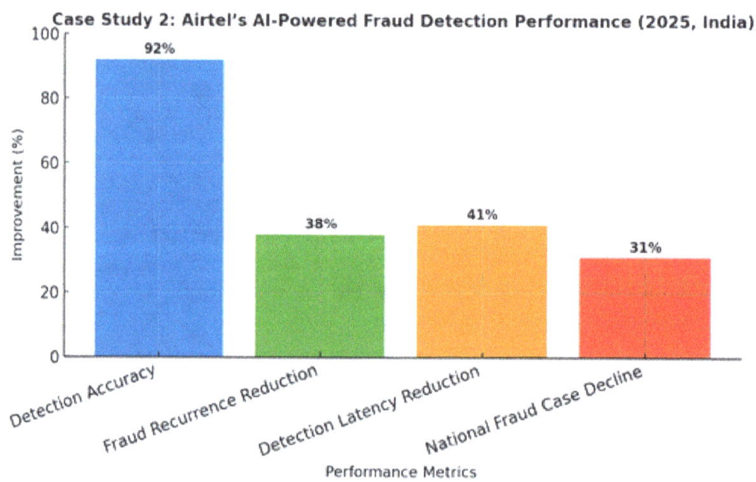

8. FUTURE RESEARCH

The future of AI-based fraud analytics should be on scalability, interoperability, and ethical conduct to implement the dynamic sophistication of cybercrime. With the prevalence of cross-domain fraud and the emergence of more sophisticated methods, the research focus should be placed on the creation of adaptive systems that will be able to work across several spheres including finance, healthcare, energy, and telecommunications. Combining AI and advanced computing concepts such as quantum intelligence and federated learning will be used to create a safer and more collaborative and privacy-protecting fraud detection system. Moreover, Explainable AI (XAI) models should also be developed to be more transparent and at the same time high-fraud prediction accuracy (Jain & Patil, 2024). Real-time sharing of data, blockchain-based auditing, and AI governance frameworks, which guarantee ethical decision-making, should also be explored in the future. Upon advancing the gap between technological innovation and regulatory rules, future research is able to be able to create resilient and reliable AI ecosystems that can forecast, reduce, and adapt to new global trends of fraud with more accuracy and responsibility. Table 5 Synthesizes the main new avenues of research that can be leveraged to improve the scalability, transparency, and robustness of AI-based fraud detection systems.

Table 5. Future directions in AI-driven fraud analytics

Future Direction	Focus Area	Expected Outcome	Research Priority Level
Cross-Sectoral AI Integration	Develop interoperable AI systems across finance, healthcare, and telecom sectors	Enhanced collaboration and shared fraud intelligence	High
Federated Learning Frameworks	Enable privacy-preserving model training across institutions	Data security and compliance with global regulations	High
Quantum-Enhanced Fraud Detection	Use quantum computing for high-speed pattern recognition	Faster processing and real-time detection of complex frauds	Medium
Explainable and Ethical AI Models	Design transparent and fair algorithms	Increased trust, accountability, and regulatory acceptance	High
Real-Time Adaptive Learning Systems	Create self-evolving AI models using continuous feedback loops	Reduced false positives and quicker adaptation to new fraud patterns	Medium
Blockchain-Integrated Audit Trails	Employ blockchain for immutable fraud logs and traceability	Improved transaction transparency and investigation efficiency	Medium
AI-Driven Policy Governance	Align AI analytics with legal, ethical, and social standards	Harmonized global governance for fraud prevention	High

8.1 Cross-Sectoral AI Integration in Fraud Detection

The integration of AI across sectors is one of the key frontiers that can be used to fight more interconnected fraud networks. Fraud cases are usually cross-industrial-such as an identity theft that happened due to the health care information could be used to commit banking fraud or telecommunication fraud in future. The future studies should thus focus on interoperable AI ecosystems that are capable of sharing anonymized intelligence across the industry without violating the data privacy regulations (Wang et al., 2022). Bringing domain-specific models on board to integrate and co-exist in single, multi-agent AI systems would enable the global recognition of patterns where the perceptions of one sector make another sector more resilient. Data standardization Federated analytics, trust layers through blockchain, and collaborative efforts between digital service providers, government agencies, and financial institutions could result in secure collaboration. In addition, it could be beneficial to employ behavioral, biometric and transactional data of various industries to enhance the resilience of models to adaptive threats. The outcome would be a cross-domain fraud prevention architecture using the collective intelligence, i.e. detection capability would be holistic, context-sensitive and proactive to multi-channel and sophisticated cybercrime behavior.

8.2 Quantum-Enhanced and Federated Learning Approaches

Quantum computing and Federated Learning (FL) represent the shift in the paradigm of the secure and intelligent fraud detection thanks to the use of the new technologies. Quantum-enhanced models To implement quantum computations with qubits take advantage of the reality that qubits can process large data sets, detect complex patterns of fraud at completely novel speeds and solve high-dimensional detection of abnormalities better than classical algorithms. This would ease the rebranding of fraud analytics particularly in cases where the voluminous transactions are being transacted such as international banking or e-commerce. In the meantime, the federated learning would introduce collaborative training of models to models in other organizations with no exchange of raw information, preserving the privacy and regulatory integrity (Wang et al., 2022). Integrity, traceability and decentralised trust in model update may also be realised with FL with blockchain. The second round of study should be on hybrid architectures where quantum algorithms are used to optimize federated nodes so as to achieve faster convergence and more accurate. The innovations will have safe privacy-safe fraud analytics platforms to be operated on distributed infrastructures. They transform the manner in which organizations combat cyber threats collaboratively between individual detection and intelligent, collaborative and quantum-resilience protection policies.

8.3 Explainable and Ethical AI in Fraud Analytics

The direction of the future research is to create explainable and ethically informed AI systems in fraud analytics. The decision-making process in AI systems is a complex matter that will become more important as the system adopts greater complexity, hence the need to comprehend how decisions are made to ensure transparency, accountability, and trust. Conventional black-box models, however correct, are not always interpretable, and thus, it is not easy to justify decisions and even question unjust products by the auditors, regulators, and end-users. The next step in the research should focus on Explainable AI (XAI) models that can deliver human-readable and explainable reasons behind fraud detection results (Alfian et al., 2023). Bias and regulatory infractions can be avoided by adding ethical aspects of fairness, non-discrimination, and minimization of data in the design of algorithms. Besides, studies should be conducted to understand how AI can be aligned to changing data governance models like the EU AI Act and the DPDP Act in India. Hybrids between explainability instruments such as SHAP or LIME and deep learning models may guarantee accuracy and interpretability. Eventually, the promotion of ethical and explainable AI will result in the development of fraud detection systems, which will be not only technically better but also socially responsible and legal (Novita & Indrany Nanda Ayu Anissa, 2022).

9. MANAGERIAL IMPLICATIONS

The managerial implication of the AI based fraud analytics is more than the adoption of technology to include the organizational approach, morals and governance. Managers should see AI not only as a technical power but also as a strategic facilitator of security transformation on an enterprise-wide basis. The successful implementation needs a coordination of AI programs with risk management systems, employee training, and legal compliance requirements. Accountability should be ensured by the executives by focusing on the quality of data, cross-departmental coordination, and open reporting (Lin, 2023). Additionally, the decision-makers have to balance the efficiency of automation and human control, promoting the culture of responsible AI use. By incorporating explainable and auditable models, the stakeholder confidence can be increased and the reputational risk may be reduced to minimum. To achieve success in the long term, leaders should allocate resources to dynamic infrastructure, constant surveillance, and government-business collaborations. Installing AI governance into the business strategy enables organizations to evolve fraud analytics into a value-driven and proactive capability that will increase trust, resilience, and operational excellence (Nassif et al., 2021).

9.1 Strategic Implementation for Organizations

In the case of organizations, fraud analytics based on AI requires a systematic, multi-level implementation that involves technology, people and processes. The first step that organizations need to undertake is to evaluate the level of data maturity and develop centralized data governance models that can facilitate safe and ethical AI integration. The interoperability between legacy systems and AI platforms should be implemented in the first place to provide the opportunity to exchange data smoothly and analyze risks in real-time. The managers should implement a staged deployment model- starting with pilot projects, reviewing the results and launching at the enterprise scale after confirmation (H. Li, 2024) . The balanced adoption of IT, compliance, and risk management teams through cross-functional collaboration is achieved. Also, AI literacy, cybersecurity awareness, and ethical risk evaluation of the workforce are necessary to be upskilled to make operations prepared. ROI can be measured by continuous monitoring based on key performance indicators (accuracy, false-positive rates, and response time), and enhance the system adaptability. A strategic alignment of AI efforts with business continuity plans ensures resiliency in the long run, competitive advantage, and assurance of stakeholders regarding the fraud defense system within the company.

9.2 Policy and Ethical Governance

The policy and ethical control will play a fundamental role in ensuring that AI-based fraud analytics would operate in good faith and with transparency. The organizations are supposed to be capable of attracting

AI ethics charters that are consistent to the world values, such as GDPR, EU AI Act, as well as India Digital Personal Data Protection Act (DPDP, 2023). Such policies will be supposed to define fairness, accountability, explainability and reduction of data. The supervisory committees in which the algorithms are analyzed should be included in the models of governance to guarantee the lack of discrimination or prejudices. Ethical governance comprises other characteristics such as model-auditing and human-in-the-loop supervision and the description of the role of AI in decision-making. In addition, data sharing and fraud intelligence processes must be controlled with the assistance of privacy-sensitive and safe systems such as federated analytics or blockchain auditing. (Duan et al., 2024) Global interoperability should be encouraged by regulators and policymakers to align compliance requirements in industries. Finally, ethical governance will help to build trust with the population and make sure that technological innovation in fraud detection should correspond to the values of society, legal requirements, and digital human rights. Table 6 Lays emphasis on the ethical and legal basis needed to have responsible AI-driven fraud prevention.

Table 6. Ethical and policy considerations for AI-based fraud analytics

Ethical Principle	**Description**	**Implementation Strategy**
Fairness	Avoid bias in AI decisions	Balanced training data, bias audits
Transparency	Explain AI decision processes	Use Explainable AI (XAI) tools
Accountability	Human oversight in automated systems	Human-in-the-loop mechanisms
Data Privacy	Protect user identity and data integrity	Federated learning, encryption
Compliance	Align with legal frameworks	GDPR, DPDP, EU AI Act adherence

9.3 Building a Culture of Continuous AI Readiness and Risk Awareness

In addition to the use of technology and governance, the success of AI-driven fraud analytics in the long term will be determined by the ability to foster a culture of lifelong AI preparedness and risk awareness among the organizations. To make sure that AI tools are applied in an effective and ethical way, managers should promote the interdisciplinary cooperation of data scientists, compliance officers, IT teams, and business strategists. Frequent training and awareness sessions are to be performed in order to improve the awareness of the employees about the AI systems, data protection roles, and the emerging patterns of fraud. The creation of internal AI competency centers may assist organizations to be on the forefront of technological change and regulatory demands (Jobin et al., 2019). Moreover, the leadership must encourage the adaptive risk management practices to incorporate the AI-driven insights in everyday decision-making to respond to the threat more quickly. Open communication, cross-functional responsibility and employee involvement brings trust to AI systems and decreases resistance to change. By embedding AI literacy and ethical consciousness into the corporate culture, the companies will be able to be innovative, become more resilient, and apply intelligent systems of fraud detection in a responsible manner. (Ravikumar et al., 2025).

10. CONCLUSION

The conclusion provided in the chapter is that AI-based fraud analytics has completely changed the landscape of cybersecurity deterrence as it makes organizations not defensive in reactive, rule-based defense structures but proactive, predictive, and adaptive. Integration of machine learning, deep learning, natural language processing, and graph neural networks have assisted the institutions to unveil complex cases of fraud that would not have been detected by the traditional systems before. Early intervention and faster response to the opening of threats through anomalies detection in real-time, behavioral trends analysis, and anticipated threats will save much money and risks linked to operations. The case study of JPMorgan

Chase (2024) and Bharti Airtel (2025) is a bright example of the real impact of the introduction of AI in any sphere of the industry, i.e., achieving the results of more than 90% detection rates, minimizing false positives, and accelerating and increasing the scale of the fraud detection system. The examples below show how the role of AI as a strategic requirement and technology innovation to achieve digital resilience has increased.

The chapter also admits that AI-based fraud analytics solutions are based on the automation/human control ratio. Algorithms are highly accurate and quick, whereas morality, contextual perception and accountability are ensured by human intellect. Through transparent governance and responsible AI models, the ethical, legal, and technical concerns, such as algorithmic discrimination, data privacy, explainability, regulatory compliance, etc. should be addressed in this way. The following development that can be made is the cross-sectoral integration, where the federated learning and quantum-enhanced analytics can facilitate the cooperation of the industries and engage privacy-respect and data confidentiality without compromising on data confidentiality.

The future is in the investment in digital infrastructure, AI able to communicate with one another, and international harmonisation of policies. The companies ought to implement explainable and auditable AI into their risk management and develop their culture of a life-long education and ethical responsibility. Finally, AI-based fraud analytics is not defence technology both as a means of defence, but as an active element in the quest to grow confident, transparent and secure in the digital economy. The societies will be able to form strong ecosystems capable of predicting, changing, and overcome the ever-changing threats of cybercrime through a mixture of technology creation and control and human intelligence. The intelligence and integrity of this kind will constitute the characteristic of the new generation of fraud prevention in the world which is becoming more and more interconnected.

REFERENCES

Abdul Salam, M., Fouad, K. M., Elbably, D. L., & Elsayed, S. M. (2024). Federated learning model for credit card fraud detection with data balancing techniques. *Neural Computing & Applications*, *36*(11), 6231–6256. DOI: 10.1007/s00521-023-09410-2

Abrol, S., & Gupta, M. (2023). Role of big data analytics in financial fraud detection-a bibliometric analysis. *Corporate Governance Insight*, *5*(1), 82–111. DOI: 10.58426/cgi.v5.i1.2023.82-111

Adeyemo, K., & Obafemi, F. J. (2024). A survey on the role of technological innovation in Nigerian deposit money bank fraud prevention. *South Asian Journal of Social Studies and Economics*, *21*(3), 133–150. DOI: 10.9734/sajsse/2024/v21i3790

Alfian, A., Ritchi, H., & Adrianto, Z. (2023). Fraud analytics practices in public-sector transactions: A systematic review. *Journal of Public Budgeting, Accounting & Financial Management*, *35*(5), 685–710. DOI: 10.1108/jpbafm-11-2022-0175

Ayinla, B. S., Asuzu, O. F., Ndubuisi, N. L., Ike, C. U., Atadoga, A., & Adeleye, R. A. (2024). Utilizing data analytics for fraud detection in accounting: A review and case studies. *International Journal of Science and ResearchArchive*, *11*(1), 1348–1363. DOI: 10.30574/ijsra.2024.11.1.0221

Bukowski, M. (2023). Combating economic cybercrime using artificial intelligence (AI). *PRZEGLĄD POLICYJNY*, *151*(3), 339–365. DOI: 10.5604/01.3001.0053.9746

Cheng, D., Xiang, S., Shang, C., Zhang, Y., Yang, F., & Zhang, L. (2020). Spatio-temporal attention-based neural network for credit card fraud detection. Proceedings of the ... AAAI Conference on Artificial Intelligence. AAAI Conference on Artificial Intelligence, 34(01), 362–369. https://doi .org/DOI: 10.1609/aaai.v34i01.5371

Chennuri, S. (2024). Advancing fraud detection in banking: Integration of data pipelines, machine learning, and cloud computing. *International Journal For Multidisciplinary Research*, *6*(6). Advance online publication. DOI: 10.36948/ijfmr.2024.v06i06.29893

Choi, D., & Lee, K. (2018). An artificial intelligence approach to financial fraud detection under IoT environment: A survey and implementation. *Security and Communication Networks*, *2018*, 1–15. DOI: 10.1155/2018/5483472

Duan, M., Zheng, T., Gao, Y., Wang, G., Feng, Z., & Wang, X. (2024). DGA-GNN: Dynamic grouping aggregation GNN for fraud detection. Proceedings of the ... AAAI Conference on Artificial Intelligence. AAAI Conference on Artificial Intelligence, 38(10), 11820–11828. https://doi .org/DOI: 10.1609/aaai.v38i10.29067

Farabi, S. F., Ro, M. P., Alam, M., Hossan, M. Z., Ariful, M., Islam, M. R., Uddin, A., Bhuiyan, M., & Biswas, M. Z. A. (2024). Enhancing credit card fraud detection: A comprehensive study of machine learning algorithms and performance evaluation. *Journal of Business and Management Studies*, *6*(3), 252–259. DOI: 10.32996/jbms.2024.6.13.21

Hamon, R., Junklewitz, H., Soler Garrido, J., & Sanchez, I. (2024). Three challenges to secure AI systems in the context of AI regulations. *IEEE Access : Practical Innovations, Open Solutions*, *12*, 61022–61035. DOI: 10.1109/access.2024.3391021

Hasan, K., Hosen, M. N., & Saha, K. (2024). Federated learning for telecom fraud detection: A privacy-preserving approach to overcoming data fragmentation and enhancing security. *European Journal of Theoretical and Applied Sciences*, *2*(6), 99–109. DOI: 10.59324/ejtas.2024.2(6).08

Henderson, R. (2020). Using graph databases to detect financial fraud. *Computer Fraud & Security*, *2020*(7), 6–10. DOI: 10.1016/s1361-3723(20)30073-7

Ikhsan, W. M., Ednoer, E. H., Kridantika, W. S., & Firmansyah, A. (2022). Fraud detection automation through data analytics and artificial intelligence. *Riset*, *4*(2), 103–119. DOI: 10.37641/riset.v4i2.166

Islam, T., Islam, S. A. M., Sarkar, A., Khan, A. J. M. O. R., Paul, R., & Bari, M. S. (2024). Artificial intelligence in fraud detection and financial risk mitigation: Future directions and business applications. *International Journal For Multidisciplinary Research*, *6*(5). Advance online publication. DOI: 10.36948/ijfmr.2024.v06i05.28496

Ismaeil, M. K. A. (2024). Harnessing AI for next-generation Financial Fraud Detection: A data-driven revolution. *Journal of Ecohumanism*, *3*(7), 811–821. DOI: 10.62754/joe.v3i7.4248

Jain, N., & Patil, S. (2024). Artificial intelligence models for fraud detection: Advancements, challenges, and future prospects. International Journal of Global Innovations and Solutions (IJGIS). https://doi.org/DOI: 10.21428/e90189c8.6d8ab5f6

Jobin, A., Ienca, M., & Vayena, E. (2019). The global landscape of AI ethics guidelines. *Nature Machine Intelligence*, *1*(9), 389–399. DOI: 10.1038/s42256-019-0088-2

Li, H. (2024). Biometric-driven digital village governance: A SWOC-enabled model with fraud prevention. *Journal of Electrical Systems*, *20*(3s), 1929–1940. DOI: 10.52783/jes.1732

Li, J., & Yang, D. (2023). Research on financial fraud detection models integrating multiple relational graphs. *Systems*, *11*(11), 539. DOI: 10.3390/systems11110539

Lin, D. (2023). An empirical analysis of machine learning for fraud detection in diverse financial scenarios. Advances in Economics. *Management and Political Sciences*, *42*(1), 202–216. DOI: 10.54254/2754-1169/42/20232110

Macedo, P. S., Coelho Inácio, H., & Vieira, S., E. (2022). A model to detect financial statement fraud in portuguese companies by the auditor. *Contaduría y Administración*, *67*(3), 346. DOI: 10.22201/fca.24488410e.2022.2987

Majumder, T. (2024). The evaluating impact of Artificial Intelligence on risk management and fraud detection in the commercial bank in Bangladesh. *International Journal of Applied and Natural Sciences*, *1*(1), 67–76. DOI: 10.61424/ijans.v1i1.75

Mazumder, S. A., & Rhaman, M. A. (2024). Patient care and financial integrity in healthcare billing through advanced fraud detection systems. Academic Journal on Business Administration. *Innovation & Sustainability*, *4*(2), 10–69593.

Mızrak, F. (2024). Integrating AI with aviation cybersecurity: The strategic role of human resources. *Business And Management Studies An International Journal*, *12*(3), 610–628. DOI: 10.15295/bmij.v12i3.2396

Mohammad, N., Prabha, M., Sharmin, S., Khatoon, R., & Imran, M. A. U. (2024). Combating banking fraud with it: Integrating machine learning and data analytics. *The American Journal of Management and Economics Innovations*, *6*(07), 39–56.

Narooka, P., Arora, S., Srivastava, S., Tiwari, M., & Yadav, S. (2025). Adaptive machine learning system for cybersecurity threats. *Journal of Discrete Mathematical Sciences & Cryptography*, *28*(5-A), 1611–1620. DOI: 10.47974/jdmsc-2161

Nassif, A. B., Talib, M. A., Nasir, Q., & Dakalbab, F. M. (2021). Machine learning for anomaly detection: A systematic review. *IEEE Access : Practical Innovations, Open Solutions*, *9*, 78658–78700. DOI: 10.1109/access.2021.3083060

Novita, N., & Indrany Nanda Ayu Anissa, A. (2022). The role of data analytics for detecting indications of fraud in the public sector. International Journal of Research in Business and Social Science (2147-4478), 11(7), 218–225. https://doi.org/DOI: 10.20525/ijrbs.v11i7.2113

Odeyemi, O., Mhlongo, N. Z., Nwankwo, E. E., & Soyombo, O. T. (2024). Reviewing the role of AI in fraud detection and prevention in financial services. *International Journal of Science and Research Archive*, *11*(1), 2101–2110. DOI: 10.30574/ijsra.2024.11.1.0279

Pan, E. (2024). Machine learning in financial transaction fraud detection and prevention. Transactions on Economics. *Business and Management Research*, *5*, 243–249. DOI: 10.62051/16r3aa10

Ranković, M., Gurgu, E., Martins, O. M. D., & Vukasović, M. (2023). Artificial intelligence and the evolution of finance: Opportunities, challenges and ethical considerations. *EdTech Journal*, *3*(1), 20–23. DOI: 10.18485/edtech.2023.3.1.2

Ravikumar, A. S., & Mamadiyarov, Z. (2025). Mitigating risks through AI-powered fraud detection systems in digital banking. In Innovating Cost-Efficient and Scalable Business Models in the Digital Era (pp. 343–376). IGI Global Scientific Publishing. https://doi.org/DOI: 10.4018/979-8-3373-2120-2.ch011

Rout, S., & Jaiswal, K. (2024). Fraud detection using deep learning. International Journal of Electrical and Data Communication, 5(1), 07–11. https://doi.org/DOI: 10.22271/27083969.2024.v5.i1a.37

S, S. G., & K, S. H. (2023). Detecting financial fraud in the digital age: The AI and ML revolution. International Journal For Multidisciplinary Research, 5(5). https://doi.org/DOI: 10.36948/ijfmr.2023.v05i05.6139

Saluja, S. (2024). Identity theft fraud- major loophole for FinTech industry in India. *Journal of Financial Crime*, *31*(1), 146–157. DOI: 10.1108/jfc-08-2022-0211

Sánchez-Aguayo, M., Urquiza-Aguiar, L., & Estrada-Jiménez, J. (2021). Fraud detection using the fraud triangle theory and data mining techniques: A literature review. *Computers*, *10*(10), 121. DOI: 10.3390/computers10100121

Sipayung, E. S. N., Yanti, H. B., & Setya, A. B. (2023). Impact of anti-fraud awareness, fraud detection procedures, and technology to fraud detection skill. In Advances in Social Science, Education and Humanities Research (pp. 783–787). Atlantis Press SARL. https://doi.org/DOI: 10.2991/978-2-494069-49-7_132

Supriyadi, H., Priyarsono, D. S., Achsani, N. A., & Andati, T. (2024). An integrated GRC approach to combating fraud in microloan services. *International Journal of Innovative Research and Scientific Studies*, *7*(4), 1580–1591. DOI: 10.53894/ijirss.v7i4.3457

Tang, J., & Karim, K. E. (2019). Financial fraud detection and big data analytics – implications on auditors' use of fraud brainstorming session. *Managerial Auditing Journal*, *34*(3), 324–337. DOI: 10.1108/maj-01-2018-1767

Villegas-Ortega, J., Bellido-Boza, L., & Mauricio, D. (2021). Fourteen years of manifestations and factors of health insurance fraud, 2006-2020: A scoping review. *Health & Justice*, *9*(1), 26. DOI: 10.1186/s40352-021-00149-3

Wang, H., Wang, W., Liu, Y., & Alidaee, B. (2022). Integrating machine learning algorithms with quantum annealing solvers for online fraud detection. *IEEE Access : Practical Innovations, Open Solutions*, *10*, 75908–75917. DOI: 10.1109/access.2022.3190897

Werder, K., Ramesh, B., & Zhang, R. (sophia). (2022). Establishing data provenance for responsible artificial intelligence systems. *ACM Transactions on Management Information Systems*, *13*(2), 1–23. DOI: 10.1145/3503488

Yigitcanlar, T., Butler, L., Windle, E., Desouza, K. C., Mehmood, R., & Corchado, J. M. (2020). Can building "artificially intelligent cities" safeguard humanity from natural disasters, pandemics, and other catastrophes? An urban scholar's perspective. *Sensors (Basel)*, *20*(10), 2988. DOI: 10.3390/s20102988

Yuhertiana, I., & Hadi Amin, A. (2024). *Artificial intelligence driven approaches for financial fraud detection: A systematic literature review*. KnE Social Sciences., DOI: 10.18502/kss.v9i20.16551

Zheng, X., Feng, C., Yin, Z., Zhang, J., & Shen, H. (2023). Research on fraud detection method based on heterogeneous graph representation learning. *Electronics (Basel)*, *12*(14), 3070. DOI: 10.3390/electronics12143070

Zhou, J., Cui, G., Hu, S., Zhang, Z., Yang, C., Liu, Z., Wang, L., Li, C., & Sun, M. (2020). Graph neural networks: A review of methods and applications. *AI Open*, *1*, 57–81. DOI: 10.1016/j.aiopen.2021.01.001

KEY TERMS AND DEFINITIONS

Artificial Intelligence (AI): The simulation of human intelligence processes by machines to perform tasks such as learning, reasoning, and problem-solving in an automated manner.

Machine Learning (ML): A subset of AI that enables systems to automatically learn from data, improve from experience, and make predictions or decisions without explicit programming.

Deep Learning (DL): A branch of ML using multi-layered neural networks to model complex relationships within large datasets for advanced pattern and anomaly detection.

Graph Neural Networks (GNNs): AI models that analyze relational data structures to detect hidden connections or fraudulent linkages among entities such as accounts or transactions.

Anomaly Detection: The process of identifying unusual patterns or behaviors in data that deviate from normal activity, often signaling potential fraud or cyber threats.

Behavioral Biometrics: The measurement and analysis of human behavioral patterns—such as typing speed, mouse movement, or navigation habits—for identity verification and fraud prevention.

Federated Learning (FL): A distributed AI approach where multiple institutions collaboratively train models without sharing raw data, preserving privacy and compliance.

Explainable AI (XAI): AI systems designed to make their decisions transparent and interpretable, ensuring accountability and user trust in automated processes.

Quantum Computing: A next-generation computing paradigm using quantum bits (qubits) to perform highly complex calculations exponentially faster than traditional computers, useful for large-scale fraud detection.

Ethical AI Governance: A structured framework ensuring fairness, transparency, and accountability in AI systems to prevent misuse, bias, or unethical outcomes in decision-making.

Data Privacy and Protection: Legal and technical measures ensuring that personal or sensitive data is securely collected, processed, and stored in compliance with regulatory frameworks like GDPR or DPDP Act.

Predictive Analytics: The application of statistical algorithms and ML techniques to forecast future fraud risks based on historical data and behavioral trends.

Cybercrime: Criminal activities carried out using digital technologies, including hacking, phishing, identity theft, ransomware, and financial fraud.

Real-Time Fraud Detection: Immediate identification and mitigation of fraudulent transactions or behaviors using AI models that continuously monitor and analyze live data streams.

Blockchain Auditing: The use of immutable, decentralized ledgers to ensure transparency and traceability of transactions in fraud prevention and compliance monitoring.

Chapter 4
Email-Based Privilege Escalation Attack Detection in Cloud Environments Using Machine Learning

B. Sreedevi
https://orcid.org/0000-0003-1225-4238
SASTRA University, India

S. Barathi
https://orcid.org/0000-0002-9471-9491
Srinivasa Ramanujan Centre, India

ABSTRACT

Cloud computing offers scalable data access and operational efficiency but introduces serious security challenges—most notably, privilege escalation attacks where insiders gain unauthorized administrative control. This project presents a machine learning-based system to detect such attacks through email analysis. Email content is transformed into numerical features using vectorization techniques. Several classifiers including Random Forest, KNN, SVM, XGBoost, and LightGBM are trained on a labeled dataset to differentiate between safe and malicious emails. An ensemble

DOI: 10.4018/979-8-3373-5992-2.ch004

voting classifier ensures higher accuracy and reduces false positives. The system performs real-time detection and generates alerts for suspicious activities, thereby enhancing cloud security against internal threats.

1. INTRODUCTION

This work addresses the challenge of detecting insider threats and privilege escalation in cloud computing by leveraging machine learning (ML), particularly ensemble models such as Random Forest, AdaBoost, and LightGBM (a gradient boosting framework). LightGBM achieved a high detection accuracy of 97% using a customised CERT (Computer Emergency Response Team) dataset. Its strengths lie in its focus on insider threats, use of a realistic dataset, and comparative analysis of multiple ML models. However, limitations include a lack of real-time detection, restricted dataset generalisation, the absence of deep learning and explainability techniques, and a narrow focus on insider threats only. The proposed extension enhances the base methodology by incorporating real-time detection, combining LightGBM with anomaly detection methods such as Isolation Forest (an unsupervised anomaly detection algorithm), applying advanced feature engineering from system behaviour and logs, introducing role-based anomaly detection, and integrating visual dashboards for improved threat monitoring and response. (Homoliak et al., 2019; Butt et al., 2023).

2. LITERATURE SURVEY

The study titled "Detection of Insider Threats using Machine Learning on the CERT Dataset" explored various supervised machine learning (ML) models to detect insider activities, including privilege escalation. Techniques such as Random Forest, Decision Trees, and Support Vector Machine (SVM) were applied to user activity data, including email usage, access logs, and device logs. While detection rates were high, the study reported challenges in real-time deployment and maintaining accuracy across varied user behaviour profiles. Research on ensemble learning for anomaly detection suggested that combining classifiers using techniques such as voting, bagging, or boosting improves the robustness and accuracy of threat detection systems. Studies noted that Random Forest and XGBoost (Extreme Gradient Boosting) yielded high precision, but required proper feature selection and tuning to avoid overfitting on imbalanced datasets. (Zou et al., 2020; Apruzzese et al., 2018).

A study conducted on cloud-based security monitoring emphasised the use of log analysis and user behaviour analytics to detect abnormal privilege access patterns. The proposed systems often relied on log aggregation tools and manual analysis, which limited real-time responsiveness. These works recommended automated detection using lightweight ML models for improved cloud performance. A research work focusing on phishing email classification using ML analysed subject lines and content to detect malicious intent. While this laid the groundwork for email-based analysis, it did not focus on identifying emails that could trigger insider-driven privilege escalation events. This creates a scope for research targeting internal threats initiated via email communication. A study titled "Real-time Threat Detection with Ensemble Machine Learning in Cloud Environments" highlighted the importance of alert generation systems triggered by model predictions. It proposed integrating classification outcomes with real-time dashboards and notification services. The study faced limitations in reducing false positives and ensuring detection scalability across multi-user systems.

Research into access control violations revealed that unauthorised privilege escalation could occur not only via direct system access, but also through indirect methods such as social engineering or malicious internal emails. While access control models have improved, they still lack context-aware detection mechanisms that understand the trigger source, such as communication content. A paper analysing false positives in privilege escalation detection found that static rule-based systems led to alarm fatigue among security teams. The authors suggested machine learning approaches for better contextual detection and outlined the need for improved datasets that reflect real-world privilege misuse scenarios.

Butt et al. (2022) present a cloud-based framework for detecting email phishing attacks based on machine learning and deep learning algorithms, demonstrating that deep learning models outperform traditional approaches in large-scale, real-time cloud environments. Oberoi (2017) conducts a comprehensive survey of major security attacks in cloud-based environments, categorizing threats such as data breaches, denial-of-service, and virtualization attacks, and emphasizing the importance of robust security mechanisms to ensure data confidentiality, integrity, and availability in cloud computing systems.

3. OBJECTIVE

The main objective is to detect and mitigate privilege escalation attacks triggered through email content by leveraging machine learning algorithms within a cloud security framework.

Specific Objectives:

1. To develop a dataset that reflects safe and suspicious email-based privilege escalation behaviour.
2. To pre-process email features (like subject keywords, script patterns, and intent indicators) into a suitable machine-learning format.
3. To apply supervised ML algorithms such as Random Forest, SVM, KNN, XGBoost, and LightGBM.
4. To compare the accuracy and performance of individual models with ensemble voting classifiers.
5. To reduce false positives and enhance the reliability of detection using ensemble approaches.
6. To enable a real-time detection and alert system that notifies cloud administrators upon detecting abnormal privilege access requests.
7. To assess the feasibility and accuracy of deploying such a system in a cloud-based infrastructure.
8. To ensure the solution is lightweight, scalable, and privacy-conscious, particularly in handling internal email communications.

3.1 Existing Work

Current research highlights that securing cloud platforms is essential but challenging, mainly because numerous applications run simultaneously on shared resources. Within this environment, a novel malware detection approach called Trend Micro Locality Sensitive Hashing (TLSH) was proposed, based on clustering techniques. To support this, researchers used the Cuckoo Sandbox, a tool that performs dynamic analysis by executing files in an isolated environment. (Glasser & Lindauer, 2013; Kandias et al., 2010).

Additionally, insider threats remain one of the most expensive and difficult types of attacks to detect, largely because insiders already have access to internal systems and understand the organisation's structure and security mechanisms. Detecting insider-based malware poses its own challenges, including highly imbalanced datasets, limited verified data (ground truth), and evolving user behaviour over time.

3.2 Disadvantages of the Existing System

Data from any provider is stored in the cloud without verifying whether the given packet data is secure or not. This causes attacks on cloud servers. Though scanning for files provides data security, it does not prevent attacks on the network.

- Uses static rule-based detection or signature-based IDS.
- Lacks behavioural analysis of users.
- Cannot adapt to new or zero-day privilege escalation techniques.
- Poor performance against insiders with legitimate access.

3.3 Proposed Work

In order to generate findings that represent real-world situations, this work assumes a realistic context for ml model training. After this, the work emphasises the differences from training under conventional ml conditions. 2) Create and analyse a user-centred insider attack detection process, including data collection, pre-processing, and ml model-based data analysis.

We develop a system where the user's data transfer is verified with the packet data and sent to the server to check the status of the packet as an attacked packet or not. Based on these details' decision is taken for data transferring or data storage.

3.4 Advantages of the Proposed System

The Time taken for prediction is less, and there is no need for any manual process in predicting. Detects four types of attacks and reduces changes of attacks on the cloud. When Data verification is done through a cloud-based platform, an attack is detected, and the security of the cloud will be improved.

3.5 Scope of the Work

The scope of this work encompasses the development of an intelligent privilege escalation attack detection system, focused on analysing email communication patterns within a cloud environment. The system leverages machine learning algorithms to identify suspicious behaviour indicative of unauthorised privilege gains. This work involves the creation of a labelled dataset consisting of email content classified as safe or malicious, which forms the basis for training and evaluating various ML models.

This work involves the implementation of multiple supervised machine learning models—including Random Forest, KNN, SVM, XGBoost, and LightGBM—combined through a voting classifier to enhance detection accuracy and minimise false positives. The models are trained on pre-processed email datasets incorporating features such as subject line cues, the presence of suspicious keywords, and structural characteristics of the emails.

This work also incorporates real-time threat detection, featuring an automated alerting system that promptly notifies administrators of potential privilege escalation attempts. Designed for scalability, the system is well-suited for deployment within cloud infrastructures and can be integrated into cloud-based email platforms or internal security dashboards. The architecture is lightweight and modular, allowing for future enhancements such as live email scanning, integration with SIEM tools, user behaviour analytics, and real-time dashboard visualisation. While the initial scope focuses on email-based detection, the underlying framework is designed to support expansion toward broader insider threat detection use cases in enterprise cloud infrastructures.

4. METHODOLOGY

Data is collected using the CERT dataset and/or cloud log simulations. Then, pre-processing techniques such as cleaning logs, extracting features like user actions, timestamps, and resource access were carried out. After this, future engineering is done by adding behavioural metrics and time-based features. Following that, model training is executed with Train LightGBM, Isolation Forest, and others. Then evaluation is made using metrics like accuracy, precision, recall, and F1-score. Finally, deployment is an optional protocol of streaming logs into the model and generating alerts (Le & Zincir-Heywood, 2019). The above methodology is represented as follows:

1. **Data Collection**
2. **Pre-processing**
3. **Feature Engineering**
4. **Model Training**
5. **Evaluation**
6. **Deployment**

4.1 Ensemble Learning

A hard voting ensemble method is used, where multiple trained classifiers vote on the final output. The majority voting approach improves prediction stability and overall model robustness.

Figure 1 shows the data flow diagram for the proposed system.

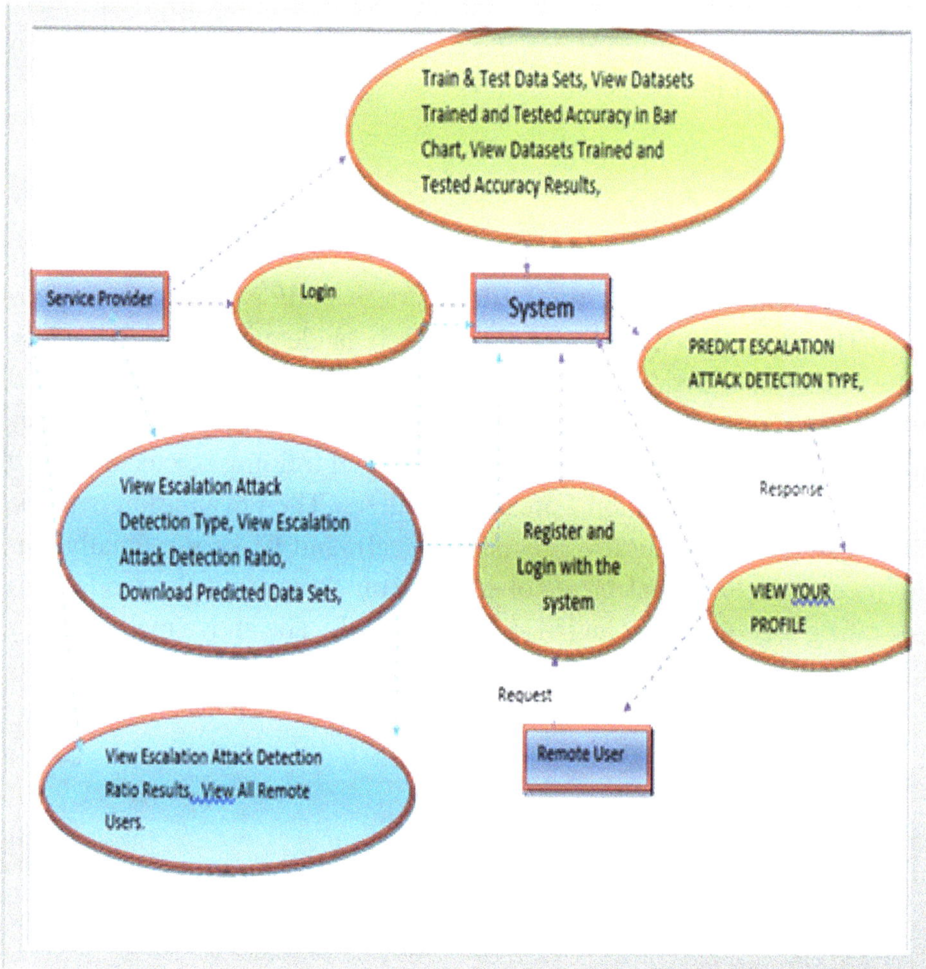

This study explores the application of ensemble machine learning techniques for detecting privilege escalation attacks initiated through insider threats in cloud environments. The research evaluates multiple classifiers and concludes that LightGBM outperforms others in terms of accuracy and robustness. The proposed system effectively identifies suspicious activities by analysing behavioural and access-related data, contributing to proactive cloud security. While LightGBM delivered the highest performance, the study emphasises the benefit of using multi-model ensembles to enhance coverage across varied attack vectors. The findings establish a foundation for developing intelligent, adaptive cloud-based security systems to counter privilege misuse. (Zou et al., 2020).

4.2 Future Enhancement

Future developments could focus on integrating the detection system with real-time monitoring tools and cloud-native security frameworks to enable immediate responses to emerging threats. Incorporation of explainable AI (XAI) techniques can enhance the transparency of detection outcomes, thereby improving the system's usability for security professionals. In addition, the use of behavioural profiling and context-aware feature engineering may strengthen detection capabilities by offering deeper insights into user actions. To improve model generalisation, it is advisable to evaluate the system across multi-tenant cloud environments and diverse email data sources. Moreover, enabling real-time email filtering and designing an intuitive user interface for threat visualisation could significantly enhance the system's operational efficiency and user adoption. The aim of this research is to detect and mitigate privilege escalation attacks within cloud infrastructures by employing advanced machine learning methods. A key focus lies in identifying insider threats who exploit their authorised access to obtain elevated privileges and carry out malicious actions.

4.2.1 Specific Objectives

1. To design and implement a machine learning-driven system capable of detecting and categorising insider threats and privilege escalation attacks.
2. To employ and evaluate ensemble learning algorithms—such as Random Forest, AdaBoost, XGBoost, and LightGBM—with the goal of enhancing detection accuracy.
3. To strengthen detection performance by combining anomaly detection techniques with traditional classification models.
4. To build a system that can be scaled or integrated into real-world cloud service monitoring platforms.

5. To provide early warning signals to security teams and reduce the mean time to detect (MTTD) privilege abuse.

4.3 PROBLEM FORMULATION

4.3.1 Background Problem

In cloud environments, privilege escalation attacks occur when a user—usually an insider—gains access to resources or data beyond their authorisation level. These attacks can be:

- Horizontal: Accessing resources meant for other users at the same level.
- Vertical: Gaining administrative/root privileges illegitimately.
- Traditional security systems often fail to detect such attacks due to:
- Insider access appears "legitimate."
- Lack of behavioural analysis.
- Inability to handle large-scale, dynamic cloud data.

4.3.2 Research Problem

How can we automatically detect and classify privilege escalation attacks—especially those performed by insiders—using machine learning, with high accuracy and low false positives, in a cloud computing environment?

4.3.3 Problem Statement

"Design and implement a machine learning-based framework that leverages classification and anomaly detection techniques to identify and mitigate privilege escalation attacks in cloud environments, particularly those arising from insider threats."

4.3.4 Challenges Identified

- Lack of labelled real-world datasets.
- Differentiating between normal behaviour and malicious behaviour by insiders.
- Building a generalizable model for different cloud setups.
- Balancing detection accuracy with performance overhead.

5. EXPERIMENTAL WORK

This section elaborates on the technical work process involved in designing, developing, and validating a machine learning system that can identify privilege escalation attacks in a cloud environment. The methodology comprises certain steps: preparing the data, creating the model, designing the system architecture, integrating the dashboard, and validating the model.

5.1 Data Collection and Preparation

Dataset Source:

The CERT Insider Threat Dataset (v6.2) developed by Carnegie Mellon Software Engineering Institute was used. It simulates the behaviour of users in a corporate environment, including malicious insiders.

Steps:

File Selection:

Merged data from multiple log types: logon.csv, device.csv, http.csv, email.csv, and file.csv.

Feature Extraction:

Extracted features: user_id, timestamp, logon type, file accessed, access time, event type, resource_id, etc.

Created behavioural features: frequency of access, file transfer rate, and session length.

Labelling:

Malicious sessions labelled as "1", benign sessions as "0". Used available annotations in CERT for labelling insider activities.

Pre-processing:

Null values are handled via imputation or removal. Categorical variables (e.g., usernames, device IDs) were encoded using Label Encoding. Normalised numeric features for model compatibility.

5.2 Model Development and Validation Strategy

Algorithms Implemented:

Random Forest (RF), AdaBoost, XGBoost, LightGBM, Isolation Forest (for unsupervised anomaly detection, integrated in the hybrid model).

Validation Strategy:

- Dataset split: 80% training, 20% testing.
- 10-fold Cross-validation for each model to ensure robustness
- Performance metrics used: Accuracy, Precision, Recall, F1-score and AUC-ROC

5.3 Architecture Design of Predictive Models

System Architecture Components:

The system architecture comprises several integral components. The Data Pipeline is responsible for ingesting user logs from a simulated cloud environment or dataset. It processes and structures these logs into a machine learning (ML)-friendly format. Following this, the Feature Engineering Layer comes into play, focusing on behavioural pattern extraction, session-based aggregation, and triggers for detecting privilege changes.

Next, the Model Training Layer trains multiple ML models using behavioural data. LightGBM serves as the primary model, while XGBoost and Isolation Forest provide secondary inputs to enhance model performance. The ensemble strategy applies a weighted voting mechanism across individual models to determine final predictions. This layer also incorporates outlier scoring to generate alerts for anomalies deemed high-risk.

At the final stage, the output layer generates a risk score ranging from 0 to 100 and categorises each instance into one of three classes: Normal, Suspicious, or Privilege Escalation.

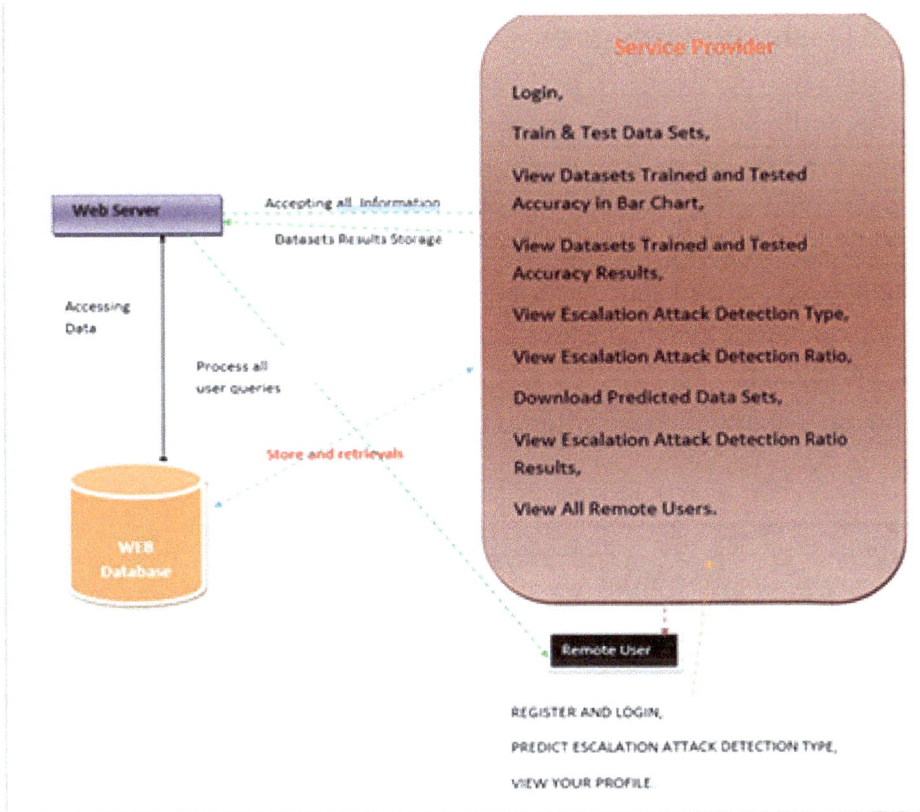

Figure 2 shows the system architecture for privilege escalation detection using ML.

5.4 Frontend Dashboard and Visualisation

5.4.1 Tools Used

The system employs a range of technologies tailored for interactive interface design and data visualisation. Streamlite is used to develop Python-based interactive dashboards, enabling users to efficiently engage with both data and model outputs. For generating insightful visualisations, Matplotlib and Seaborn are utilised to produce detailed plots. Additionally, Grafana can be optionally integrated to support real-time log visualisation, especially when Elastic Search is part of the system architecture.

5.4.2 Dashboard Features

The dashboard provides real-time visualisation of user-specific risk scores, offering immediate insight into potential threats. It includes a variety of graphical representations, such as daily suspicious event trends, user activity timelines, and a heatmap highlighting privilege escalation attempts. To support focused monitoring and in-depth analysis, the interface includes filtering capabilities based on time range, user identity, and activity type.

Figure 3 shows the user login interface.

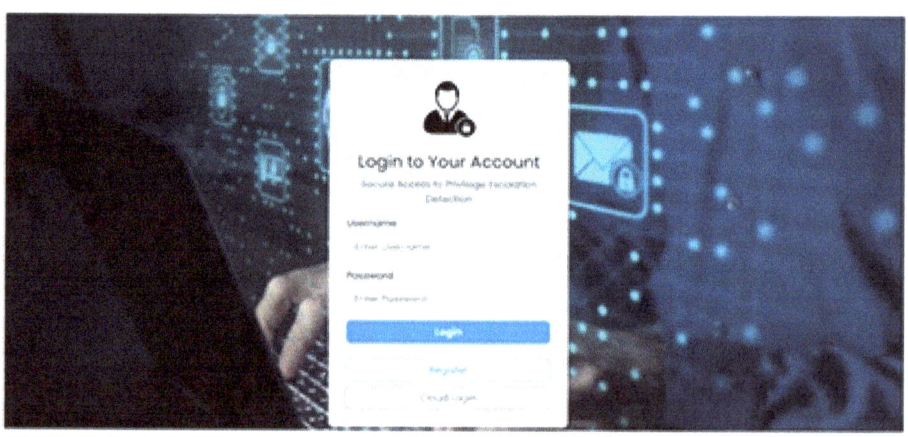

Figure 4 shows the cloud login interface.

Figure 5 provides a remote user profile dashboard with certain features.

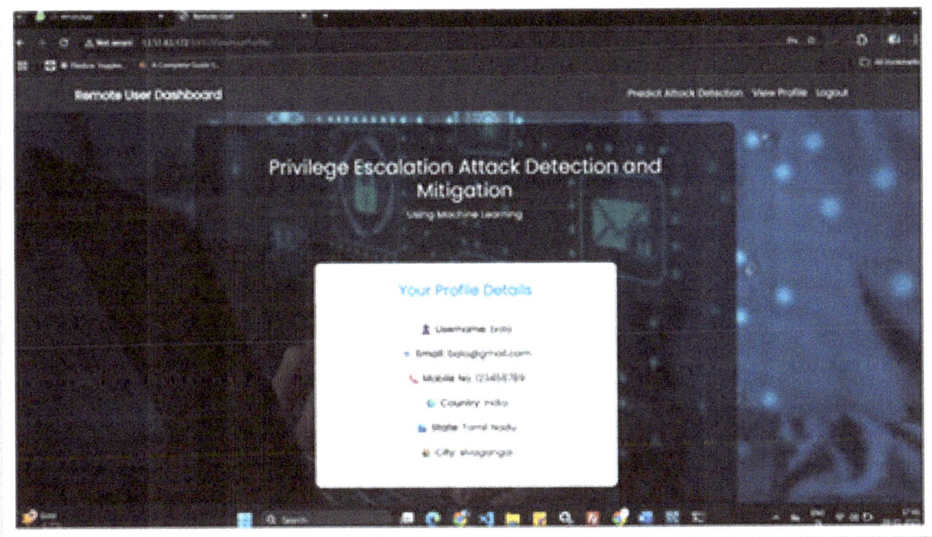

5.5 Model Performance Analysis and Comparative Study

Table 1.

Model	Accuracy(%)	Precision	Recall	F1-Score	AUC-ROC
Random Forest	86.00	0.84	0.83	0.83	0.89
AdaBoost	88.00	0.85	0.87	0.86	0.90
XGBoost	88.27	0.86	0.87	0.86	0.91
LightGBM	97.00	0.96	0.97	0.96	0.98
Isolation Forest (unsupervised)	79.34	-	-	-	0.82

Table 1 elaborates the model performance analysis and comparative study for the experiments conducted.

5.5.1 Observations

LightGBM is found to consistently achieve superior performance across all evaluation metrics, highlighting its effectiveness in modelling behavioural data. AdaBoost and XGBoost exhibit comparable performance, demonstrating strong reliability, particularly when applied to balanced datasets, and thus serve as dependable secondary models. In contrast, Isolation Forest, as an unsupervised algorithm, shows promise in detecting zero-day anomalies—those not previously observed—though it tends to be less effective in scenarios involving known threats. Notably, the hybrid ensemble of LightGBM and Isolation Forest enhances early detection capabilities, particularly in cases involving novel behavioural patterns, making it a valuable asset for proactive anomaly detection strategies.

6. RESULTS AND DISCUSSIONS

This section provides the experimental results of the machine learning models used to detect privilege escalation attacks in cloud environments.

The results are evaluated using standard performance metrics. Additionally, it showcases the role of the frontend interface in visualising alerts and outcomes.

6.1 Evaluation Metrics and Results

To assess the effectiveness of the proposed system, the following evaluation metrics were used:

Evaluation Metrics:

- **Accuracy**: Measures overall correctness of the model
- Formula: **Accuracy = (TP + TN) / (TP + TN + FP + FN)**
- **Precision**: Measures the proportion of positive identifications that were actually correct.
- Formula: **Precision = TP / (TP + FP)**
- **Recall (Sensitivity)**: It measures the percentage of actual positives that were accurately identified.
- Formula: **Recall = TP / (TP + FN)**
- **F1-Score**: Harmonic mean between precision and recall, which gives a balance between them.
- Formula: **F1 = 2 × (Precision × Recall) / (Precision + Recall)**
- **AUC-ROC**: It is expanded as the Area under the Receiver Operating Characteristic curve. It measures the classifier's ability to distinguish between classes — the higher the value, the better the model's performance.

Figure 6 shows the trained model accuracy and alerts the user.

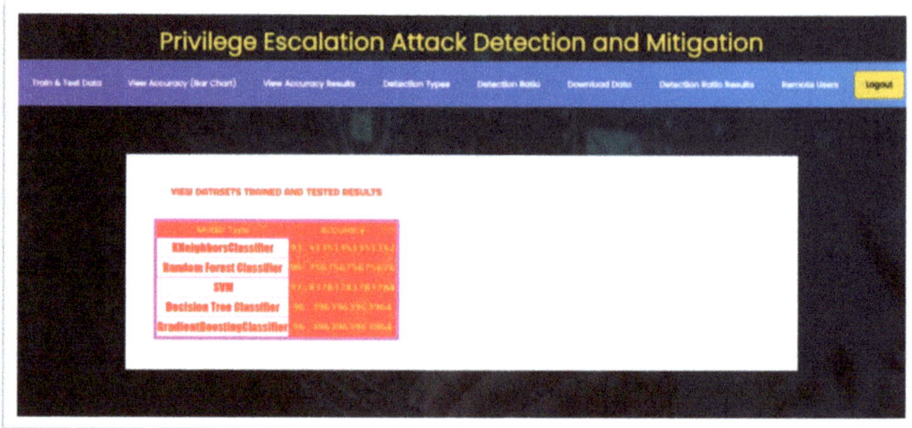

6.2. Result of Machine Learning Models

Table 2.

Model	Accuracy(%)	Precision	Recall	F1-Score	AUC-ROC
Random Forest	86.00	0.84	0.83	0.83	0.89
AdaBoost	88.00	0.85	0.87	0.86	0.90
XGBoost	88.27	0.86	0.87	0.86	0.91
LightGBM	**97.00**	0.96	0.97	0.96	0.98
Isolation Forest (unsupervised)	79.34	-	-	-	0.82

Table 2 shows the results for each ML model trained on the CERT insider threat dataset and tabulated below.

6.2.1 Key Observations

- LightGBM achieved the highest accuracy and AUC-ROC, confirming its superior ability to detect insider threats and privilege escalation.

- AdaBoost and XGBoost were reliable but slightly less accurate.
- Isolation Forest, when unsupervised, was useful for anomaly detection but not as precise as classification.

Figure 7 shows the bar chart for visualisation.

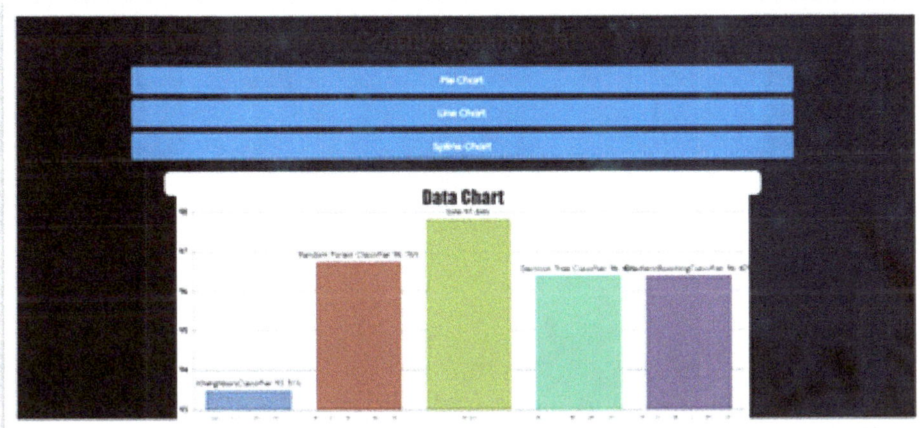

Figure 8 is a pie chart for visualisation.

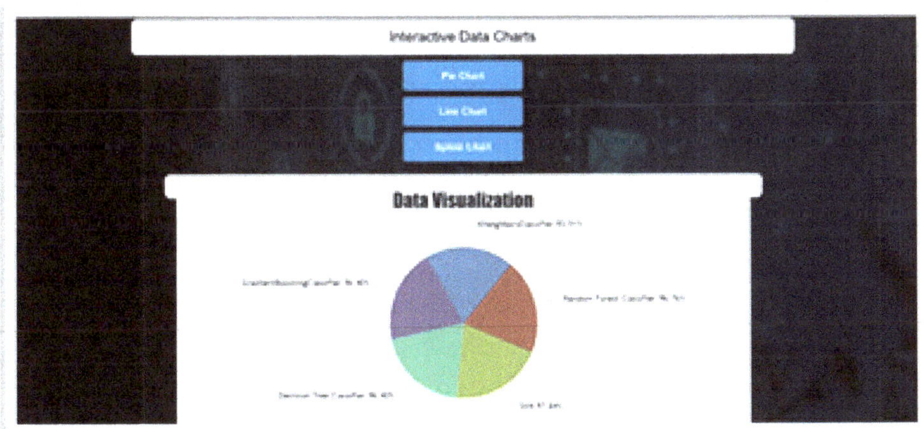

Figure 9 shows a spline chart for visualisation.

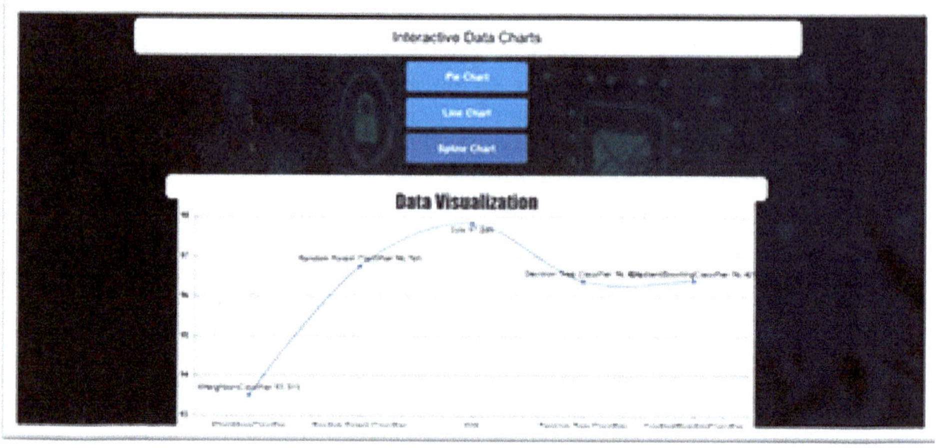

6.3 Front End

A user-friendly frontend dashboard was developed to visualise and interact with the prediction results. The frontend acts as an interface for security analysts to monitor potential insider threats and take necessary action.

Technologies Used:

- **Streamlit (Python)** – for building the web-based UI.
- **Plotly / Seaborn / Matplotlib** – for creating dynamic plots and charts.

6.3.1 Key Features of the Frontend

The system includes several key functionalities to improve security monitoring and user behaviour analysis. The Real-time Risk Score Display shows scores for each user session, with alerts being triggered when scores exceed a configurable threshold. An Activity Timeline provides a visual representation of suspicious user behaviour, featuring interactive filters that allow filtering by user ID, date range, and type of activity, such as login events, file access, or privilege changes. In terms of Graphical Insights, the system includes bar and line graphs that display daily privilege escalation attempts, along with heatmaps that highlight high-risk users or peak times during the day. Additionally, the Export and Logging features enable users to export flagged incidents for auditing purposes, while a log viewer offers access to raw user events and alerts for deeper investigation.

Figure 10 shows the administrator panel for the remote users.

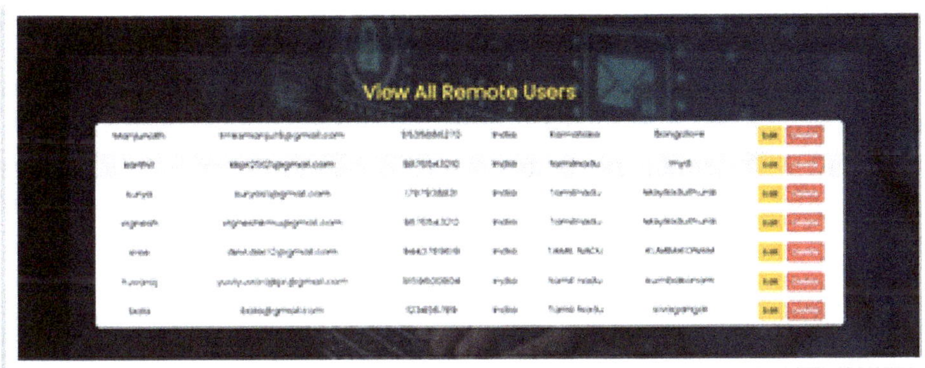

Figure 11 shows the escalation attack.

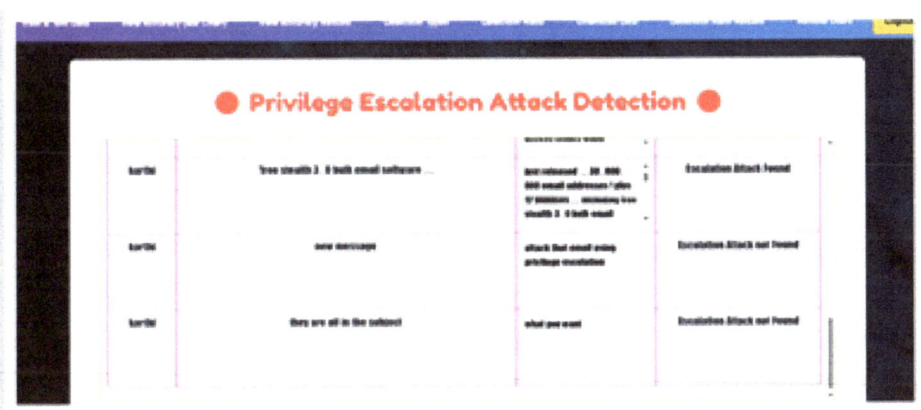

7. CONCLUSION AND FUTURE WORK

7.1 Conclusion

This research focuses on the detection and mitigation of privilege escalation attacks in cloud environments using machine learning techniques, specifically, insider threats. Using the CERT Insider Threat dataset, a series of models was designed and tested for classifying anomalous user behaviour related to potential privilege escalation. Of the applied algorithms—Random Forest, AdaBoost, XGBoost, and LightGBM—only the LightGBM demonstrated superior performance with 97% accuracy rate, the highest F1-score, and AUC. (Homoliak et al., 2019; Ajmal et al., 2022).

Some of the major achievements are:

1. Effective data aggregation across various sources, such as logon events, file access, and emails.
2. Adoption of an ensemble learning technique for enhanced prediction accuracy and robustness.
3. Creation of a Streamlit frontend dashboard for real-time alerting and visualisation.

This system represents a scalable, extensible, and high-accuracy solution for real-world clouds in fighting insider threats and privilege misuse.

7.2 Future Work

Although the initial results are encouraging, there is still room for improvement to boost overall performance as stated below:

Integration with Real-Time Cloud Systems: The model can be extended to operate on live cloud infrastructure (e.g., AWS CloudTrail or Azure Monitor logs).

Deep Learning Approaches: To make temporal behaviour analysis, we can experiment with LSTM or Transformer-based models.

Unsupervised & Semi-supervised Learning: This can be utilised to handle zero-day threats or rare attack patterns not seen during training.

Explainability & Transparency: The use of SHAP or LIME provides explainable AI outputs to aid human analysts.

Multi-Language Log Support: To enhance log parsing to support internationalised systems with varied formats.

REFERENCES

Ajmal, A., Ibrar, S., & Amin, R. (2022). Cloud computing platform: Performance analysis of prominent cryptographic algorithms. *Concurrency and Computation*, *34*(15), e6938. DOI: 10.1002/cpe.6938

Apruzzese, G., Colajanni, M., Ferretti, L., Guido, A., & Marchetti, M. (2018). On the effectiveness of machine and deep learning for cybersecurity. *10th International Conference on Cyber Conflict (CyCon)* (pp. 371–390). IEEE. https://doi.org/DOI: 10.23919/CYCON.2018.8405026

Butt, U. A., Amin, R., Aldabbas, H., Mohan, S., Alouffi, B., & Ahmadian, A. (2022). Cloud-based email phishing attack using machine and deep learning algorithm. *Complex & Intelligent Systems*, •••, 1–28. DOI: 10.1007/s40747-022-00788-9 PMID: 35668732

Butt, U. A., Amin, R., Mehmood, M., Aldabbas, H., Alharbi, M. T., & Albaqami, N. (2023). Cloud security threats and solutions: A survey. *Wireless Personal Communications*, *128*(1), 387–413. DOI: 10.1007/s11277-022-09754-1

Glasser, J., & Lindauer, B. (2013). *Bridging the gap: A pragmatic approach to generating insider threat data. IEEE Security and Privacy Workshops*. IEEE., DOI: 10.1109/SPW.2013.24

Homoliak, I., Toffalini, F., Guarnizo, J. D., Elovici, Y., & Ochoa, M. (2019). Insight into insiders and IT: A survey of insider threat taxonomies, analysis, modeling, and countermeasures. *ACM Computing Surveys*, *52*(2), 1–40. DOI: 10.1145/3303771

Kandias, M., Virvilis, N., & Gritzalis, D. (2010). The insider threat in cloud computing. In *Critical Information Infrastructure Security* (pp. 230–241). Springer., DOI: 10.1007/978-3-642-16806-2_21

Le, D. C., & Zincir-Heywood, A. N. (2019, April). Machine learning based insider threat modelling and detection. In *2019, IFIP/IEEE Symposium on Integrated Network and Service Management (IM)* (pp. 1–6). IEEE. https://doi.org/DOI: 10.23919/INM.2019.8719981

Oberoi, P. (2017). Survey of various security attacks in cloud-based environments. *International Journal of Advanced Research in Computer Science*, *8*(9), 405–410. DOI: 10.26483/ijarcs.v8i9.5012

Touqeer, H., Zaman, S., Amin, R., Hussain, M., Al-Turjman, F., & Bilal, M. (2021). Smart home security: Challenges, issues and solutions at different IoT layers. *The Journal of Supercomputing*, *77*(12), 14053–14089. DOI: 10.1007/s11227-021-03795-y

Zou, S., Sun, H., Xu, G., & Quan, R. (2020). Ensemble strategy for insider threat detection from user activity logs. *Computers, Materials & Continua*, *65*(2), 1321–1334. DOI: 10.32604/cmc.2020.010563

Chapter 5
The Rise of Deepfake Fraud:
Legal Challenges and AI-Driven Detection Strategies

Kaveri Sharma
https://orcid.org/0000-0001-7957-2252
Turon University, Karshi, Uzbekistan

Yunfei Li
Department of Business Sciences, University Giustino Fortunato, Benevento, Italy

Ubaldo Comite
Faculty of Economy, Department of Business Sciences, University of Calabria, Italy

ABSTRACT

Deepfake technology, enabled by advanced AI models like GANs and diffusion networks, has created a new frontier of digital fraud. Its misuse spans financial scams, executive impersonation, political disinformation, and reputational sabotage, producing media nearly indistinguishable from reality. Legal systems remain fragmented and reactive, with inconsistent definitions, weak penalties, and difficulties in establishing liability among creators, platforms, and AI developers. The global spread of deepfakes

DOI: 10.4018/979-8-3373-5992-2.ch005

complicates enforcement, while regulators must balance intervention with freedom of expression. This paper analyzes comparative legal responses in the European Union, United States, India, and China, alongside technological defenses such as AI classifiers, blockchain verification, and biometric tools. It advocates for harmonized laws, stronger detection, and corporate accountability to confront evolving risks.

1. INTRODUCTION

1.1 The Emergence of Deep-Fake Technology

The advent of deepfake technology represents one of the most consequential disruptions in the digital era. Deepfakes, short for "deep learning" + "fake," are synthetic media created using advanced machine learning techniques, particularly Generative Adversarial Networks (GANs) and more recently, diffusion models. Unlike traditional photo or video editing tools, which required significant human intervention and often left detectable artifacts, deepfakes automate the production of hyper-realistic images, voices, and videos that are virtually indistinguishable from authentic recordings (Chesney & Citron, 2019; Mirsky & Lee, 2021).

Originally developed for research and entertainment purposes, deepfakes have quickly proliferated into areas of high risk. Open-source platforms and low-cost software have democratized access to generative AI tools, allowing even non-experts to produce convincing synthetic media. As accessibility has grown, so too has the misuse of this technology, ranging from identity theft and executive impersonation in financial fraud to political disinformation campaigns and cyber-harassment (Vaccari & Chadwick, 2020).

1.2 Real-World Manifestations of Deepfake Fraud

The malicious use of deepfakes is no longer hypothetical. Several high-profile cases illustrate the gravity of the problem. In 2019, a UK-based energy firm lost nearly €220,000 when fraudsters used a deepfake audio to impersonate the voice of the CEO of its German parent company, instructing a wire transfer (Stupp, 2019). Similar scams have been reported in Asia, where executives were tricked into transferring millions of dollars based on fabricated voice calls (Noto, 2024).

Beyond financial fraud, deepfakes have been deployed in political contexts. For example, manipulated videos of global leaders have circulated during election campaigns, threatening democratic processes and amplifying disinformation (Sandoval et al., 2024). Deepfakes are also weaponized in gendered harassment, with women disproportionately targeted through non-consensual pornographic deepfakes (Cheng, 2024). The scale and diversity of these incidents demonstrate that deepfake fraud is not confined to one domain but spans financial, political, social, and personal spheres, making it a multidimensional threat.

1.3 Legal Frameworks: Lagging Behind Technology

Despite the exponential rise of deepfake-related crimes, legal systems worldwide have struggled to keep pace. Laws addressing fraud, impersonation, or defamation predate deepfake technology and are often inadequate to capture its unique attributes. For example, while the European Union's AI Act proposes restrictions on high-risk AI systems and mandates transparency in synthetic content, it does not yet provide detailed enforcement mechanisms specific to deepfakes (Ebers et al., 2021). In the United States, the regulatory approach remains fragmented, with a patchwork of state-level laws (e.g., Virginia and Texas banning deepfake election disinformation) but no comprehensive federal legislation. India, under the Information Technology Act (2000) and proposed Digital India Bill, has yet to formulate specific statutory provisions on deepfake fraud (Vajiram Content Team, 2023).

These gaps create significant enforcement challenges. Courts struggle with evidentiary issues, as distinguishing authentic from synthetic media requires advanced forensic tools not always available to investigators. Moreover, jurisdictional issues complicate matters, since deepfakes are disseminated globally across decentralized platforms. The absence of uniform definitions and penalties further enables perpetrators to exploit legal loopholes, making deepfake fraud one of the most difficult crimes to prosecute effectively.

1.4 Ethical Dilemmas and Competing Rights

The regulation of deepfakes also raises ethical and constitutional dilemmas. At the heart of the debate lies the tension between freedom of expression and the need to prevent harm. Generative AI, including deepfakes, has legitimate applications in film, education, and accessibility. Overly broad bans risk stifling innovation and infringing upon artistic or satirical expression. Conversely, insufficient regulation exposes individuals and institutions to reputational harm, financial loss, and democratic destabilization (Chesney & Citron, 2019).

This ethical balancing act complicates policymaking. Unlike traditional fraud or defamation, deepfake misuse blurs lines between satire, parody, misinformation, and malicious manipulation. Determining intent is often subjective, yet it is essential for legal accountability. Consequently, regulatory frameworks must evolve with nuance, targeting malicious intent while protecting legitimate expression.

1.5 AI-Driven Detection Strategies: a Technological Counterbalance

While legal systems grapple with regulation, technological communities are developing AI-driven detection strategies. Detection tools based on machine learning classifiers analyze inconsistencies in pixelation, audio frequencies, or facial micro-expressions to identify synthetic media (Mirsky & Lee, 2021). More advanced methods employ blockchain-based verification systems, embedding immutable records of authentic content at the point of creation, and biometric verification technologies, which use multi-factor authentication to confirm speaker or actor identities (Rana et al., 2022).

However, detection faces a perpetual arms race. As generative models improve, they reduce detectable artifacts, making even state-of-the-art classifiers less reliable over time. Research shows that detection accuracy can fall below 60% when confronted with next-generation diffusion-based deepfakes (Bendiab et al., 2025). This underscores the need for continuous investment in detection R&D and collaboration between AI researchers, regulators, and private firms to maintain technological resilience.

1.6 Objectives of the Study

Although deepfake fraud has garnered significant academic and media attention, existing scholarship remains fragmented across technical, legal, and ethical silos. Most studies focus either on algorithmic detection techniques (Rana et al., 2022) or on legal frameworks for online harms, with limited integration of the two. Few comparative analyses exist that bridge the gap between technological countermeasures and legal responses, particularly across diverse jurisdictions.

This study seeks to fill this gap by adopting a comparative, interdisciplinary approach. Specifically, it aims to:

i. To analyze the evolution and manifestations of deepfake fraud, with a focus on financial, political, and reputational harms.
ii. To evaluate the adequacy of legal frameworks in addressing deepfake misuse across the EU, US, India, and China.
iii. To assess emerging AI-driven detection strategies, including classifiers, blockchain verification, and biometric tools.
iv. To develop an integrated framework for legal-technical governance of deepfake fraud.

By sitting down fraud within the broader discourse of AI governance and digital security, this chapter contributes to both legal scholarship and technological research.

1.7 Structure of the Chapter

The remainder of this chapter is structured as follows: Section 2 provides a literature review of theoretical foundations, legal responses, and technological innovations surrounding deepfake fraud. Section 3 outlines the methodology, including doctrinal legal analysis and secondary case studies. Section 4 presents the results, offering comparative insights into regulatory landscapes and detection tools. Section 5 provides a discussion that situates these findings within broader ethical and policy debates. Finally, Section 6 concludes with recommendations for harmonizing law and technology in addressing the deepfake threat.

2. LITERATURE REVIEW

2.1 Theoretical Foundations: Digital Fraud, AI Governance, and Cyberlaw

Deepfake fraud sits at the intersection of cybercrime, AI governance, and digital rights law. From a fraud perspective, deepfakes exemplify a new class of deception that leverages synthetic identities to manipulate decision-making, akin to but more advanced than phishing or identity theft. AI governance frameworks emphasize transparency, accountability, and human oversight, yet struggle to adapt to generative models that create convincingly false representations (Cath, 2018). In the legal domain, cyberlaw has historically addressed harms through statutes on impersonation, defamation, and data protection, but these provisions are often inadequate to capture the unique synthetic realism of deepfakes.

Theoretical debates also highlight responsibility gaps: should liability rest with the deepfake creator, the hosting platform, or the developers of generative AI models? Scholars argue that without a shared responsibility framework, regulatory interventions will remain reactive and fragmented (Chesney & Citron, 2019; Dabas, 2024). This tension underscores the need for interdisciplinary approaches that merge legal reasoning with technical realities.

2.2 Evolution of Deepfake Technology: From GANs to Diffusion Models

Deepfakes are enabled by GANs, introduced by Goodfellow et al. (2014), which pit a generator against a discriminator to iteratively improve synthetic media realism. While GANs powered early deepfakes, recent breakthroughs in diffusion models (e.g., Stable Diffusion, DALL·E, MidJourney) have dramatically enhanced fidelity and accessibility (Ramesh et al., 2022).

The democratization of these tools has lowered entry barriers. Open-source repositories and "deepfake-as-a-service" platforms allow non-technical users to create synthetic voices and videos within minutes (Mirsky & Lee, 2021). Studies show that by 2023, over 85,000 deepfake videos were circulating online, with exponential growth projected (Bendiab, 2025). Importantly, while research initially emphasized benign uses-such as entertainment or accessibility-misuse has quickly dominated, from financial scams to gender-based harassment (Cheng, 2024).

The literature underscores a critical arms race dynamic: as generative models improve, detection systems degrade, requiring perpetual innovation in forensic science (Rana et al., 2022).

2.3 Deepfake Fraud in Practice: Financial, Political, and Social Harms

Empirical studies document the diverse harm caused by deepfakes. In the financial sector, manipulated audio and video have been used to authorize fraudulent transfers by impersonating executives (Stupp, 2019). A recent case in Hong Kong involved a deepfake video call that defrauded a company of USD 25 million, demonstrating the escalating stakes (Noto, 2024).

In the political domain, deepfakes have amplified disinformation campaigns, especially around elections. Vaccari and Chadwick (2020) argue that deep-fake disinformation undermines democratic trust by blurring distinctions between truth and fabrication. The U.S. 2020 elections and the 2019 Indian elections both saw deepfake videos used for political propaganda (Sandoval et al., 2024).

At the societal level, deepfakes have disproportionately harmed women, who are targeted in non-consensual pornographic content. A study by Cheng (2024) revealed that over 90% of deepfakes online are pornographic, raising serious concerns about digital safety and gender-based violence.

The literature highlights that these harms are not isolated but mutually reinforcing financial losses, reputational damage, and political instability converge to create systemic risks.

2.4 Legal Responses: Fragmented and Reactive

The rise of deepfakes has created profound challenges for regulators and policymakers worldwide. Unlike traditional digital manipulation, deepfakes employ advanced artificial intelligence techniques, producing synthetic media that is almost indistinguishable from authentic content. This technological sophistication has outpaced the ability of legal systems to respond, resulting in fragmented, reactive, and largely insufficient regulatory frameworks. Scholars across jurisdictions converge on the assessment that laws addressing deepfakes remain piecemeal, jurisdictionally inconsistent, and reactive rather than anticipatory (Łabuz, 2023). The following analysis examines legal responses in the European Union, the United States, India, and China, highlighting the comparative strengths and limitations of each, before drawing broader conclusions on the inadequacies of current frameworks.

2.4.1 European Union

The European Union has taken some of the most ambitious steps toward regulating artificial intelligence broadly, with implications for deepfakes. The proposed EU Artificial Intelligence Act (2022) classifies deepfakes under the category of "high-risk AI systems." Under this framework, developers and distributors of deepfake technologies must adhere to transparency obligations, such as clearly labeling synthetic media and ensuring traceability mechanisms. These requirements reflect a proactive recognition of the potential harms posed by deepfakes in political manipulation, financial fraud, and reputational damage (Ebers et al., 2021).

However, legal scholars note significant shortcomings in this approach. Enforcement mechanisms under the AI Act are uneven, as responsibility for oversight rests with national regulatory authorities, leading to potential disparities in enforcement across member states. Furthermore, penalties for non-compliance are not harmonized, leaving gaps that can be exploited by perpetrators or corporations operating across borders (Łabuz, 2023). Another limitation is that the Act focuses on ex ante compliance obligations rather than ex post remedies, meaning that victims of deepfake harms may still face difficulties obtaining redress once damage has occurred. The EU framework is therefore an important step toward codifying deepfake governance but remains incomplete in addressing cross-border enforcement and victim protection.

2.4.2 United States

In contrast to the EU's supranational effort, the United States lacks federal legislation specifically targeting deepfakes. Instead, regulation has been left largely to the states, producing a patchwork of legal responses. States such as Virginia and Texas have enacted statutes addressing deepfakes in particular contexts, such as election-related disinformation and non-consensual deepfake pornography. These laws criminalize the creation or distribution of synthetic media that aims to mislead voters or exploit individuals sexually without consent.

While these state-level initiatives mark an acknowledgment of the deepfake threat, critics argue that the fragmented approach leaves significant loopholes. A perpetrator in one state may operate across multiple jurisdictions, complicating enforcement and leaving victims without clear avenues for legal remedy. Moreover, federal regulatory silence has meant that platforms hosting deepfake content—many of which operate nationally and internationally face no uniform obligations to remove or label such content. The reliance on existing doctrines such as defamation, fraud, or copyright infringement is ill-suited to the unique challenges of synthetic media, particularly given evidentiary hurdles in proving falsity and intent. In sum, U.S. regulation of deepfakes exemplifies a reactive and decentralized model that risks undermining consistent enforcement and victim protection.

2.4.3 India

India, as one of the world's largest digital markets, faces growing challenges related to deepfakes but has yet to enact a dedicated legal framework addressing the phenomenon. Instead, deepfakes are subsumed under broader provisions of the Information Technology Act (2000). Section 66D of the Act criminalizes "cheating by impersonation using computer resources," which may apply to deepfake-based fraud or identity theft. Similarly, Section 67 addresses the transmission of obscene material in electronic form, potentially encompassing non-consensual sexual deepfakes (Vajiram Content Team, 2023).

While these provisions can be invoked to prosecute certain deepfake offenses, their generality highlights the absence of a targeted statute. The lack of specific recognition of synthetic media fraud results in doctrinal ambiguity, with courts left to interpret outdated statutory language in light of new technological harms. This not only undermines evidentiary admissibility—since deepfakes challenge traditional notions of digital authenticity—but also raises questions about jurisdictional clarity, as deepfakes are often disseminated transnationally. Furthermore, India lacks clear regulatory obligations on platforms to detect or remove deepfake content, relying instead on general intermediary liability rules. Consequently, victims often face prolonged litigation with uncertain outcomes, underscoring the insufficiency of India's current legal approach.

2.4.4 China

China represents a unique case of proactive but highly surveillance-oriented regulation. In 2019, the Cyberspace Administration of China (CAC) introduced rules mandating that all deepfake content be clearly labeled as synthetic. The regulations also hold platforms accountable for ensuring compliance, requiring them to remove or flag unlabeled deepfakes. This approach aims to curb the spread of misinformation and prevent reputational and political harms associated with synthetic media (Latham & Watkins LLP, 2023).

While scholars acknowledge the effectiveness of China's framework in addressing deepfakes at scale, concerns remain regarding its broader implications for human rights and freedom of expression. By embedding deepfake governance within an already expansive surveillance apparatus, China's regulatory approach risks conflating legitimate creative uses of synthetic media—such as satire or art—with malicious applications.

Moreover, critics argue that the emphasis on state control and censorship undermines individual autonomy and raises questions about proportionality. Nonetheless, China's proactive stance contrasts with the reactive postures of other jurisdictions, demonstrating both the promise and perils of stringent deepfake regulation.

2.4.5 Comparative Analysis

Across these jurisdictions, comparative analyses confirm that most laws subsumed deepfakes under broader cybercrime or media laws, rather than treating them as distinct threats. This lack of specificity undermines the legal system's ability to address the unique evidentiary and jurisdictional challenges posed by synthetic media. For instance, existing obscenity or fraud statutes may capture certain deepfake harms, but they often fail to account for the distributed and transnational nature of deepfake dissemination. Moreover, without clear statutory definitions, courts face difficulties in adjudicating whether a given piece of content qualifies as a deepfake, creating uncertainty in evidence admissibility.

Another recurring challenge lies in cross-border enforcement. Deepfake content is frequently created in one jurisdiction, hosted in another, and consumed globally. Without harmonized legal frameworks, perpetrators can exploit jurisdictional gaps to evade accountability. The EU's AI Act, for example, cannot bind non-EU actors unless they operate within the EU market, while the U.S. state-level model offers little protection for victims abroad. India's reliance on general IT provisions illustrates the inadequacy of retrofitting old statutes to new technological realities, while China's surveillance-heavy model raises normative questions about whether regulatory efficiency can justify restrictions on civil liberties.

The fragmented nature of legal responses also reveals a reactive tendency. Rather than anticipating harms, most jurisdictions legislate only after deepfake scandals emerge—whether in the form of political disinformation campaigns, celebrity pornographic deepfakes, or financial fraud. This leaves societies vulnerable to the next wave of deepfake innovations, such as real-time synthetic voice cloning or interactive AI avatars. The law's reactive character thus creates a persistent lag between technological capabilities and regulatory safeguards.

The comparative evidence demonstrates that legal responses to deepfakes remain fragmented, reactive, and insufficient. The EU offers a promising model of proactive regulation through the AI Act but faces issues of enforcement consistency. The United States, hampered by federal inaction, relies on a patchwork of state laws that fail to address cross-jurisdictional harms. India relies on outdated IT Act provisions, leaving deepfake victims vulnerable to evidentiary and procedural uncertainties. China, while proactive, adopts a surveillance-heavy model that sacrifices individual rights for regulatory efficiency. Taken together, these cases reveal that the global legal order has yet to develop a harmonized, anticipatory, and rights-sensitive framework for governing deepfakes. Until such frameworks emerge, perpetrators will continue to exploit gaps in jurisdictional authority and enforcement, leaving societies exposed to the multifaceted harms of synthetic media.

2.5 AI-Driven Detection Research

Parallel to legal debates, technical scholarship has advanced AI-driven detection strategies. Early efforts focused on neural network classifiers that detect pixel-level inconsistencies, blinking patterns, or frequency mismatches (Mirsky & Lee, 2021). More recent methods employ multimodal forensic tools, integrating audio, video, and text signals for higher accuracy (Rana et al., 2022)

Emerging approaches include:

i. Blockchain-based authenticity markers, embedding immutable metadata to verify original content (Bendiab et al., 2025).
ii. Watermarking techniques, inserting invisible signals into synthetic media (Yu et al., 2021).
iii. Biometric authentication, cross-verifying speaker/actor identity against registered data.

However, detection faces challenges of accuracy, explainability, and scalability. Studies indicate that detection systems degrade rapidly as new generative models emerge, falling below 60% accuracy in some benchmarks (Zhou et al., 2023). Scholars emphasize the need for continuous R&D investment and public–private partnerships to sustain resilience.

2.6 Ethical and Constitutional Debates

Literature also explores the ethical dilemmas surrounding deepfake regulation. On one hand, deepfakes enable artistic, educational, and accessibility benefits (e.g., restoring voices for the speech-impaired). On the other hand, misuse undermines trust in media ecosystems. This duality complicates constitutional debates on free expression versus harm prevention (Chesney & Citron, 2019).

Scholars warn of over-regulation risks, where broad bans stifle innovation and legitimate uses, and under-regulation risks, where inaction erodes democratic trust (Dabas, 2024). Calls for algorithmic accountability stress transparency in AI models, auditability of training datasets, and human oversight in enforcement (Cath, 2018).

2.7 Gaps in Existing Literature

Synthesizing across domains, the literature reveals four critical gaps:

i. **Integration gap**: Most studies examine either legal frameworks or technical detection, with limited interdisciplinary synthesis.
ii. **Comparative gap**: Few works conduct detailed cross-jurisdictional analysis beyond Western contexts.
iii. **Scalability gap**: Detection research rarely addresses real-time, global deployment challenges.
iv. **Governance gap**: Limited exploration of global norms and cross-border enforcement mechanisms.

This study addresses these gaps by integrating comparative legal analysis with technical assessment, focusing on the EU, US, India, and China, while proposing a regulatory risk matrix that links fraud typologies to policy priorities.

3. METHODOLOGY

3.1 Research Design

This study adopts an interdisciplinary methodology that bridges legal scholarship and technical research to investigate the phenomenon of deepfake fraud. The design rests on three pillars: comparative legal analysis, doctrinal review, and technical assessment. Comparative legal analysis evaluates statutes, regulations, and judicial decisions across key jurisdictions-United States, European Union, India, and China-chosen for their diverse regulatory approaches and geopolitical influence. The doctrinal review scrutinizes legal concepts such as intent, liability, and evidence admissibility in the context of synthetic media. In parallel, a technical assessment surveys state-of-the-art detection methods, with emphasis on neural network classifiers, blockchain-based authenticity markers, and multimodal forensic tools.

This combination provides both breadth (cross-jurisdictional comparisons) and depth (intra-jurisdictional doctrinal reasoning), enabling a holistic understanding of how law and technology interact in addressing deepfake fraud.

3.2 Data Sources

The research relies exclusively on secondary data to ensure reliability and traceability. Legal data sources include:

i. Statutes, such as the Information Technology Act (India, 2000), the EU AI Act (2022 draft), and the U.S. Communications Decency Act (Section 230).
ii. Judicial responses, including U.S. state-level deepfake cases and European Court of Justice decisions on digital impersonation.
iii. Regulatory documents from agencies such as the Ebers et al. (2021), and Chinese Cyberspace Administration.

Technical data sources include:

i. Peer-reviewed articles from journals in AI, computer vision, and cybersecurity.
ii. Benchmarking reports on deepfake detection accuracy (e.g., Media Forensics Challenge datasets).
iii. White papers from technology firms experimenting with blockchain watermarking and biometric verification.

Triangulation across legal and technical sources enhances the validity and robustness of findings.

3.3 Comparative Legal Analysis

The comparative analysis covers four jurisdictions:

i. **United States**: A patchwork of state-level deepfake laws addressing election disinformation (e.g., Texas, Virginia) and pornography-related offenses.
ii. **European Union**: The AI Act (2022) and GDPR provisions on identity and data protection.
iii. **India**: The Information Technology Act (2000) and the proposed Digital India Bill, with indirect application to deepfakes.
iv. **China**: 2019 regulations requiring labeling of synthetic media and platform accountability.

By comparing these frameworks, the study evaluates convergence (shared principles) and divergence (context-specific gaps), providing insights into the feasibility of global harmonization.

3.4 Technical Assessment

To assess AI-driven detection strategies, this study reviews the three main categories of methods:

i. **Neural network classifiers**: Machine learning models that identify artifacts in images, audio, or video. Benchmarks were drawn from studies using datasets such as FaceForensics++.
ii. **Blockchain-based authenticity markers**: Immutable verification of original content metadata, reducing reliance on detection after dissemination.
iii. **Multimodal forensic tools**: Cross-verification of audio, video, and textual cues to improve detection reliability.

The evaluation considered accuracy, explainability, scalability, and ethical implications, recognizing that technical detection is not value-neutral but raises questions of surveillance and privacy.

3.5 Analytical Framework

The methodology applies a three-stage analytical framework:

i. **Stage 1**: Map the manifestations of deepfake fraud (financial, political, reputational, and social harms).
ii. **Stage 2**: Analyze legal responses and gaps across jurisdictions.
iii. **Stage 3**: Assess technical detection tools, examining their capacity to mitigate fraud and their ethical trade-offs.

Figure 1. Deepfake Fraud Analysis Framework

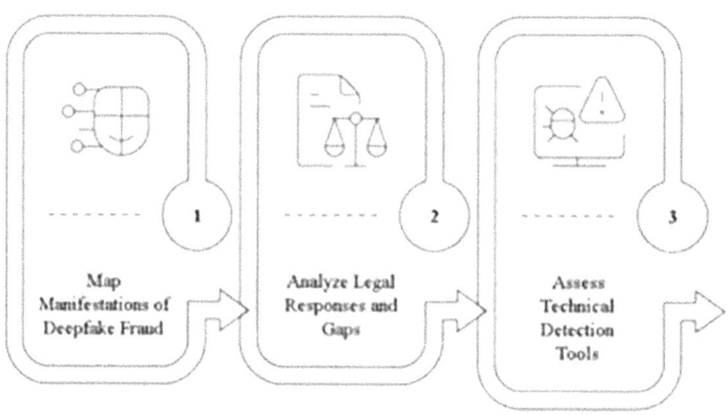

Findings from these three stages are synthesized to propose a regulatory risk matrix that links specific fraud scenarios to policy priorities and detection feasibility.

3.6 Ethical Considerations

While this study did not involve primary participants, ethical scholarship was maintained by:

i. Using only open-access and credible secondary sources.
ii. Avoiding misrepresentation of statutes or detection accuracy.
iii. Acknowledging the dual-use nature of detection technologies, which may also be weaponized for surveillance.

3.7 Limitations

The methodology is subject to three main limitations. First, reliance on secondary data may omit emerging unpublished regulatory developments. Second, comparative legal analysis is restricted to four jurisdictions, potentially limiting generalizability. Third, the evaluation of detection methods is descriptive rather than experimental, due to resource constraints. Nonetheless, these limitations are offset by the breadth of sources and interdisciplinary synthesis, ensuring meaningful insights.

Table 1. Overview of Jurisdictions and Detection Methods Analyzed

Jurisdiction	Key Legal Instruments	Enforcement Challenges	Detection Methods Surveyed
United States	State laws (TX, VA), no federal law	Fragmentation; intent proof	Classifiers; biometric verification
European Union	AI Act (2022 draft), GDPR	Enforcement gaps; lack of penalties	Blockchain authenticity; watermarking
India	IT Act (2000), Digital India Bill (proposed)	Outdated provisions; limited capacity	Multimodal forensics; classifiers
China	2019 Deep Synthesis Rules	Overregulation; human rights concerns	Platform-embedded detection

4. RESULTS

4.1 Comparative Legal Findings

The analysis of legal frameworks across four jurisdictions-United States, European Union, India, and China-reveals that regulation remains fragmented, reactive, and inconsistent. While each jurisdiction has initiated measures to address synthetic media, most rely on pre-existing cybercrime, defamation, or data protection laws rather than deepfake-specific legislation.

Table 2. Comparative Legal Approaches to Deepfake Regulation (2020–2024)

Jurisdiction	Regulatory Instruments	Coverage	Key Strengths	Key Weaknesses
United States	Patchwork of state laws (e.g., TX, VA bans on election deepfakes; CA ban on pornographic deepfakes); Section 230 CDA	Limited to elections, pornography, harassment	Addresses targeted harms	No federal law; evidentiary challenges; loopholes in Section 230
European Union	AI Act (2022 draft); GDPR (identity/data protection); DSA (2022)	Deepfakes labeled as "high-risk AI"; transparency mandates	Comprehensive framework; labeling obligations	No dedicated enforcement mechanisms; penalties vague
India	IT Act (2000), IPC provisions, proposed Digital India Bill	Impersonation, obscenity, cyber fraud	Legal foundation for prosecutions	Outdated statutes; no explicit deepfake provisions; weak institutional capacity
China	Deep Synthesis Regulations (2019), Cybersecurity Law	Requires labeling; platforms accountable	Proactive; enforcement clear	Raises surveillance & rights concerns; innovation risks

The results indicate that China's approach is the most direct, mandating content labeling and platform accountability, but at the cost of civil liberties. The EU provides the broadest governance framework through the AI Act and GDPR yet lacks robust enforcement mechanisms. The US remains fragmented, with state-level laws filling the federal gap. India shows the widest gap, relying on outdated provisions that fail to address synthetic realism directly.

4.2 Case Analyses of Deep-Fake Fraud

Real-world incidents illustrate the systemic risks of deep fakes across financial, political, and social domains.

Table 3. Selected Deepfake Fraud Cases (2019–2024)

Year	Domain	Incident	Outcome/Impact
2019	Financial	UK energy firm executive voice deepfaked, €220,000 fraud (Stupp, 2019)	Successful fraud; first corporate case reported
2020	Political	Deepfake of Indian politician circulated during election	Spread misinformation; raised electoral integrity concerns
2021	Gendered Harassment	Non-consensual pornographic deepfakes of celebrities	Online harassment; reputational harm; platforms slow to act
2022	Financial	Deepfake impersonation scam in Hong Kong, USD 25 million fraud (Noto, 2024)	Highlighted cross-border enforcement gaps
2023	Disinformation	Synthetic video of Ukrainian President urging surrender	Viral spread; countered by official denial
2024	Corporate Fraud	Deepfake CEO video call duped multinational into transferring USD 11 million	Demonstrates sophistication of deepfake fraud

i. Financial fraud cases reveal the direct economic costs of deepfakes, with losses in the millions.
ii. Political deepfakes threaten democratic legitimacy, fueling disinformation campaigns.
iii. Gendered harassment cases highlight the disproportionate targeting of women, underscoring gendered digital harms.
iv. Corporate impersonation scams demonstrate that organizational cybersecurity policies remain ill-prepared for synthetic media threats.

4.3 AI Detection Strategies: Efficacy and Limitations

The technical assessment of AI-driven detection tools reveals progress, but also critical limitations.

Table 4. AI Detection Methods and Limitations

Detection Strategy	Mechanism	Strengths	Limitations
Neural Network Classifiers	Identify pixel inconsistencies, blinking patterns, frequency mismatches	Widely tested; benchmark datasets available	Accuracy degrades with new generative models; explainability issues
Blockchain Authenticity Markers	Immutable metadata embedded at content creation	Tamper-proof verification; strong for provenance	Requires adoption at creation stage; scalability concerns
Multimodal Forensics	Cross-verifies audio, video, text	Higher accuracy (up to 85% in lab tests)	Computationally expensive; limited real-time deployment
Watermarking	Invisible digital signatures embedded in AI output	Easy to enforce via policy mandates	Can be removed or obfuscated; requires compliance
Biometric Authentication	Compares with registered identities	Strong individual verification	Raises privacy and surveillance concerns

Figure 2. Growth of Reported Deepfake Incidents (2018–2024)

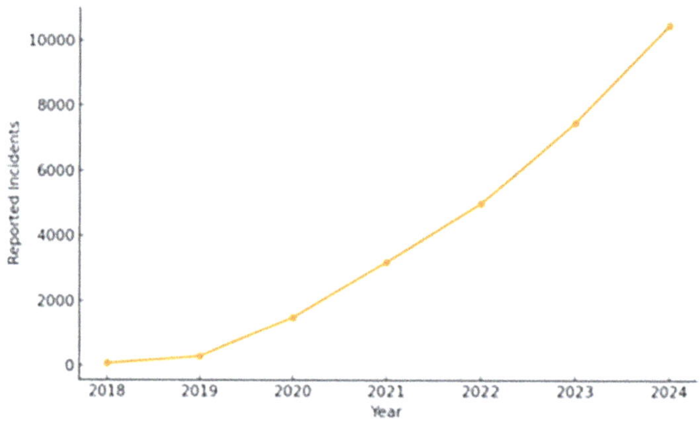

Detection technologies provide promising countermeasures, yet the arms race dynamic undermines their reliability. Classifiers degrade in accuracy as deepfakes evolve; blockchain solutions require global adoption; watermarking depends on compliance by AI developers. No single method is sufficient-rather, a layered detection ecosystem combining technical, legal, and institutional safeguards is required.

4.4 Consolidated Results Overview

The results point to several consolidated insights:

i. **Regulatory fragmentation** undermines enforcement: most jurisdictions treat deepfakes under broad cybercrime laws rather than dedicated statutes.
ii. **Fraud cases are escalating in sophistication and cost**, moving from small-scale impersonations to multi-million-dollar corporate scams.
iii. **Technological countermeasures exist but are partial**, facing scalability and explainability challenges.
iv. **The gap between generative speed and legal response** is widening: deepfakes can be produced and disseminated within hours, while regulatory action takes months or years.

Together, these findings underscore the urgent need for integrated legal-technical frameworks, harmonized international governance, and continuous R&D in AI detection systems.

5. DISCUSSION

The results reveal that deepfake fraud is expanding rapidly, exposing weaknesses in legal frameworks and technological countermeasures. To contextualize these findings, this section synthesizes them through theoretical, comparative, and ethical lenses. It also introduces new contributions: a typology of deepfake fraud scenarios and a regulatory risk matrix designed to guide interventions.

5.1 Legal Frameworks: Fragmented and Reactive

The comparative analysis confirms scholarly critiques that current laws addressing deepfakes are reactive rather than anticipatory (Łabuz, 2023). The U.S. illustrates the pitfalls of a fragmented state-level approach, where laws differ widely in scope and enforcement, leaving loopholes exploitable by perpetrators. The EU's AI Act represents a more systematic attempt, but its broad classification of deepfakes as "high-risk AI" lacks specificity in penalties and implementation. India's reliance on provisions of the IT Act (2000) underscores the risks of outdated frameworks, while China's mandatory labeling regime demonstrates proactivity but raises surveillance and human rights concerns (Latham & Watkins LLP, 2023).

From a theoretical perspective, institutional theory suggests that legal systems evolve under pressure from social and technological changes (DiMaggio & Powell, 1991). Yet the speed of deepfake innovation outpaces legal adaptation, producing a governance lag. Without harmonization and dedicated statutes, enforcement will remain inconsistent, undermining deterrence.

5.2 Technological Detection: Arms Race Dynamics

AI-driven detection tools-classifiers, blockchain verification, multi-modal forensics-show promise but remain partial and unstable. Detection algorithms rapidly degrade as generative models evolve; blockchain-based authenticity requires adoption at the point of content creation; watermarking mandates depend on compliance by developers. Scholars characterize this as an "arms race" between generative and forensic AI (Rana et al., 2022).

This arms race has two implications. First, technological solutions alone cannot guarantee resilience-legal mandates must reinforce their adoption. Second, continuous R&D investment and collaboration across academia, industry, and government are critical to sustain detection capabilities. Without this, detection will lag further behind generation, widening the gap.

5.3 Ethical Dilemmas and Competing Rights

The findings reinforce the ethical dilemmas surrounding deepfake regulation. While malicious deepfakes cause demonstrable harm-financial loss, reputational damage, democratic erosion-there are also legitimate uses in film, education, and accessibility. Broad bans risk over-regulation, stifling creativity and innovation (Dabas, 2024). Conversely, under-regulation fosters normative ambiguity, where malicious actors exploit legal gaps.

Balancing these competing rights requires a nuanced governance model: one that targets malicious intent while preserving legitimate expression. The ethical principle of proportionality-ensuring interventions are targeted and not excessive-should guide regulatory design. This aligns with broader debates in AI governance, which emphasize accountability, transparency, and fairness (Cath, 2018).

5.4 Typology of Deepfake Fraud Scenarios

A major contribution of this study is the development of a typology of deepfake fraud, categorizing incidents into four core domains.

Table 5. Typology of Deepfake Fraud Scenarios

Category	Example	Primary Harm	Regulatory Challenge
Financial Fraud	CEO voice/video impersonation scams	Monetary loss, corporate liability	Jurisdictional enforcement; evidentiary admissibility
Political Disinformation	Deepfake election propaganda	Democratic instability, public trust erosion	Freedom of expression vs. misinformation control
Gendered Harassment	Non-consensual pornographic deepfakes	Reputational damage, psychological harm	Definitional gaps; weak platform accountability
Reputational/ Corporate Harm	Fake speeches of executives	Brand damage, market manipulation	Attribution of liability; cross-border dissemination

This typology underscores that deep-fake fraud is not monolithic. Each category carries distinct harms and regulatory challenges, necessitating context-specific interventions.

5.5 Regulatory Risk Matrix

Building on the typology, this study introduces a regulatory risk matrix that maps fraud types against urgency and detection feasibility.

Table 6. Regulatory Risk Matrix for Deepfake Fraud

Fraud Type	Urgency of Intervention	Detection Feasibility	Recommended Intervention
Financial Fraud	High	Medium (voice/video classifiers improving but imperfect)	Mandated corporate compliance audits; AI-assisted forensic capacity
Political Disinformation	Very High (election sensitivity)	Low (difficult to trace intent, viral spread rapid)	Pre-election monitoring, rapid response task forces, platform accountability
Gendered Harassment	High	Medium (biometric verification, watermarking)	Stronger platform liability, fast-track judicial remedies
Corporate/ Reputational Harm	Medium	Medium-High (blockchain provenance feasible for official media)	Mandated watermarking for corporate comms; liability-sharing frameworks

Figure 3. Regulatory Risk Matrix for Deepfake Fraud

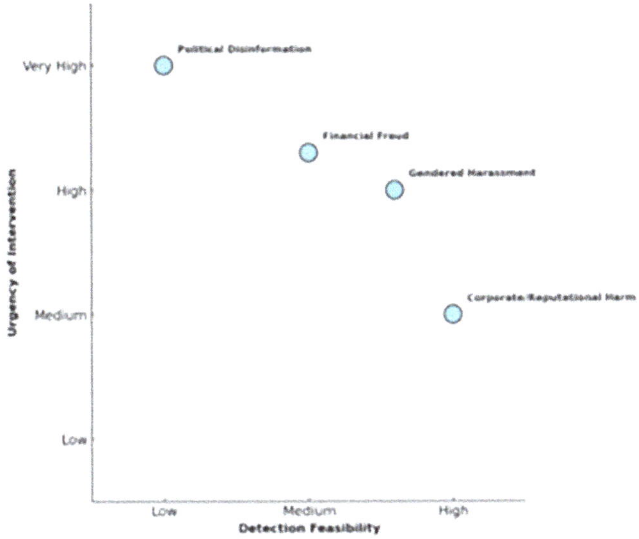

The matrix provides a prioritization tool: policymakers can focus first on high-urgency, low-feasibility scenarios (e.g., political disinformation), while building long-term capacity for others. It also highlights that no single intervention suffices-a mix of legal reforms, platform regulation, and technical safeguards is essential.

5.6 Originality and Contribution

This study advances scholarship by offering an integrated synthesis of legal and technical domains. Three contributions stand out:

i. **Interdisciplinary framework**: By juxtaposing legal regulation with AI detection strategies, the study bridges two previously siloed literatures.
ii. **Typology and risk matrix**: The chapter proposes new conceptual tools for categorizing fraud scenarios and prioritizing regulatory responses.
iii. **Practical roadmap**: Recommendations for watermarking mandates, cross-border enforcement, and ethical regulatory sandboxes provide actionable insights for policymakers and practitioners.

These contributions move the debate beyond description toward actionable governance strategies.

5.7 Implications for Global Governance

The global nature of deepfakes necessitates international cooperation. Just as money laundering and cybercrime spurred transnational frameworks (e.g., FATF, Budapest Convention), deepfake fraud requires harmonized norms. The results suggest three pillars for global governance:

i. **Shared definitions** of synthetic media and malicious intent.
ii. **Cross-border enforcement coalitions**, involving agencies like Interpol and ITU.
iii. **Global technical standards** for watermarking and AI transparency.

Figure 4. Pillars of Deepfake Governance

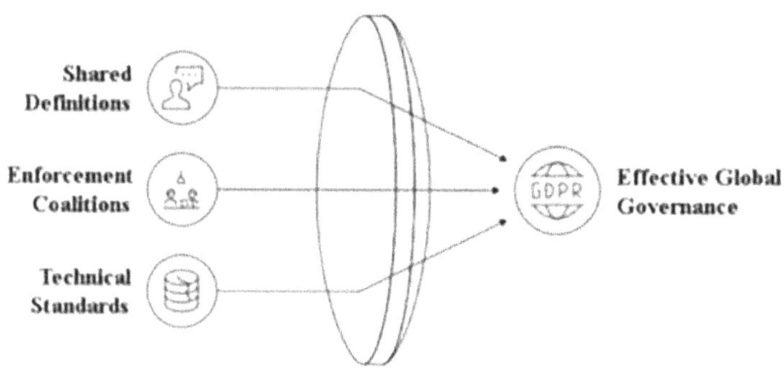

Absent such harmonization, perpetrators will exploit jurisdictional inconsistencies, undermining national-level reforms.

5.8 Practical Implications for Institutions

The emergence of deepfakes as a pervasive digital threat has far-reaching consequences for multiple institutional stakeholders. Governments, corporations, digital platforms, and the research community each face distinct challenges and responsibilities in addressing the risks posed by synthetic media. The findings of this study underline the urgent need for differentiated yet complementary strategies across these domains.

5.8.1 Implications for Governments

For governments, the most pressing implication is the establishment of dedicated legislation specifically tailored to deepfakes. Current reliance on broad cybercrime or media laws is inadequate, as it leaves gaps in areas such as definitional clarity, evidence admissibility, and jurisdictional enforcement. Dedicated statutes can provide precise definitions of synthetic media, categorize harmful uses, and stipulate penalties aligned with the severity of the offense. Equally important is the need for enhanced forensic capacity. National law enforcement agencies must be equipped with advanced digital forensics laboratories capable of distinguishing authentic from manipulated content. This requires investment in technical expertise, inter-agency collaboration, and international partnerships, given the inherently transnational nature of deepfakes. Governments also need to balance regulation with fundamental rights, ensuring that laws do not stifle legitimate uses of synthetic media in art, satire, or education.

5.8.2 Implications for Corporations

Corporations face unique reputational and operational risks from deepfake misuse, ranging from executive impersonation to fraudulent communications. As such, businesses must adopt robust compliance policies that clearly define protocols for identifying, reporting, and responding to deepfake incidents. Employee training is a crucial element of this framework, as awareness and vigilance at the organizational level can significantly reduce susceptibility to deepfake-driven phishing or impersonation attacks. Moreover, companies should consider watermarking official communications, particularly financial statements, press releases, and strategic announcements, to safeguard the authenticity of corporate messaging. By embedding authenticity markers within communications, corporations not only protect themselves but also signal credibility to stakeholders. Beyond individual firms, industry-wide coalitions can play a vital role in setting best practices and coordinating responses to large-scale deepfake threats.

5.8.3 Implications for Digital Platforms

Digital platforms, as primary conduits for the dissemination of deepfake content, hold a pivotal position in mitigating harm. The findings indicate that proactive detection and takedown mechanisms are essential. Platforms must invest in AI-based detection systems capable of real-time monitoring and flagging of synthetic content. These obligations should be paired with clearly defined liability frameworks, ensuring that platforms bear responsibility when negligent practices enable the viral spread of harmful deepfakes. At the same time, transparency and accountability mechanisms—such as public reporting on the volume and type of deepfake removals—can enhance trust among users and regulators alike. By shifting from reactive moderation to proactive governance, platforms can help curb the weaponization of synthetic media.

5.8.4 Implications for Researchers and Technologists

Finally, the findings carry significant implications for researchers and technologists. Despite advances in detection tools, the constant evolution of generative models makes it difficult to achieve long-term effectiveness. As a result, investment in explainable, scalable detection technologies is a top priority. Detection tools must not only identify manipulated media but also provide interpretable explanations that can withstand judicial scrutiny in courts of law. Furthermore, scalability is critical: tools must be capable of handling vast volumes of content across languages, formats, and platforms. The research community also has an obligation to collaborate with policymakers and industry stakeholders, ensuring that technological innovations are integrated into broader governance frameworks. Ethical considerations must remain central, as overly intrusive detection systems may compromise privacy or lead to disproportionate surveillance.

Taken together, the practical implications of deepfakes demand a multi-stakeholder response. Governments must legislate and build forensic capabilities; corporations must embed compliance and authenticity safeguards;

platforms must assume proactive responsibilities; and researchers must advance detection in ways that are both scalable and explainable. Only through coordinated action across these institutional domains can societies effectively address the risks of deepfake technologies while safeguarding democratic values, economic stability, and individual rights.

6. CONCLUSION AND POLICY RECOMMENDATIONS

6.1 Consolidated conclusions

This study has examined the rise of deepfake fraud as both a technological and legal challenge. The findings reveal that deepfakes-enabled by GANs, diffusion models, and widely accessible AI tools-pose multidimensional risks across financial, political, corporate, and personal domains. Fraudulent cases ranging from multi-million-dollar impersonation scams to election disinformation campaigns highlight the urgency of intervention.

Comparative legal analysis showed that regulatory frameworks remain fragmented and reactive. The United States relies on a patchwork of state laws; the European Union has advanced a broad AI governance framework, yet enforcement remains uncertain; India's IT Act is outdated; and China enforces mandatory labeling, though at the expense of civil liberties. Meanwhile, AI-driven detection strategies-neural classifiers, blockchain authenticity markers, multimodal forensics, watermarking, and biometric verification-offer promising tools but remain limited in scalability, accuracy, and explainability.

The research contributions of this chapter include: (1) an interdisciplinary framework combining legal and technical perspectives, (2) a typology of deepfake fraud scenarios, and (3) a regulatory risk matrix mapping urgency and feasibility to intervention strategies. These tools advance the debate from descriptive analysis to actionable solutions, offering a roadmap for governments, platforms, and corporations.

6.2 Policy Recommendations

Based on the findings, this chapter advances five key policy recommendations:

1. Establish global norms for synthetic media regulation

The global nature of deepfakes requires harmonized international standards. Just as the Budapest Convention unified approaches to cybercrime, deepfake regulation should adopt:

i. A shared legal definition of deepfakes and malicious intent.
ii. Cross-border enforcement mechanisms through Interpol, UN ITU, or OECD frameworks.
iii. Global technical standards for watermarking, provenance tracking, and algorithmic transparency.

Without international convergence, perpetrators will exploit jurisdictional inconsistencies, undermining national reforms.

2. Mandate watermarking and algorithmic transparency

Governments should require AI developers to embed invisible watermarking protocols in all synthetic media outputs. These digital signatures can facilitate authenticity checks while preserving legitimate applications. At the same time, algorithmic transparency mandates should compel companies to disclose model training data, risk assessments, and detection compatibility. This fosters accountability without stifling innovation.

3. Enhance digital forensics and institutional capacity

Regulators and enforcement agencies need greater capacity to detect and prosecute deepfake crimes. This requires:

i. Investment in AI-assisted forensic laboratories capable of handling real-time detection.
ii. Training programs for judges, investigators, and corporate compliance officers.
iii. Public–private partnerships to ensure that state-of-the-art detection systems are accessible beyond elite institutions.
iv. Enhanced forensic capacity reduces the enforcement gap between rapid deepfake dissemination and slow institutional response.

4. Promote regulatory sandboxes and ethical AI deployment

Given the evolving nature of deepfakes, regulatory sandboxes can provide controlled environments for testing detection technologies, balancing innovation and oversight. This approach allows policymakers to pilot biometric verification, blockchain authenticity markers, and multimodal forensic tools while monitoring their ethical and privacy implications. Lessons from these sandboxes can guide scalable, responsible deployment.

5. Increase public awareness and resilience

Deepfake fraud is amplified by public unawareness. Governments and civil society must invest in awareness campaigns that teach individuals how to identify manipulated media, verify sources, and report suspicious content. Embedding digital literacy in educational curricula and workplace compliance training can enhance resilience, reducing the social engineering leverage that makes deepfakes effective.

Figure 5. Strategies for Synthetic Media Regulation

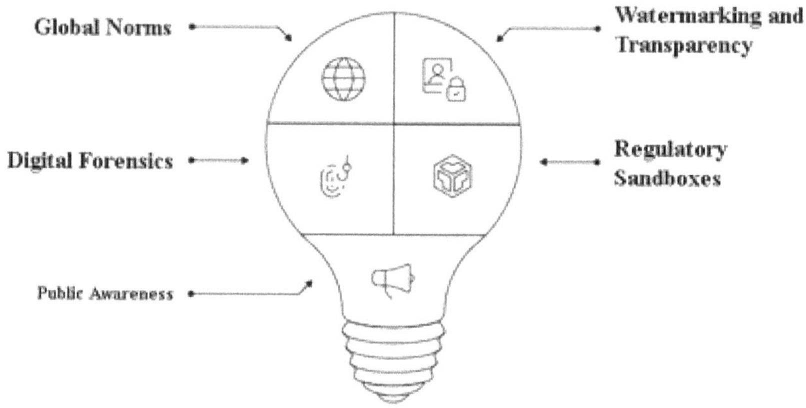

6.3 Future Directions

While this study provides a foundational synthesis, further research is needed. Longitudinal studies should track the effectiveness of legal reforms, while experimental research should benchmark next-generation detection tools. Interdisciplinary collaborations between computer scientists, legal scholars, ethicists, and policymakers will be vital. In particular, integrating explainable AI (XAI) into detection systems and designing global governance mechanisms remain urgent priorities.

Deepfakes represent both the promise and peril of generative AI. They exemplify how technological innovation can simultaneously enhance creativity and undermine trust. Addressing this paradox requires interdisciplinary governance, where legal reforms, technological safeguards, and ethical frameworks converge.

This chapter demonstrates that deepfake fraud is not merely a technical challenge but a societal governance issue. By adopting global norms, mandating watermarking, strengthening forensic capacity, piloting ethical AI, and enhancing public awareness, stakeholders can transform the current fragmented response into a coherent, proactive defense.

In conclusion, deepfake fraud underscores the broader lesson of the digital age: that governance must evolve as rapidly as innovation. Only through integrated legal–technical solutions can societies preserve democratic trust, safeguard individuals, and ensure that AI-driven creativity serves humanity rather than undermines it.

REFERENCES

Bendiab, G., Haiouni, H., Moulas, I., & Shiaeles, S. (2025). Deepfakes in digital media forensics: Generation, AI-based detection and challenges. *Journal of Information Security and Applications*, *88*, 103935. Advance online publication. DOI: 10.1016/j.jisa.2024.103935

Cath, C. (2018). Governing artificial intelligence: Ethical, legal and technical opportunities and challenges. *Philosophical Transactions. Series A, Mathematical, Physical, and Engineering Sciences*, *376*(2133), 20180080. Advance online publication. DOI: 10.1098/rsta.2018.0080 PMID: 30322996

Cheng, X. (2024). The Gendered Impact of Deepfake Technology: Analyzing Digital Violence Against Women in South Korea. *Lecture Notes in Education Psychology and Public Media*, *75*, 80–85. DOI: 10.54254/2753-7048/75/20241102

Chesney, R. M., & Citron, D. K. (2019). Deep fakes: A looming challenge for privacy, democracy, and national security. *California Law Review*, *107*, 1753–1819. https://www.californialawreview.org/print/deep-fakes-a-looming-challenge-for-privacy-democracy-and-national-security/

Dabas, P. (2024, November 28). *The impact of deepfake technology: Legal risks and regulatory solutions*. Mondaq. https://www.mondaq.com/india/new-technology/xxxxx

Ebers, M., Hoch, V. R. S., Rosenkranz, F., Ruschemeier, H., & Steinrötter, B. (2021). *The European Commission's proposal for an Artificial Intelligence Act—A critical assessment by members of the Robotics and AI Law Society (RAILS)*. J, 4(4), 589–603. https://doi.org/DOI: 10.3390/j4040043

Goodfellow, I. J., Pouget-Abadie, J., Mirza, M., Xu, B., Warde-Farley, D., Ozair, S., Courville, A., & Bengio, Y. (2014). *Generative adversarial networks*. arXiv. https://arxiv.org/abs/1406.2661

Łabuz, M. (2023). Regulating deep fakes in the Artificial Intelligence Act. [ACIG]. *Applied Cybersecurity & Internet Governance*, *2*(1). Advance online publication. DOI: 10.60097/ACIG/162856

Latham & Watkins LLP. (2023, August 16). *China's new AI regulations* (Client Alert No. 3110). https://www.lw.com/

Mirsky, Y., & Lee, W. (2021). *The creation and detection of deepfakes: A survey*. ACM Computing Surveys, 54(1). *Article, 7*, 1–41. DOI: 10.1145/3425780

Noto, G. (2024, May 17). *Scammers siphon $25M from engineering firm Arup via AI deepfake "CFO"*. CFO Dive. https://www.cfodive.com/

Powell, W. W., & DiMaggio, P. J. (Eds.). (1991). *The new institutionalism in organizational analysis*. University of Chicago Press.

Ramesh, A., Dhariwal, P., Nichol, A., Chu, C., & Chen, M. (2022). *Hierarchical text-conditional image generation with CLIP latents*. arXiv. https://doi.org//arXiv.2204.06125DOI: 10.48550

Rana, M. S., Nobi, M. N., Murali, B., & Sung, A. H. (2022). Deepfake detection: A systematic literature review. *IEEE Access : Practical Innovations, Open Solutions, 10*, 25494–25513. DOI: 10.1109/ACCESS.2022.3154404

Sandoval, M. P., de Almeida Vau, M., & Solaas, J.. (2024). Threat of deepfakes to the criminal justice system: A systematic review. *Crime Science, 13*, 41. Advance online publication. DOI: 10.1186/s40163-024-00239-1

Stupp, C. (2019, August 30). *Fraudsters used AI to mimic CEO's voice in unusual cybercrime case*. The Wall Street Journal. https://www.wsj.com/

Vaccari, C., & Chadwick, A. (2020). Deepfakes and Disinformation: Exploring the Impact of Synthetic Political Video on Deception, Uncertainty, and Trust in News. *Social Media + Society, 6*(1). Advance online publication. DOI: 10.1177/2056305120903408

Vajiram Content Team. (2023, November 15). *Digital India Bill*. Vajiram & Ravi. https://vajiramandravi.com/current-affairs/digital-india-bill/

Chapter 6

The Evolving Cyber Threat Landscape in India:
Trends and Implications

Pallavi Kudal
https://orcid.org/0000-0001-9382-804X
Balaji Institute of International Business, Sri Balaji University, Pune, India

Rahul Waghmare
Balaji Institute of International Business, Sri Balaji University, Pune, India

ABSTRACT

India's rapid digital transformation, driven by fintech, e-governance, and smartphone penetration, has created vast opportunities but also heightened cyber risks. A 278% rise in state-sponsored attacks and incidents reported by 83% of organizations makes India one of the most targeted nations. Threats are evolving—from Ransomware-as-a-Service and state-backed espionage to supply chain exploits and disinformation campaigns. Systemic vulnerabilities such as outdated infrastructure, weak regulations, talent shortages, and poor cyber hygiene amplify risks. Businesses suffer financial and reputational losses, governments face threats to critical

DOI: 10.4018/979-8-3373-5992-2.ch006

infrastructure, and citizens encounter identity theft and fraud. Combating these challenges requires stronger public-private partnerships, AI-driven detection, resilient infrastructure, legislative reforms, and widespread cyber literacy. Building cybersecurity talent and awareness is vital to mitigate human-factor risks. India's digital future is promising, but securing it demands collaboration, innovation, and proactive defense is essential.

INTRODUCTION

India is undergoing rapid digital transformation since launch of Digital India Program in the yrear 2015. India is determined to make a digitally empowered society by rapid adoption of fintech solutions, e-governance platforms, and smartphones. Digital transformation is indeed revolutionizing the way individuals and businesses interact with technology. In past decade, fintech has become an integral part of the Indian economy, providing citizens with accessible financial services and facilitating transactions with ease. This boom is evidenced by widespread proliferation of digital payment platforms like Paytm, PhonePe, and Google Pay, which have become the most common way to make payments across the nation. These platforms leverage mobile technology, which has seen unprecedented growth in India, with the country boasting over 1.15 billion mobile subscribers as of December 2024 according to Telecom regulatory Authority of India. Alongwith digital transformation, e-governance, too, is transforming the public administration landscape, offering citizens streamlined access to government services and information. Initiatives like the Aadhaar project and the Digital India campaign aim to enhance transparency and efficiency in governance, further embedding digital practices into everyday life (Sharma, Jamwal, & Agrawal, 2025).

However, this digital revolution brings its own set of challenges. In past few years India has seen steep rise in cyberattacks. Between October 2023 and September 2024, India experienced more than 369 million malware incidents—averaging approximately 702 potential threats each minute. This surge highlights a deeper, systemic challenge, with cybercriminals employing advanced tactics and aggressively targeting any available vulnerabilities (Tripwire, 2024, May 6). In the first half of 2024, India witnessed

593 cyberattacks targeting essential sectors like education, government, and technology. A recent study highlights that 83% of organizations in India reported cyber incidents in the past year, underscoring the pervasive nature of these threats. In 2024, cyberattacks on banks and financial firms more than doubled. In 2024, 21% of all reported cyber incidents in India targeted healthcare. Why? Because healthcare data is valuable and vulnerable (Doyle, 2025).The complexity of the cyber threat landscape is illustrated by high-profile incidents such as the ransomware attack on the All India Institute of Medical Sciences (AIIMS), which disrupted healthcare services and highlighted vulnerabilities in essential systems (Cull, Peria, & Verrier, 2017). Figure 1 shows the trend of increase in cyber security market in India from 2019 to 2023, this growth clearly shows the increase in cyber threats and common man's need to get access to cyber security.

India's cyber threat environment is complex, with a wide range of players and driving forces. For example, state-sponsored cyberwarfare entails geopolitical tensions in which countries target one another's digital assets in an effort to obtain a strategic edge. Such assaults have the potential to destabilize economic systems, compromise private information, and interfere with vital infrastructure. An effective illustration of how cybercriminals can take advantage of flaws in healthcare systems to demand ransoms and cause extensive disruption is the AIIMS ransomware attack (Taheri, Hosany, & Altinay, 2019).

Furthermore, cyberthreats are increasingly targeting Indian individuals, startups, and small enterprises. Because they frequently lack strong cybersecurity defenses, these organizations are prime targets for cybercriminals. Such attacks can have disastrous financial repercussions, including data breaches, monetary losses, and harm to one's reputation. Securing third-party vendors and partners is crucial because of the interconnectedness of contemporary business ecosystems, which means that breaches in one entity can have a ripple effect on supply chains (Massei, Kindberg, & Licoppe, 2015).

Strategic responses to the changing cyber threat landscape are critical as India continues its digital transformation. This chapter will examine the main weaknesses, new trends, and ramifications of cyberthreats in India. It will examine the difficulties that different stakeholders—such as companies, the government, and citizens—face and offer tactical suggestions to improve cybersecurity resilience. The chapter highlights the value of taking proactive steps to combat cyberthreats, such as investing in resilient systems, adopting national and international best practices, and updating laws to stop new and existing threats (Palvia, Aeron, Gupta, & Mahapatra, 2018).

India's digital transformation is a double-edged sword, offering immense opportunities while presenting significant cybersecurity challenges, all stakeholders must work together, be innovative, and exercise leadership in order to secure the digital future. India can create strategic responses that protect its digital assets and guarantee the ongoing expansion of its digital economy by comprehending the trends, vulnerabilities, and ramifications of cyber threats (Nurdiawati, Mir, & Al-Ghamdi, 2025).

Figure 1. Value of cybersecurity market in India from 2019 to 2023 (in billion US dollars)

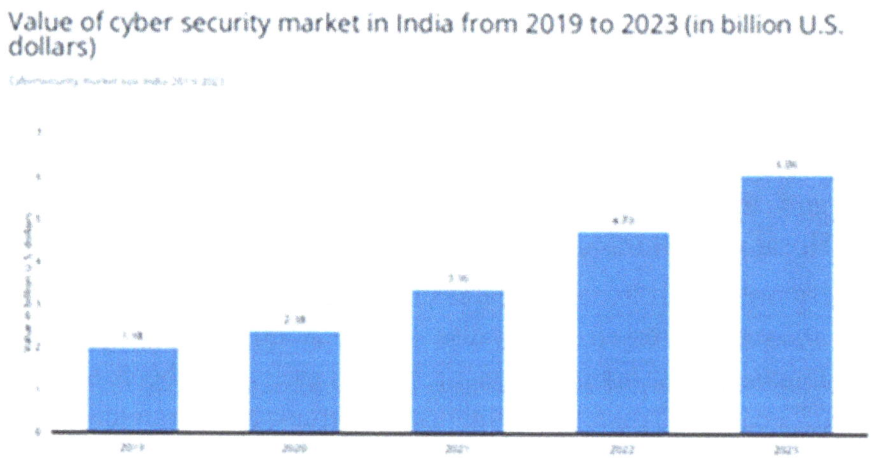

(Statista, 2024)

EMERGING TRENDS IN CYBER THREATS

In 2024, cybercriminals have become increasingly sophisticated, shifting from traditional online fraud to more manipulative and emotionally charged schemes like fake wedding invitations and very famous "digital arrests." These evolving threats are not just a matter of numbers; they reflect how fast cybercrime is adapting, while we remain unprepared.

Fraudsters today are exploiting both technology and human psychology. Scams like the so-called "digital arrests," where criminals impersonate law enforcement to extort money, have become alarmingly effective. Similarly, fake wedding invitation scams on platforms like WhatsApp attack users' trust and curiosity. In just one year, Indians lost over 120 crore to such digital arrest scams—a staggering figure that highlights just how deep this problem runs (Livemint, 2024).

RANSOMWARE AS A SERVICE (RAAS)

In recent years, Ransomware as a Service (RaaS) has emerged as a formidable threat to cybersecurity in India, reflecting a broader global trend. RaaS platforms operate similarly to legitimate software businesses, providing ransomware tools and services to cybercriminals, thus making it easier for individuals with little technical expertise to launch sophisticated attacks. The rise of RaaS can be attributed to the increasing sophistication and accessibility of cyber tools, which have democratized the ability to conduct cyberattacks (Bhardwaj, 2024). In India, several high-profile ransomware incidents have underscored the urgency of addressing this threat.

For instance, the ransomware attack on the AIIMS hospital in New Delhi serves as a stark reminder of the vulnerabilities within critical infrastructure. The attack disrupted hospital operations, highlighting the potential consequences of ransomware on essential services (R Reghunadhan, 2018). According to a report by Economic Times, India has seen a 278% surge in state-sponsored cyberattacks, with ransomware being a predominant method (Economic Times, 2023). This surge indicates not only the prevalence of RaaS but also its attractiveness to various threat actors, ranging from organized crime groups to state-sponsored entities.

STATE-SPONSORED ATTACKS AND GEOPOLITICAL RISKS

Statistics show that over 83% of organizations in India have reported ransomware incidents, reflecting the widespread impact of this threat. The financial sector, in particular, has been heavily targeted, with ransomware attacks resulting in significant monetary losses and reputational damage. Moreover, the proliferation of smartphones and the rapid adoption of digital payment systems have further widened the attack surface for cybercriminals, making India an attractive target for RaaS operators (A Bhardwaj, 2024).

State-sponsored cyber warfare is another critical trend impacting India's cybersecurity landscape. Geopolitical tensions often manifest in the digital realm, where nations engage in cyber espionage, sabotage, and other hostile activities. India, with its strategic position and growing digital infrastructure, finds itself at the crossroads of such cyber conflicts. The narrative of emerging threats under the Digital India scheme has been extensively analyzed, highlighting the intricate web of international cyber relations (R Reghunadhan, 2018).

One notable example is the cyberattack on India's power grid, which was attributed to a state-sponsored group with geopolitical motives. This incident emphasized the vulnerabilities of critical infrastructure to cyber warfare, where the intent is not just disruption but also intimidation and strategic gain (S Patil, 2022). The United Nations Group of Governmental Experts (UNGGE) initially showed promise in establishing cyber norms, but its efforts have faltered, leaving countries like India to navigate these threats independently (S Patil, 2022).

The geopolitical risks associated with state-sponsored cyber warfare are compounded by the complexity of attribution. Determining the origin of an attack is often challenging, leading to diplomatic tensions and the potential for escalation. As noted by Ramakrishnan and Tandon (2018), underestimating the threat of state-sponsored cyber warfare can have severe consequences, necessitating robust defensive measures and international cooperation.

SMALL BUSINESSES AND STARTUPS AS TARGETS OF CYBER ATTACK

Small businesses and startups in India are increasingly being targeted by cyber threats, a trend driven by their relatively weaker cybersecurity defenses. These enterprises often lack the resources to implement comprehensive security measures, making them attractive targets for cybercriminals (R Reghunadhan, 2018). With the rise of digital entrepreneurship and the proliferation of fintech solutions, startups are becoming integral to India's digital economy, yet their vulnerabilities pose significant risks.

Pharming, a technique that involves redirecting users to fraudulent websites, is one method used to exploit small businesses (UP Ramakrishnan, JK Tandon, 2018). Cybercriminals employ tactics like changing the hosts file on a victim's computer to execute such attacks, highlighting the need for heightened awareness and preventive measures. The consequences of these attacks include data breaches, financial losses, and reputational damage, which can be devastating for startups striving to establish themselves in competitive markets.

Furthermore, the assessment of cyber threats in emerging economies like India underscores the risks faced by small businesses (G Bhardwaj, R Gupta, AP Srivastava, 2021). These enterprises often operate with limited cybersecurity expertise, making them susceptible to various forms of cyberattacks. Therefore, addressing the vulnerabilities of small businesses is crucial for safeguarding India's digital ecosystem and fostering sustainable economic growth.

THREATS VIA THIRD-PARTY VENDORS AND SUPPLY CHAINS

The interconnectedness of modern businesses has given rise to threats via third-party vendors and supply chains. These threats are particularly relevant in India, where a significant portion of operations depends on external partners and suppliers. Cybercriminals exploit weaknesses within these networks, leading to breaches that can have cascading effects across organizations (AK Shanker, G Usha, 2017).

Recent breaches have demonstrated the susceptibility of supply chains to cyber threats. For example, a breach involving a third-party vendor led to the compromise of sensitive data for multiple companies, illustrating the broader impact of such incidents (G Kaur). The Information Technology Act's amendments in 2008 aimed at strengthening legal provisions to combat emerging cyber threats; however, the dynamic nature of threats necessitates continuous updates and enforcement (G Kaur).

The standards deployed to mitigate cybersecurity threats within supply chains validate the need for comprehensive approaches to address these vulnerabilities (LL Dhirani, E Armstrong, T Newe, 2021). Organizations must implement rigorous vetting processes and establish robust cybersecurity protocols to protect against threats originating from third-party vendors. As noted by Shafqat and Masood (2016), the global cyber threat landscape requires agile adaptation, making it imperative for Indian enterprises to align with international standards and best practices.

The evolving cyber threat landscape in India presents a complex array of challenges, from the growing prevalence of RaaS to the geopolitical risks of state-sponsored cyber warfare. Small businesses and startups, along with third-party vendors and supply chains, face significant vulnerabilities that necessitate proactive measures and strategic responses. As India continues its digital transformation, addressing these emerging trends is crucial for securing the digital future and fostering a resilient cyber ecosystem.

The insights provided by the references underscore the multifaceted nature of cyber threats and the importance of adopting comprehensive strategies to mitigate risks. By enhancing cybersecurity infrastructure, building talent, and aligning with global standards, India can navigate the complexities of the cyber threat landscape and safeguard its digital assets. As Oyewole et al. (2024) emphasize, leveraging technologies like big data analytics and artificial intelligence will be key to enhancing cyber defense capabilities and ensuring the security of India's digital endeavors.

KEY EMERGING THREATS IN INDIA'S CYBER ECOSYSTEM

1. **Digital Arrest Scams** Criminals impersonate law enforcement officers to scare victims into paying bogus fines. These scams are effective due to the misuse of authority and public unawareness.
2. **Ransomware Attacks** Attacks like the one on C-Edge Technologies in August 2024 disrupted payment systems in nearly 300 banks. Previous hits like the 2023 AIIMS attack also exposed healthcare vulnerabilities.
3. **Supply Chain Exploits** The 2020 SolarWinds breach demonstrated how a compromised vendor can expose numerous key institutions, including MeitY and NIC.
4. **State-Sponsored Espionage** Incidents like the 2020 Mumbai power grid cyberattack, allegedly state-backed, underscore vulnerabilities in critical infrastructure.
5. **Deepfake Manipulations** In 2024, a fake explicit video of actress Rashmika Mandanna went viral, illustrating the dangers of AI-powered misinformation.
6. **IoT Exploitation** With a 59% rise in IoT-related attacks in 2024, unsecured smart devices have become easy targets for cybercriminals.
7. **Cryptocurrency-Based Fraud** A major Bitcoin scam in Bengaluru revealed collusion between hackers, police, and cybersecurity experts, showing how cryptocurrency fraud is evolving.
8. **Dark Web Dealings** The breach of 750 million telecom users' data being sold online is just one example of how the dark web supports illegal activities.

THE CURRENT CYBERSECURITY FRAMEWORK IN INDIA

To address these growing threats, India has laid down several legislative, institutional, and strategic measures:

1. **Legislative Tools** o Information Technology Act, 2000: The Information Technology Act, 2000, is India's primary legislation dealing with cy-

bercrime and electronic commerce. It provides a legal framework for online transactions and aims to facilitate lawful digital transactions while curbing cybercrimes. It is the cornerstone of India's cybersecurity legal framework. o Digital Personal Data Protection Act, 2023: The Digital Personal Data Protection Act (DPDP Act) is a comprehensive legal framework in India for protecting digital personal data, balancing individual rights with lawful processing needs. It establishes obligations for data fiduciaries (entities processing data) and rights for individuals (data principals). The Act, notified on August 11, 2023, is designed to regulate how digital personal data is handled within India, and in some cases, even outside India if it pertains to offering goods or services to individuals within India.

2. **Institutional Framework** o CERT-In: The Indian **Computer Emergency Response Team (CERT-In) under Ministry of Electronics and Information Technology**, Government of India has been designated to serve as National agency for incident response under Section 70B of the Information Technology Act, 2000. CERT-In operates 24x7 incident response Help Desk for providing timely response to reported cyber security incidents. CERT-In provides Incident Prevention and Response services as well as Security Quality Management Services. CERT-In is regularly carrying out awareness activities to educate the users about **cyber security best practices to protect them against cyber security threats**. CERT-In also publishes awareness booklets and posters through its website and social media handles on a regular basis to promote cyber awareness across the country (**Press Information Bureau 2024**) o NCIIPC: NCIIPC stands for National Critical Information Infrastructure Protection Centre. It is an organization of the Government of India responsible for protecting critical information infrastructure from cyber threats. It acts as the nodal agency for this purpose and is a unit of the National Technical Research Organisation (NTRO). It focusses on securing critical sectors like power, telecom, and banking. o I4C: Indian Cybercrime Coordination Centre (I4C) is an initiative of the Ministry of Home Affairs, Government of India to deal with cyber crime in the country in a coordinated and comprehensive manner. I4C focuses on tackling all the issues related to Cybercrime for the citizens, which includes

improving coordination between various Law Enforcement Agencies and the stakeholders, driving change in India's overall capability to tackle Cybercrime and to improve citizen satisfaction levels. Indian Cybercrime Coordination Centre scheme was approved on 05th October 2018. Since its roll out, it has worked towards enhancing the nation's collective capability to tackle cybercrimes and develop effective coordination among the Law Enforcement Agencies. The I4C was dedicated to the Nation on 10th January 2020 by Hon'ble Home Minister. o Cyber Swachhta Kendra and Cyber Surakshit Bharat: Cyber Swachhta Kendra (CSK) and Cyber Surakshit Bharat are both government initiatives aimed at improving cybersecurity in India. CSK, also known as the Botnet Cleaning and Malware Analysis Centre, focuses on detecting, analyzing, and mitigating botnet infections and malware. Cyber Surakshit Bharat, on the other hand, is a capacity-building program designed to equip government officials with the knowledge and skills to address cyber threats. Both these initiatives promote awareness and hygiene across citizen and government domains. o NCRF: The Indian government has developed the National Cybersecurity Reference Framework (NCRF), a guideline that sets the standard for cybersecurity in India. The framework focuses on critical sectors and provides guidelines to help organisations develop strong cybersecurity systems. It can serve as a template for critical sector entities to develop their own governance and management systems. The government has identified telecom, power, transportation, finance, strategic entities, government entities, and health as critical sectors. The NCRF is non-binding in nature, meaning its recommendations will not be binding. It recommends enterprises allocate at least 10% of their total IT budget towards cybersecurity, with monitoring by top-level management or the board of directors. The framework may suggest that national nodal agencies evolve platforms and processes for machine-processing data from different sources to ensure proper audits and rate auditors based on performance (CyberPeace Foundation, 2023).

3. **Strategic and Sectoral Initiatives** o National Cyber Security Policy (2013): The National Cyber Security Policy (NCSP) 2013, released by the Indian government, is a comprehensive framework designed to protect India's cyberspace and critical information infrastructure

from cyber threats. It aims to create a secure cyber ecosystem, enhance the nation's ability to respond to cyberattacks, and promote cyber-security awareness. o SEBI's Cybersecurity Framework: In order to strengthen the cybersecurity measures in Indian securities market, and to ensure adequate cyber resiliency against cybersecurity incidents/ attacks, Securities and Exchange Board of India (SEBI) has released the Cybersecurity and Cyber Resilience Framework (CSCRF). The CSCRF aims to provide standards and guidelines for strengthening cyber resilience and maintaining robust cybersecurity of SEBI regulated entities (KPMG Assurance and Consulting Services LLP, 2024).

- o Telecom (Critical Infrastructure) Rules, 2024: The Telecommunications (Critical Telecommunication Infrastructure) Rules, 2024 aim to enhance the security and resilience of critical telecommunication networks in India. These rules, notified under the Telecommunications Act, 2023, designate specific networks as Critical Telecommunication Infrastructure (CTI) based on their potential impact on national security, economy, public health, or safety. The rules outline measures for protecting CTI, including requirements for data and network access, incident reporting, and the appointment of a Chief Telecommunication Security Officer.

KEY VULNERABILITIES IN THE INDIAN CYBER ECOSYSTEM

In recent years, it is heartening to see a massive increase in cyber threats in India, paralleling its rapid digital transformation. As the nation embraces digital solutions across various sectors, the vulnerabilities within its cyber ecosystem have become a matter of policy concern. These vulnerabilities include infrastructural weaknesses, regulatory framework deficiency, workforce skills, and digital literacy. In this section, we explore these vulnerabilities in detail, shedding light on the factors that contribute to the precarious state of cybersecurity in India.

India's cyber infrastructure is a complex web of outdated systems and modern technology and it often lacks the necessary encryption and security protocols. Many organizations continue to rely on ols security systems, which might have done good earlier but are inefficients to handle threats today. Wireless Sensor Networks (WSNs), as described by Butun, Österberg, and Song (2019), represent a promising technology but it is highly vulnerable due to its widespread application. The reliance on such technologies without adequate security measures exposes critical data and systems to potential breaches.

India's regulatory and legal frameworks have also not been able to keep pace with the evolving cyber threat landscape. Current laws are outdated and lack the necessary provisions to address modern cybersecurity challenges. Saba et al. (2019) highlight the concept of vulnerability in medical contexts, and it can be applied to the regulatory sector whose outdated policies fail to protect against new and emerging threats.

Absence of mandatory enforcement mechanisms further compounds this issue. There is a pressing need for updated cybersecurity laws that can effectively address the nuances of digital threats and establish clear accountability for breaches.

Apart from regulatory issues, India faces a significant shortage of trained cybersecurity professionals, which greatly impacts its ability to defend against cyber threats. Rufat et al. (2015) discuss vulnerability to digital presence and identified that lack of skilled professionals is a major siurse of vulnerability. The demand for cybersecurity expertise much more than the present supply.

Moreover Indian education system has been slow to adapt to the growing need for cybersecurity training, which has resulted in a workforce that is ill-prepared to tackle the complexities of modern cyber threats. This shortage is not only a national concern but even a global concern, as India plays a significant role in the global tech ecosystem.

Another important issue is digital illiteracy, where a significant portion of the population lacks the knowledge and skills necessary to protect themselves online. Schilling et al. (2020) detail vulnerability comprising of sensitivity, adaptive capacity, and exposure, which highlights the nature of digital illiteracy. Poor cyber hygiene practices, such as using weak passwords or failing to update software, contribute towards increasing risk of cyber attacks.

The cybersecurity issues in India exist not only among individuals but are equally commmon amongst organisations where employees may unknowingly compromise security through negligence or lack of awareness. The implications of such behaviors may lead to data breaches and financial losses.

All these vulnerabilities in India's cyber ecosystem have significant implications for citizend, businesses and government of the country. These vulnerabilities lead to data loss, reputational damage, and financial repercussions (Bracken-Roche et al., 2017).

For businesses, these vulnerabilities can result in substantial financial losses due to data breaches and legal penalties. The government's ability to safeguard national security and critical infrastructure is compromised as these vulnerabilities leave sensitive information exposed to potential attacks.

Citizens face risks such as privacy violations, fraud, digital exploitation and increasing possibility of cyber threats. The key vulnerabilities in India's cyber ecosystem require urgent attention and strategic responses. From outdated infrastructure and regulatory gaps to workforce shortages and digital illiteracy, these vulnerabilities are interconnected and demand a comprehensive approach to cybersecurity.

Hence the road ahead for India's cybersecurity journey is fraught with challenges but also opportunities for innovation, collaboration, and leadership.

RECOMMENDATIONS

To strengthen India's cybersecurity posture, a multi-pronged approach is essential. Following are the few points which can help create a civil infrastructure around cybersecurity. Launching nationwide cyber literacy programs in local languages will empower vulnerable groups such as rural users and senior citizens. Enforcing IoT security standards with a focus on security-by-design, firmware updates, and encryption is critical. Adoption of AI-based threat detection systems can enable real-time monitoring and improve forensic capabilities. CERT-In should be strengthened with upgraded tools and regional hubs to enable swift responses. Regulations to detect and penalize deepfake misuse must be introduced. Establishing district-level cyber cells equipped with trained personnel can ensure localized incident handling. A cybersecurity certification mandate for supply chain partners will enhance ecosystem integrity. To curb crypto-related crimes, cryptocurrency regulations should include mandatory KYC, transaction tracking, and dedicated forensics units. Regular cybersecurity audits, especially in critical sectors like banking and healthcare, must become mandatory and include stress and penetration tests. Startups should be supported through training and subsidized security tools. Dark web monitoring tools must be deployed to identify and act against emerging threats. Implementing multi-factor authentication (MFA) should be mandated for all major digital platforms. Further, cybersecurity awareness in educational institutions must be promoted through national programs, while data localization laws should be strictly enforced to ensure sensitive data remains within national borders.

CONCLUSION

India's cyber threat landscape is evolving rapidly, shaped by increased digitalization, the rise of sophisticated cyberattacks, and growing geopolitical tensions. From ransomware-as-a-service (RaaS) and deepfake scams to vulnerabilities in supply chains and critical infrastructure, the nature and scale of threats have broadened significantly. While India's strides in digital transformation are commendable, they also expose systemic weaknesses—ranging from outdated infrastructure and regulatory gaps to a shortage of skilled professionals and widespread digital illiteracy.

Addressing these multifaceted challenges requires a comprehensive, forward-looking strategy that integrates robust legal frameworks, widespread cyber literacy, real-time threat intelligence, and international collaboration. Strengthening institutional mechanisms like CERT-In and I4C, along with enforcing sector-specific regulations such as SEBI's CSCRF and the Digital Personal Data Protection Act, will be crucial to building national resilience.

A secure digital future for India hinges on proactive governance, technological innovation, and a collective commitment from all stakeholders—government, industry, academia, and citizens. As cyber threats grow in complexity and impact, India must transition from reactive responses to a culture of cybersecurity by design, ensuring that digital progress does not come at the cost of national security and citizen trust.

REFERENCES

KPMG Assurance and Consulting Services LLP. (2024, August 20). *SEBI CSCRF – Our point of view*. KPMG in India.

Bhardwaj, A. (2024). *5G: The Emerging Cybersecurity Threat Landscape for India. In 5G and Fiber Optics Security Technologies for Smart Grid Cyber Defense*. IGI Global.

Bhardwaj, G., Gupta, R., Srivastava, A. P., & Singh, S. V. (2021, April). Cyber Threat Landscape of G4 Nations: Analysis of Threat Incidents & Response Strategies. In 2021 2nd International Conference on Intelligent Engineering and Management (ICIEM) (pp. 75-79). IEEE.

Bracken-Roche, D., Bell, E., Macdonald, M. E., & Racine, E. (2017). The concept of 'vulnerability' in research ethics: An in-depth analysis of policies and guidelines. *Health Research Policy and Systems*, *15*, 1–18.

Butun, I., Österberg, P., & Song, H. (2019). Security of the Internet of Things: Vulnerabilities, attacks, and countermeasures. *IEEE Communications Surveys and Tutorials*, *22*(1), 616–644.

Cull, R., Peria, M. M. S. M., & Verrier, J. (2017). *Bank ownership: Trends and implications*. International Monetary Fund.

CyberPeace Foundation. (2023) *National Cyber Security Reference Framework – Need of the hour*. CyberPeace. https://www.cyberpeace.org/resources/blogs/national-cyber-security-reference-framework-need-of-the-hour

Dhirani, L. L., Armstrong, E., & Newe, T. (2021). Industrial IoT, cyber threats, and standards landscape: Evaluation and roadmap. *Sensors (Basel)*, *21*(11), 3901.

Doyle, K. (2025, June 3). *The Rising Tide: Understanding the Surge in Cyber Attacks in India*. Tripwire. Retrieved from https://www.tripwire.com/state-of-security/rising-tide-understanding-surge-cyber-attacks-india

Economic Times. (2023, May 9). India sees sharp increase in cyberattacks in Q1 2023: report. The Economic Times Tech. Retrieved from https://economictimes.indiatimes.com/tech/technology/sharp-increase-in-cyberattacks-in-india-in-q1-2023-report/articleshow/100096450.cms?from=mdr

Kaur, G. Emerging Trends in Cyber Crime in India.

Livemint. (2024, November 29). Mint Quick Edit: Cyber cons go from digital arrests to wedding scams. LiveMint. Retrieved from https://www.livemint.com/opinion/quick-edit/mint-quick-edit-cyber-cons-go-from-digital-arrests-to-wedding-scams-digital-arrest-whatsapp-invite-malware-scam-crime-11732775304080.html

Massei, G., Kindberg, J., Licoppe, A., Gačić, D., Šprem, N., Kamler, J., & Náhlik, A. (2015). Wild boar populations up, numbers of hunters down? A review of trends and implications for Europe. *Pest Management Science*, *71*(4), 492–500.

Nurdiawati, A., Mir, B. A., & Al-Ghamdi, S. G. (2025). Recent advancements in prospective life cycle assessment: Current practices, trends, and implications for future research. Resources. *Environmental Sustainability*, •••, 100203.

Oyewole, A. T., Okoye, C. C., Ofodile, O. C., & Ugochukwu, C. E. (2024). Cybersecurity risks in online banking: A detailed review and preventive strategies application. *World Journal of Advanced Research and Reviews*, *21*(3), 625–643.

Palvia, S., Aeron, P., Gupta, P., Mahapatra, D., Parida, R., Rosner, R., & Sindhi, S. (2018). Online education: Worldwide status, challenges, trends, and implications. *Journal of Global Information Technology Management*, *21*(4), 233–241.

Patil, S. (2022). India's cyber security landscape. In *Varying Dimensions of India's National Security: Emerging Perspectives* (pp. 75–90). Springer Nature Singapore.

Press Information Bureau. (2024, July 17). *India leads discussions on cybersecurity at Global Digital Summit 2024*. https://www.pib.gov.in/PressReleaseIframePage.aspx?PRID=2109192

Ramakrishnan, U. P., & Tandon, J. K. (2018). The evolving landscape of cyber threats. *Vidwat*, *11*(1), 31–35.

Reghunadhan, R. (2018). Cyber threat landscape of digital India: A critical perspective. *Journal of Polity and Society*, *10*(1&2), 37–50.

Rufat, S., Tate, E., Burton, C. G., & Maroof, A. S. (2015). Social vulnerability to floods: Review of case studies and implications for measurement. *International Journal of Disaster Risk Reduction*, *14*, 470–486.

Saba, L., Saam, T., Jäger, H. R., Yuan, C., Hatsukami, T. S., Saloner, D., & Wintermark, M. (2019). Imaging biomarkers of vulnerable carotid plaques for stroke risk prediction and their potential clinical implications. *Lancet Neurology*, *18*(6), 559–572.

Schilling, J., Hertig, E., Tramblay, Y., & Scheffran, J. (2020). Climate change vulnerability, water resources and social implications in North Africa. *Regional Environmental Change*, *20*, 1–12.

Shafqat, N., & Masood, A. (2016). Comparative analysis of various national cyber security strategies. *International Journal of Computer Science and Information Security*, *14*(1), 129–136.

Shanker, A. K., & Usha, G. (2017, April). Cyber threat landscape in cyber space. In *2017 International Conference of Electronics, Communication and Aerospace Technology (ICECA)* (Vol. 1, pp. 375–380). IEEE.

Sharma, V., Jamwal, A., Agrawal, R., & Pratap, S. (2025). A review on digital transformation in healthcare waste management: Applications, research trends and implications. *Waste Management & Research*, *43*(6), 828–849.

Statista. (2024). Cyber security in India. https://www.statista.com/study/85981/cyber-security-in-india/

Taheri, B., Hosany, S., & Altinay, L. (2019). Consumer engagement in the tourism industry: New trends and implications for research. *Service Industries Journal*, *39*(7–8), 463–468.

Tripwire. (2024, May 6). Rising tide: Understanding the surge in cyber attacks in India. The State of Security. https://www.tripwire.com/state-of-security/rising-tide-understanding-surge-cyber-attacks-india

Chapter 7
Policies Against Fraud and Cybercrime:
Strategic, Legal, and Technological Approaches

Radha Ranjan
https://orcid.org/0009-0009-1550-7780
Amity University, Patna, India

Naveen Nandal
https://orcid.org/0009-0007-2272-7437
JIMS, India

Ankit Kumar
https://orcid.org/0009-0001-8249-4969
Sandip University, Sijoul, India

Anupam Sinha
Amity Law School, India

Shagufta Parween
https://orcid.org/0000-0002-5221-4137
Chaitanya Bharathi Institute of Technology, India

S. Srinivas Kumar
Jain University, India

Bhoopathy Rajan
https://orcid.org/0000-0003-2175-6328
Sree Rama Engineering College, India

ABSTRACT

In an age of rapid digitisation, fraud and cybercrime have transformed into intricate risks affecting individuals, enterprises, and governments. The expansion of e-commerce, online banking, and mobile payments

DOI: 10.4018/979-8-3373-5992-2.ch007

has heightened hazards like ransomware, identity theft, phishing, and money laundering, with anticipated losses estimated at USD 10.5 trillion per year by 2025. This paper presents a comprehensive framework that integrates strategic policies, robust regulatory measures, and cutting-edge technologies—AI, machine learning, blockchain, and behavioural analytics—to identify and mitigate fraud. It analyses international rules (e.g., GDPR, CCPA, EU AI Act, FATF AML) and transnational collaboration, supplemented by case studies from the banking, e-commerce, and governmental sectors. Challenges such as adversarial AI, algorithmic bias, and disconnected response systems are tackled, with resilience techniques encompassing adversarial training and privacy-preserving analytics.

1. INTRODUCTION

1.1 Background: The Rising Threat of Fraud and Cybercrime

In recent years, fraud and cybercrime have become significant risks to economic stability, institutional trust, and individual security globally. The global annual cost of cybercrime is anticipated to reach USD 10.5 trillion by 2025, a significant increase from roughly USD 3 trillion in 2015, so establishing it as the world's third-largest economy, following the United States and China (Cybersecurity Ventures, 2025; BD Emerson, 2025). Annual losses exceed USD 1 trillion, mostly impacting industries such as banking, healthcare, and retail (BD Emerson, 2025). The increasing severity of cyberattacks is demonstrated by a 14 percent increase in occurrences in the UK in 2024, with fraud comprising 41 percent of all offences and damages totalling £1.1 billion (Levy, 2025). The World Economic Forum's worldwide Risks Report (2023) identifies cybercrime as a leading worldwide risk for the forthcoming decade, projecting economic damages to exceed USD 9 trillion in 2024 (WEF, 2023). The global average cost of a data breach has increased to between USD 4.5 million and USD 4.9 million, varying by industry, with financial institutions and healthcare at the higher end of the spectrum (BD Emerson, 2025; Indusface, 2025). Simultaneously, Artificial Intelligence (AI) is reshaping the cyber threat landscape: organised crime syndicates are progressively utilising AI, deepfakes, and generative technologies to develop complex fraud schemes; Europol of the European Union cautions that AI is amplifying organised crime, facilitating voice cloning, deepfake fraud, and extortion (Europol, 2025). In Karnataka, India, cybercriminals utilised AI to execute scams, resulting in significant financial losses amounting to Rs 938 crore from January to May 2025, a notable increase from prior years (Times of India, 2025). These data points highlight the increasing operational, financial, and reputational risks facing organisations and governments. Conventional defences manual surveillance, rule-based filters, and local jurisdictional regulations are inadequate against internationally dispersed, technologically advanced criminal networks. Consequently, there is a distinct necessity to reevaluate cybercrime prevention using a more cohesive, anticipatory, and systemic perspective.

1.2 Rationale for a Multi-Dimensional Approach

The increasing complexity of cybercrime and fraud requires a comprehensive response that integrates strategic strategy, strong legal frameworks, and advanced technological instruments. Each dimension addresses a distinct aspect of the issue, and their integration produces synergies essential for efficient prevention, detection, and intervention.

- **Strategic Policy**: Macro-level coordination, transnational frameworks, and flexible policymaking facilitate resilience and uniformity across jurisdictions. The recently approved United Nations Convention against Cybercrime (2024), scheduled for signing in October 2025, illustrates attempts to enhance international cooperation, although persistent criticisms over human rights protections (UN Cybercrime Convention, 2024).
- **Legal Frameworks**: National and sector-specific legislation, like the GDPR, PSD2, FATF standards, and AI governance instruments, define accountability, apply data protection requirements, and define legal liability, while concurrently balancing investigative power and civil rights.

- **Technology**: Artificial Intelligence (AI), Machine Learning (ML), blockchain technology, and behavioural analytics enhance threat detection and response through automation, pattern recognition, real-time evaluation, and anomaly identification. Research indicates that the integration of federated learning with Explainable AI (XAI) can improve efficiency and clarity in fraud detection while maintaining privacy (Awosika et al., 2023).

The absence of integration among these dimensions creates vulnerabilities: fragmented incident response, inadequate legal uniformity, and technology implementations lacking of governance, risking misuse or neglect of fundamental ethical issues. A multi-faceted model where policy directs implementation, regulation facilitates responsible utilisation, and technology actualises prevention is crucial for establishing reliable, adaptive, and secure anti-fraud systems.

1.3 Research Objectives and Scope

This chapter aims to establish a thorough framework that integrates the strategic, legal, and technological aspects in combating fraud and cybercrime. The primary objectives are as follows:

1. **Demonstrate the need for multi-dimensional strategies** by illustrating the constraints of individual approaches and highlighting how integration may improve resilience.
2. **Analyse key strategic and legal mechanisms**, involving international agreements, domestic rules, and exceptional governance practices, while identifying their advantages and limitations.
3. **Review and evaluate technological tools** such as AI/ML, federated learning, blockchain, and XAI in real-world fraud detection systems.
4. **Highlight emerging threats,** especially those leveraging AI deepfakes, adversarial attacks, AI-driven crime tools and discuss defence mechanisms.
5. **Propose a cohesive governance model** that integrates public-private collaboration, legal compliance, and human & AI coordination.

6. **Offer forward-looking recommendations** that address evolving challenges, including quantum-resistant AI, federated threat intelligence, and global harmonization.

The chapter targets interdisciplinary thinkers, including policy-makers, compliance and legal professionals, cybersecurity leaders, AI researchers, and postgraduate students in law, public administration, and information systems. It examines the integration of theory and practice, offering both ideas and practical frameworks supported by empirical evidence and real-world applications.

2. UNDERSTANDING THE MODERN FRAUD AND CYBERCRIME LANDSCAPE

2.1 Definitions and Classifications of Fraud and Cybercrime

Cybercrime include offences aimed at information systems, networks, or the data contained therein, usually for financial profit or disruption. It includes a range from illegal system access and data expropriation to cyber-facilitated fraud and espionage. The United Nations' classification (2000) defines cybercrime into five primary categories: unauthorised access, data/program damage, sabotage, data interception, and espionage-like activities. Fraud, a distinct category, includes deception aimed at achieving financial or personal advantage for the offender. Internet fraud includes phishing, romance scams, pig-butchering frauds, and identity theft ((Internet fraud, 2025)). In addition, crimeware malware designed to automate fraudulent activities including identity theft or financial fraud has emerged as a significant transformed resource inside cybercriminal networks (Sood & Enbody, 2013). Ad fraud, characterised by bots, click farms, and domain spoofing, continues to be an attractive cybercriminal enterprise valued at USD 19 billion in 2017 and anticipated to escalate to USD 44 billion by 2022. The emergence of Cybercrime-as-a-Service (CaaS) introduces further complexity, allowing non-technical individuals to conduct advanced assaults using acquired tools and services. The intersection of cybercrime techniques, fraud categories, and criminal resources such as crimeware and ad fraud underpins the comprehension of dangers in digital banking and e-commerce.

2.2 Emerging Threat Trends in Digital Finance and E-Commerce

The digital transformation of financial services and commerce has expanded the cyber threat surface dramatically:

- **Account Takeover (ATO) Fraud**: In 2025, ATO became a major threat, enabled by cyberattacks on mobile wallets, peer-to-peer (P2P) applications, and cryptocurrency platforms. Fraudsters employ credential stuffing, AI-driven phishing, and deepfake speech impersonations to avoid security measures (FinTalk, 2025).
- **AI-Enhanced Social Engineering**: Artificial intelligence capabilities have empowered criminals to create exceptionally persuasive frauds. Voice cloning and deepfake technology have facilitated the impersonation of individuals to deceive banks, illustrated by a case in Hong Kong resulting in losses of USD 25 million (Hoover, 2025). Artificial intelligence is amplifying fraudulent strategies on a large scale, while institutions find it challenging to adapt accordingly.
- **Ransomware, Double- and Triple-Extortion**: Financial organisations face ransomware that not only encrypts data but also involves the extortion of customer and partner information (double/triple extortion). The MOVEit breach illustrates extensive implications throughout the sector. Current defences encompass zero-trust architecture and immutable backups.
- **API Exploits & Embedded Finance**: The integration of embedded banking and e-commerce through APIs has engendered vulnerabilities—such as compromised authorisation, exposed tokens, and inadequate validations providing financial services a recurrent target.
- **Smishing and Mobile Phishing**: A major smishing campaign conducted by Chinese-speaking organisations compromised around

115 million U.S. credit cards in 2025, employing localised SMS phishing and geofencing evasion strategies (Levy, 2025).
- **Scams as Investment Bait**: In the Gurgaon region of India, over 40% of 16,000 cyber fraud incidents in 2025 were to fraudulent investment schemes distributed through WhatsApp, fake trading applications, and social networking platforms. Ghost accounts were essential for laundering illegal revenues.

These advancements highlight the rapidly changing characteristics of fraud in digital finance and e-commerce, with artificial intelligence, mobile networks, social media platforms, and integrated APIs all being exploited.

2.3 Criminal Actors, Tactics, and the Cybercrime Economy

Modern cybercriminal ecosystems are structured, specialized, and increasingly commercialized:

- **Organized Crime and Identity Fraud**: Organised crime syndicates commit cyber fraud, including identity theft, romance scams, and phishing, as sources of revenue. Complex operations utilise social engineering and network impersonation on social media to mislead victims.
- **Crimeware and CaaS Marketplaces**: Crimeware tools are marketed on underground markets, allowing non-technical criminals to execute automated schemes. These instruments include malware, phishing kits, botnets, and ad fraud tools.
- **Cybercrime-as-a-Service (CaaS)**: CaaS minimises challenges, such as facilitating the deployment of plug-and-play ransomware or phishing operations. The CaaS economy is supported by illegal marketplaces and privacy services, hence transforming cybercrime.
- **Technological Arms Race**: AI-enabled phishing, social engineering, and deepfakes have become readily available. Fraudsters employ these technologies to amplify lying while avoiding detection. AI tools are employed to produce extensive fraudulent customer interactions and bypass outdated systems.

- **Geopolitical Dimensions**: Fraudulent operations in unstable or poorly governed regions intensify global cybercrime. INTERPOL has classified them as a "global crisis," with activities extending across several countries through digital networks.

This ecosystem is driven by advanced technology, specialisation, and interconnected criminal networks, making even local fraud a worldwide issue.

2.4 Economic and Social Impact of Fraud

The impact of fraud and cybercrime is significant financially, societally, and institutionally:

- **Global Financial Costs**: Cybercrime is anticipated to result in yearly costs of USD 10.5 trillion by 2025, positioning it as a major worldwide economic threat. Smaller organisations frequently experience losses ranging from USD 100,000 to USD 500,000 each event, including recovery costs, downtime, legal expenses, and reputational harm (Buckman, 2025).
- **Personal-Level and Business Losses**: In 2024, the U.S. FTC recorded 6.47 million cybercrime complaints, with 40% related to fraud and 18% connected to identity theft. Identity fraud frequently includes credit card schemes and internet payment fraud. In the UK, fraud constituted 41% of all crimes and resulted in £1.1 billion in losses in 2024, reflecting a 14% increase from 2023.
- **Sustained Financial Harm**: Over 60% of small enterprises affected by cyberattacks have been forced to cease operations after six months because of financial strain. Healthcare breaches increased by 25% from 2023 to 2024, highlighting significant sector risks.
- **Societal & Economic Strain**: In addition to direct losses, fraud reduces confidence, diverts law enforcement resources, and transfers risk to victims. In Gurgaon, India, fraudsters manipulated trust networks through WhatsApp and social media, causing significant financial loss and psychological distress. The continued existence of

scam centres in Southeast Asia compromises regional governance and economic stability.

3. STRATEGIC AND POLICY FRAMEWORKS

3.1 The Role of Strategic Policies in Fraud Prevention

Strategic strategies provide essential direction to synchronise organisational conduct, technological implementation, and intersectoral cooperation for an integrated response to fraud and cybercrime. Strategic policies facilitate proactive security by integrating resilience at the system level, a notion referred to as "systems defence" by the World Economic Forum (WEF), rather than relying on reactive, fragmented measures. Instead of depending exclusively on user awareness, upstream policy measures require technology suppliers to highlight security-by-design principles, including phishing-resistant MFA and real-time fraud detection, as standard requirements (Joshi et al., 2025). Governments can leverage state procurement authority such as the U.S. federal government's annual purchasing power of around USD 760 billion—to influence market behaviours towards security-compliant items. Strategic procurement functions as an effective lever. Policy instruments may establish accountability for insecure software and provide incentives for manufacturers conforming to security requirements, promoting a comprehensive transition to enhanced digital infrastructure safety. The Role of Strategic Policies in Fraud Prevention with essential steps is shown in Figure 1.

Strategic policies fulfil multiple essential role:

Figure 1. The role of strategic policies in fraud prevention

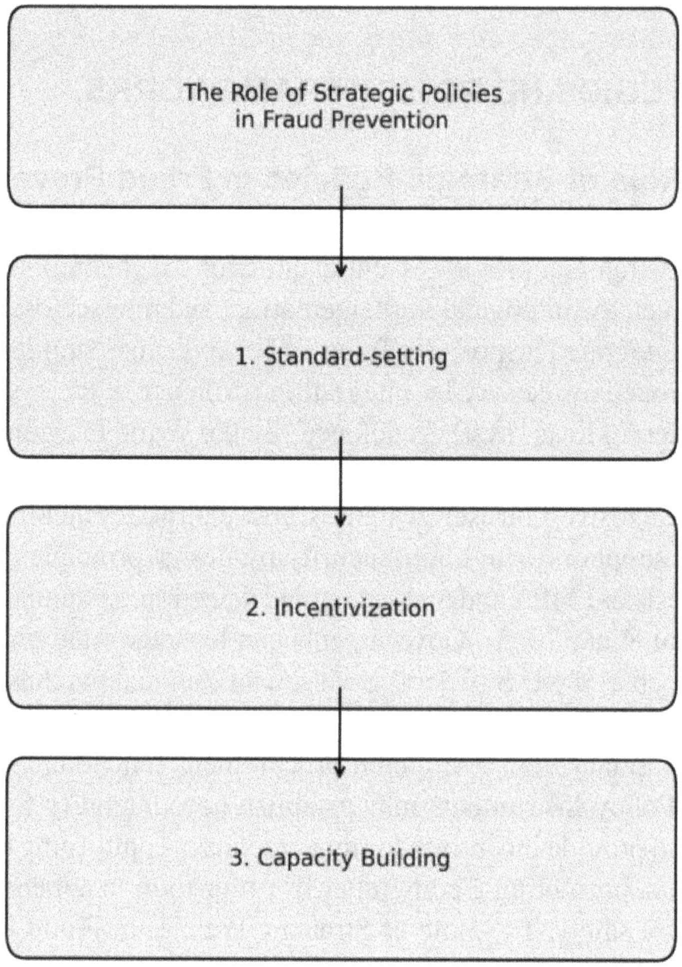

1. Standard-setting: Establishing basic security standards through regulation (e.g., "shadow banking" systems for resilience, as illustrated by the EU DORA program) (Financial Times, 2024).
2. Incentivization: Encouraging vendors to include security features from the ground up through procurement and risk-based rewards
3. Capacity building: Directing resources toward stakeholder training, research, and innovation.

4. Stress testing: Periodic evaluation of frameworks through pressure tests and real-world incident response simulations (Alicia, 2025).

These strategic layers provide an effective basis for operational execution, regulatory compliance, and technological integration.

3.2 International Cybersecurity and Anti-Fraud Strategies

Numerous international frameworks aim to standardise legal norms, promote cross-border cooperation, and enhance cyber resilience.

3.2.1 Multilateral Treaties and Conventions

- The Budapest Convention on Cybercrime (2001) is the inaugural international treaty aimed at standardising cybercrime legislation, improving investigation methodologies, and boosting collaboration among member governments. By mid-2025, 80 governments had ratified the agreement, while Ireland and South Africa had signed but not approved it; India remains a non-signatory due to concerns regarding sovereignty.
- Emerging frameworks such as the UN Cybercrime Convention aim to standardise worldwide practices while safeguarding civil rights, although widespread implementation is still in development (Kudriasova, 2025).

3.2.2 Regional and Collaborative Mechanisms

- The European Electronic Crime Task Force (EECTF), established in 2009, consolidates public bodies, financial institutions, academic entities, and security companies to share knowledge and formulate strategic responses throughout Europe.
- The African Union Convention on Cyber Security and Personal Data Protection (AU-CPSD) establishes an interconnected legal and capacity-building framework for African member states, despite on-

going variations in legal systems and resource limitations (Bouke et al., 2023).

- The OIC-CERT, with 27 member states and coordinated by Cyber Security Malaysia, provides emergency assistance and policy direction among Islamic nations.

3.2.3 Capacity Maturity Models

The Cybersecurity Capacity Maturity Model for Nations (CMM), created through international collaboration, allows nations to evaluate and enhance their cybersecurity preparedness across policy, legal, technical, and organisational aspects. Public-Private Operational Collaboratives Collaborations such as the WEF's Systemic Defence and the Counter Ransomware Initiative comprising 56 participating nations aimed at ceasing ransom payments and exchanging cyber strategies and Visa's USD 12 billion investment in fraud detection and response illustrate strategic alignment across sectors (Graff, 2024). These worldwide policies collectively offer frameworks for policy alignment, capacity improvements and coordinated efforts crucial for addressing transnational cyber-enabled fraud.

3.3 Cross-Border Policy Challenges and Jurisdictional Gaps

Despite advancements, the enforcement of policies across borders continues to face significant legal, ethical, and technical challenges.

3.3.1 Jurisdictional Complexity

Different legal systems, definitions of cybercrime, and enforcement capacities limit prosecution. Jurisdiction determination may rely on factors such as the offender's nationality, the crime's location, or the victim's impact concepts represented in the principles of nationality, passive personality, and protective jurisdiction (United Nations Office on Drugs and Crime, 2013).

3.3.2 Mutual Legal Assistance (MLA) Constraints

Requests for Mutual Legal Assistance depend on sluggish, bureaucratic procedures. Delays in response to a hack that produces volatile digital evidence can lead to data loss. The establishment of Joint Investigation Teams (JITs) presents potential benefits but frequently encounters delays in beginning and challenges in coordination (Eurojust, 2020).

3.3.3 Transnational Cybercrime Enforcement Challenges

Cybercriminals can exploit inconsistencies in national laws to avoid prosecution, for as by operating from jurisdictions with inadequate cyber legislation. Territorial sovereignty concerns increase coordination challenges, obstructing prompt investigations and extraditions. The legal uncertainty regarding the location of offenses whether determined by server location, data storage, or resultant impacts generates uncertainties in international law.

Addressing these challenges requires:

1. **Harmonized legal definitions** of cyber-enabled fraud across treaties.
2. **Expedited MLA mechanisms** and better resourcing for JITs.
3. **Regional agreements** for quick response especially important where digital evidence is permanent.

3.4 Risk Management and Governance Principles

Sound governance and risk management are critical to translating policy into effective anti-fraud action:

3.4.1 Integrated Governance Models

Organisations need to consolidate cybersecurity and fraud prevention teams, establishing common objectives, key performance indicators, and communication tools. Thomson Reuters highlights the necessity of cross-training and alignment across these teams for effective real-time threat identification and preventive defence (Meda, 2024).

3.4.2 Risk-Based Regulatory Compliance

Regulators are progressively mandating zero-trust security models, continuous monitoring, and quick incident response planning, in accordance with frameworks such as NIS2 (EU), DORA, Circia, and U.S. critical infrastructure requirements.

3.4.3 White-Box Evaluation & Stress Testing

Legal requirements and internal regulations necessitate periodic performance evaluations and simulated fraud event practices. Baker & McKenzie advise conducting pressure tests on fraud control systems to evaluate their durability and reactivity (Alicia, 2025).

3.4.4 Performance Metrics and Accountability

Shared organisational metrics such as average time to discover breaches, fraud reduced and stakeholder trust enhance accountability and strategy alignment among teams and agencies. Integrating governance into policy and practice guarantees that the organisational structure, conduct, and resource distribution are aligned for ongoing fraud resilience and adaptability.

4. LEGAL AND REGULATORY LANDSCAPE

4.1 Key International Regulatory Frameworks (GDPR, PSD2, FATF, etc.)

Several international regulatory frameworks define the essential legal foundations for addressing fraud and cybercrime, including privacy, financial integrity, and transnational collaboration.

4.1.1 GDPR (General Data Protection Regulation)

Established in 2018, the GDPR imposes strict rules on the processing of personal data within the European Union and extends its applicability worldwide to entities managing data of EU residents. It enforces substantial penalties reaching €20 million or 4% of a company's annual global revenue for infractions like inadequate transparency, insufficient user permission, or inadequate security measures (European Data Protection Board, 2024). Significant penalties, exemplified by the €1.2 billion punishment imposed on Meta in 2023, illustrate the authority of regulatory enforcement. The GDPR establishes concepts such as privacy by design, data minimisation, and accountability. However, objections have arisen: small and medium firms (SMEs) perceive compliance as difficult, and others believe that GDPR may impede prompt fraud detection by limiting inter-organizational data sharing especially when such sharing is legally restricted (Doherty, 2025). In addition, variations in enforcement attributable to delays in cross-border cases and the "one-stop shop" mechanism have resulted in reports that large technology companies can circumvent prompt responsibility. Recent decisions in Germany or by the European General Court indicating that mere loss of data control may warrant compensation, even in the absence of concrete damage, could broaden the extent of responsibility, especially for organisations facing compliance challenges. Reuters, 2025.

4.1.2 PSD2 (Payment Services Directive 2)

Introduced in 2018, PSD2 updated Europe's payment ecosystem by adding strong customer authentication (SCA), open APIs, and secure communication standards, considerably increasing fraud protection in online transactions. PSD2 requires multi-factor authentication (two of knowledge, possession, or inherence) for most electronic payments, allowing more secure authorization and lowering fraud risk. It also requires enhanced openness and accelerated event reporting to increase confidence in financial institutions (Sollitto, 2024). This has transformed fraud prevention techniques and consumer experience for merchants.

4.1.3 FATF (Financial Action Task Force)

The FATF establishes international benchmarks for preventing money laundering (AML) and terrorist financing, that involve hazards associated with fraud. Despite lacking regional enforceability, FATF proposals incentivise member nations to implement comprehensive risk-based frameworks, utilise transaction monitoring systems, and promote cross-border information exchange.

These frameworks collectively embody a confluence of privacy, financial integrity, and collaboration. GDPR safeguards personal data and influences fraud-prevention technologies, PSD2 strengthens payment infrastructure, and FATF promotes global oversight and cross-border enforcement.

4.2 National Laws and Sector-Specific Compliance Requirements

At both national and sectoral levels, customised law strengthens these international principles and adapts them to local settings.

4.2.1 UK – Data Protection Act (2018)

The UK's Data Protection Act 2018 enacts GDPR, establishes specific regulations for law enforcement and intelligence agencies, and confers enforcement authority to the Information Commissioner's Office (ICO). The Act imposes criminal penalties for unauthorised access to or misuse of data.

4.2.2 National Enforcement Disparities & Challenges

In the EU, enforcement inconsistencies are influenced by the varying national Data Protection Authorities (DPAs). Western European nations have been more aggressive in imposing fines, approaching €500 million by early 2020; However, the rate of enforcement has fluctuated, and smaller Data Protection Authorities encounter backlogs (Daigle & Khan, 2020).

The "one-stop shop" system occasionally causes delays in procedures, thereby reducing the effectiveness of deterrence (Burgess, 2020).

4.2.3 AI Governance Regulations

New AI legislation, including the EU AI Act, highlight openness, accountability, and the reduction of bias in automated systems utilised for fraud prediction or screening. An increasing focus on explainable AI (XAI) signifies a need for auditability and legal transparency.

4.2.4 Law Enforcement Coordination

In August 2025, Indian authorities organised an inter-agency coordination meeting with the Chandigarh Police, Reserve Bank of India (RBI), telecom companies, and banks to address AI-driven cyber fraud. The session handled significant issues such as KYC deficiencies, postponed sharing of data, and insufficient weekend assistance, while instituting quarterly coordination and standardised procedures (Times of India, 2025).

4.3 Data Protection, Privacy, and AI Governance Regulations

Emerging technologies, including AI-driven fraud detection systems, must balance security effectiveness with privacy and ethical responsibilities as the Figure 2 shows Data Protection, Privacy, and AI Governance Regulations.

Figure 2. Data protection, privacy, and AI governance regulations

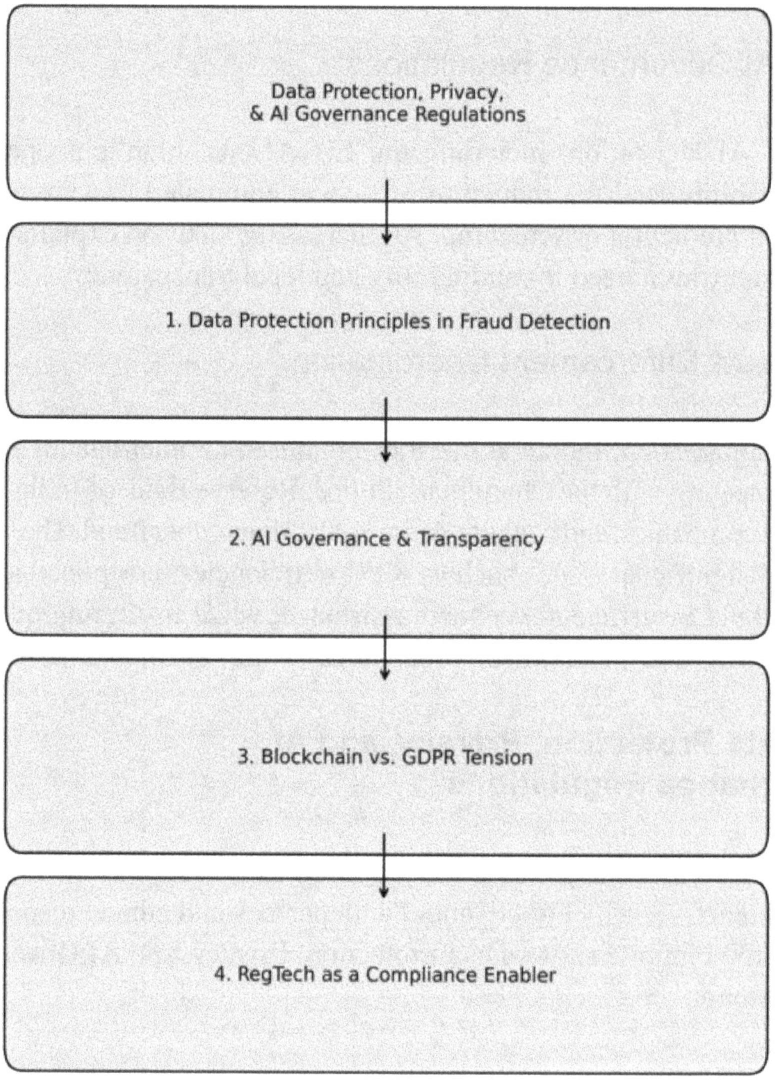

- Data Protection Principles in Fraud Detection: The GDPR specifies purpose limitation and data minimisation, necessitating that fraud detection solutions gather only essential consumer data and explicitly notify users regarding monitoring activities (DataDome, 2025).

Organisations must integrate privacy by design and default, meticulously documenting data flows to comply with GDPR rules.

- AI Governance & Transparency: Systems utilising AI need to conform to evolving requirements for accountability and bias reduction. The GDPR's focus on openness and the necessity for AI choices to be interpretable suggests the adoption of rule-based or hybrid methodologies to ensure compliance (Kingston, 2018).
- Blockchain vs. GDPR Tension: Public blockchain systems provide issues for GDPR compliance due to its immutability, which obstructs the "right to be forgotten," confusing delineation of responsibilities between data controllers and processors, and ambiguous territorial application (Belen-Saglam et al., 2023).
- RegTech as a Compliance Enabler: Regulatory Technology (RegTech) assists organisations in fulfilling GDPR's accountability requirements through compliance dashboards, metadata tracking, and automated reporting. However, interoperability and validation deficiencies remain, constraining efficiency (Ryan et al., 2020).

These factors highlight persistent conflicts between innovation and legal structures. Artificial intelligence and new technologies can improve fraud detection.

4.4 Legal Gaps and Challenges in Enforcement

Despite robust frameworks, significant gaps and enforcement challenges persist across jurisdictions:

- **Resource Constraints and Slow Investigations:** Enforcement of GDPR has frequently been complicated by insufficient resources and complex cross-border coordination. The ICO's poor response during the COVID-19 outbreak attracted criticism, underscoring operational difficulties in upholding data privacy (Burgess, 2020).
- **Technological Conflicts with Legal Principles:** Modern cloud systems frequently breach GDPR stipulations due to anti-patterns such as unlimited data retention, absence of removal dates, and opaque

decision-making procedures, hence making compliance fundamentally challenging (Shastri et al., 2019).

- **Balancing Fraud Detection & Privacy Rights:** The dual objectives of user protection and fraud detection may conflict GDPR's strong individual safeguards might occasionally delay essential fraud notifications or data sharing with law enforcement. The integration of prompt fraud action with the safeguarding of privacy presents a complex legal challenge.

Although the legal framework addressing fraud and cybercrime is advanced and continually developing, practical enforcement remains inadequate compared to technology advancements and operational requirements.

5. TECHNOLOGICAL FOUNDATIONS FOR AI-DRIVEN FRAUD DETECTION

5.1 Evolution of Fraud Detection Technologies

Fraud detection has progressed markedly over the past few decades, transitioning from rule-based systems anchored in predetermined criteria to intelligent, AI-driven adaptive models. Initial systems utilised expert systems that contained specialised knowledge in "if-then" rules for identifying anomalous patterns. These programs proved competent in familiar circumstances but encountered difficulties with innovative or complex types of fraud. With the emergence of data mining and statistical analysis, financial institutions commenced employing data mining techniques to categorise, cluster, and identify irregularities in transaction data, establishing the foundation for modern machine learning methodologies. With the escalation in data volumes and complexity, machine learning (ML) provided enhanced adaptability, facilitating dynamic models that integrate evolving patterns without the necessity of explicit programming. Modern systems frequently include various AI/ML models hybrid methodologies that can more efficiently identify both established and innovative fraud trends. Real-time data processing, pattern recognition, and adaptive learning have become standard, facilitating rapid and precise responses to emerging threats (Jarugula, 2025).

5.2 AI and Machine Learning Approaches

Artificial Intelligence and Machine Learning currently form the foundation of the majority of advanced fraud detection systems. These techniques are classified into three major categories:

5.2.1 Supervised Learning Models

Supervised learning develops models utilising labelled instances transactions identified as fraudulent or lawful. Prevalent algorithms encompass Random Forests, XGBoost, Support Vector Machines (SVMs), and deep neural networks. tested supervised models such as XGBoost and Random Forests on credit card fraud data, with AUROC scores over 0.98, so demonstrating robust performance when accurate labels are accessible.

5.2.2 Unsupervised and Anomaly Detection

In the absence of abundant labelled data, unsupervised algorithms excel. Methods such as autoencoders, One-Class SVMs, and clustering identify abnormal behaviour without prior categorisation. Investigations utilising autoencoders and RBMs identified abnormal transactions in credit card data with strong recall, demonstrating potential for finding previously unrecognised fraud patterns(Niu et al., 2019) Anomaly detection techniques, including isolation forests, local outlier factor, and one-class SVMs, are widely utilised to discover statistical outliers.

5.2.3 Hybrid Approaches

Hybrid models integrate supervised and unsupervised methodologies to leverage the advantages of each. An excellent model is a Mixture of Experts (MoE) that integrates RNNs, Transformers, and autoencoders. This model dynamically evaluates expert predictions, attaining 98.7%

accuracy, 94.3% precision, and 91.5% recall on synthetic transaction datasets, thereby greatly outperforming baseline models. Such systems more effectively adapt to emerging fraud strategies while maintaining detection accuracy and generalisability.

5.3 Behavioural Analytics and Pattern Recognition

In addition to statistical modelling, behavioural analytics monitoring user interactions with systems has gained significant importance. Identifying patterns in user behaviour uncovers complex variations that traditional models may overlook. Integrating Behavioural Analytics with Cyber Threat Intelligence (CTI) enables organisations to transition from reactive post-hoc detection to proactive defence. Analysts can analyse user behaviour trends and identify anomalies, such as atypical login timings, navigation behaviours, or interaction patterns, thereby discovering dangers prior to their escalation (Dahl et al., 2025). Behavioural biometrics, such as mouse movement, typing cadence, and device usage, enhance detection capabilities. Major companies such as Mastercard utilise this data to differentiate authentic users from fraudsters, thereby preventing identity theft and first-party fraud.

5.4 Blockchain and Distributed Ledger Technologies

Blockchain and distributed ledger technology (DLT) have distinctive attributes immutability, transparency, and decentralised trust that enhance fraud detection systems. One method entails utilising supervised learning on blockchain transaction graphs. Ostapowicz and illustrated the application of classifiers such as Random Forest and XGBoost for the identification of fraudulent accounts on Ethereum, attaining high recall and precision even inside decentralised, pseudonymous contexts (Ostapowicz & Żbikowski, 2019).. Additional study investigates blockchain-facilitated machine learning collaboration: introduced a framework that integrates blockchain with smart contracts to securely distribute machine learning models among organisations. This technique attained strong detection performance (~98.9% accuracy) while maintaining privacy through incentivised, secure model upgrades (Pranto et al., 2022). Despite these benefits, blockchain presents obstacles, mostly concerning GDPR compliance and privacy integration. Current research highlights privacy-preserving methodologies such as federated learning and zero-knowledge proofs to guarantee secure and compliant implementations.

5.5 Threat Intelligence Sharing Platforms

Efficient fraud detection transcends individual systems to encompass inter-entity threat intelligence transmission. Threat Intelligence Platforms (TIPs) consolidate, refine, and distribute threat data, enhancing an organization's overall security posture. Wikipedia, 2025. The fundamental standards of contemporary CTI sharing are STIX and TAXII. STIX (Structured Threat Information eXpression) establishes a standardised lexicon for articulating threats indicators, tactics, methods, and procedures (TTPs). TAXII (Trusted Automated eXchange of Indicator Information) is the communication protocol that facilitates the automated and secure exchange of STIX data between tools and teams (Anomali, 2024). STIX/TAXII were initially created by the U.S. Department of Homeland Security and MITRE, subsequently embraced by OASIS for global standardisation. Real-world platforms such as Microsoft Sentinel utilise integrated TAXII connectors to automatically ingest threat data, hence enhancing analysts' efficiency in addressing and responding to incoming threats (Microsoft, 2025). These platforms facilitate real-time, organised intelligence sharing, enabling institutions to identify fraud tendencies across several targets or areas, thus enhancing collective resilience.

6. ADVERSARIAL THREATS TO AI MODELS

6.1 Understanding Adversarial AI Attacks

Adversarial Machine Learning (AML) refers to intentional acts by adversaries aimed at manipulating AI systems, particularly machine learning models, to yield incorrect predictions. These attacks capitalise on weaknesses in model assumptions, especially when models assume that training and test data conform to the same statistical distribution, which attackers might intentionally damage.

AML attacks typically take the following forms:

- **Evasion attacks**: Small, frequently undetectable alterations (perturbations) to inputs that result in misclassification widely illustrated in image and audio contexts, although equally alarming for financial systems.
- **Data poisoning attacks**: Contamination of training data may lead the model to acquire inaccurate or harmful patterns, perhaps establishing backdoors that promote misbehaviour upon activation.
- **Privacy and inference attacks**: Utilising machine learning algorithms to deduce training data or sensitive attributes, potentially compromising data confidentiality or exposing vulnerabilities (Pelekis et al., 2025).

As AI infiltrates critical industries such as financial fraud detection, understanding these adversarial techniques is vital for creating robust systems.

6.2 Model Evasion and Data Poisoning in Fraud Detection

6.2.1 Evasion Attacks in Fraud Detection

In fraud detection, evasion attempts involve the selective modification of transaction attributes to prevent the AI model from identifying fraudulent activity. For instance, attackers may alter transaction metadata (e.g., timestamp, amount, geolocation) to remain within standard parameters or replicate authentic user activity. These evasion strategies target vulnerabilities in the model's decision boundary.

6.2.2 Data Poisoning Attacks

Data poisoning is a significant threat in contexts where models are perpetually updated or retrained using real-time data. In this context, adversaries may introduce fake "fraudulent" or innocent samples that reduce model performance. Recent research presents FRAUD-RLA, an adversarial approach based on reinforcement learning targeting credit card fraud detection systems. This attack enhances deceptive tactics with restricted understanding of the foundational framework, illustrating the viability of advanced poisoning in financial contexts (Lunghi et al., 2025).

6.2.3 Unifying Attacks and Threat Modelling

Detailed analyses of AML underscore interconnected vulnerabilities including both evasion and poisoning. This literature highlights that systems optimised for high accuracy might show weakness when faced with threatening cases or contaminated training datasets.

6.3 Hardening AI Models: Robust Training and defence Mechanisms

To counter adversarial threats, several defence strategies have been developed:

- Adversarial Training: Adversarial training, a prevalent defence mechanism, includes adversarial cases into the training process, enabling the model to learn to withstand such changes. This technique modifies model loss functions to equilibrate performance on both clean and threatening data (Neptune.ai, 2023). Despite its efficiency, it is limited by the predicted attack types models might fail when faced with innovative, unencountered adversarial techniques.
- AML Tools and Benchmarks: Cutting-edge AML frameworks are developing, providing open-source tools and benchmarks for robustness analysis across various domains, including image recognition and financial systems. Practitioners can utilise these tools to evaluate model robustness against recognised adversarial attacks.

- Generative Adversarial Networks (GANs) for Defence: GANs fulfil a dual role in fraud detection: they can emulate adversarial behaviours for model training and function as detection instruments themselves. Fraud protection systems employing GANs can reduce false-positive rates by 50%, hence enhancing detection robustness (BankInfoSecurity, 2025). GANs facilitate both defensive simulation and anomaly detection.

6.4 Explainable AI for Trust and Compliance

Explainable AI (XAI) offers transparency and interpretability in model decisions critical for trust and compliance in regulated environments.

6.4.1 XAI in Fraud Detection Systems

Effective fraud-detection algorithms must conform to regulatory mandates, including GDPR, and facilitate oversight by auditors and compliance personnel. Methods like SHAP and LIME provide post-hoc elucidations for understanding the impact of features on model outputs. Hybrid frameworks that integrate interpretable models with these strategies attain both superior performance and explainability.

6.4.2 XAI in Federated Learning Models

The integration of Explainable Artificial Intelligence (XAI) with Federated Learning (FL) reduces data privacy concerns while improving transparency. Federated Learning facilitates collaborative model training without the exchange of raw data, while Explainable Artificial Intelligence guarantees that the resulting predictions are interpretable and reliable.

6.4.3 Transparency vs. Adversarial Exposure

Although XAI enhances oversight, it may also expose the model's inner mechanisms to adversaries, enabling them to reverse-engineer trigger features and avoid detection. Designers have to combine transparency with strategic opacity to prevent inadvertently assisting attackers.

6.4.4 Regulatory Accountability and Explainability

Opaque AI determinations limit legal transparency. Leaders like Jamie Dimon of JPMorgan underscore the necessity for transparency in AI systems, especially within the financial sector. The upcoming EU AI Act establishes mandates for explainability and human oversight in high-risk sectors, hence enhancing the significance of XAI in legal adherence.

7. GLOBAL CASE STUDIES & LESSONS LEARNED

7.1 Banking Sector Case Studies

7.1.1 JPMorgan Chase—AI-Powered Real-Time Fraud Reduction

JPMorgan Chase deployed AI-driven tools that analyse transactional behaviours and customer profiles instantaneously. Through the integration of machine learning models, including behavioural biometrics, and the alignment with current fraud infrastructure, the bank reportedly realised a 60% decrease in credit card fraud within six months of using (SuperAGI, 2025). The system's capacity to process millions of transactions and swiftly identify irregularities demonstrates superior operational efficiency and concrete financial advantage.

7.1.2 Secure Bank Corp via AIVEDA

Secure Bank Corp, facing increasing fraud and decreasing client trust, implemented AIVEDA's AI suite, which includes decision trees, random forests, neural networks, and real-time monitoring using SIEM and intrusion detection systems. In a single quarter, fraudulent transactions decreased by 70%, while consumer satisfaction rose by 25% (AIVeda, 2024). This demonstrates how multi-model integration and real-time alerting may quickly re-establish trust and operational stability.

7.1.3 Indian Banking Sector—AI for Phishing & Money Laundering Detection

Research from IIM Ahmedabad highlights the implementation of AI techniques, including neural networks, anomaly detection, and predictive analytics, in Indian banks. These solutions addressed money laundering, phishing, and illegal transaction schemes, conforming to RBI regulatory standards. The findings demonstrate significant decreases in fraud and enhanced regulatory compliance (Dubey, 2022).

7.2 E-Commerce Fraud Prevention Success Stories

7.2.1 TickPick & Riskified—Recovering Revenue via Adaptive AI

Riskified's "Adaptive Checkout" solution employs artificial intelligence to evaluate transaction risk, resulting in approvals, decreases, or requests for more verification. When executed by TickPick, a high-ticket e-commerce company, it recouped USD 3 million in income from transactions previously misidentified as fraudulent within three months. This highlights the significance of precision-oriented AI in minimising false decreases that result in revenue loss and reduced client goodwill.

7.2.2 Contrastive Learning for E-Commerce Fraud Detection

A recent scholarly investigation established a SimCLR-based contrastive learning model for identifying unlabelled fraud in e-commerce datasets. The model, evaluated on actual eBay data, outperformed conventional unsupervised methods such as k-means clustering and isolation forests in terms of accuracy, precision, recall, and F1 measures (Li et al., 2025). This indicates the potential of innovative unsupervised deep learning methodologies in e-commerce settings characterised by a lack of labelled data.

7.3 Public-Private Partnership Models in Fraud Prevention

7.3.1 Chandigarh, India—Multi-Stakeholder Coordination

In response to an increase in AI-driven fraud, phishing, and mule-account frauds, Chandigarh Police organised a high-level meeting with the RBI, telecommunications providers, and public and private banking institutions. The partnership resulted in standards for prompt subscriber data sharing, swift SIM deactivation, and account suspension. Quarterly meetings and stakeholder commitment to the Chakshu reporting platform were instituted. This case illustrates how operational alignment among sectors enhances proactive detection and response.

7.3.2 Indian Armed Forces—Cybersecurity PPP Doctrine

The Indian Armed Forces have recently established a Joint Doctrine for Cyberspace Operations, expressly recognising the involvement of private-sector partners in cybersecurity. This theory enhances national cyber resilience through integrating private expertise in threat detection and resilience development.

7.4 Cross-Border and Transnational Cybercrime Investigations

1. Operation Jackal III—Targeting West African Syndicates: Interpol's Operation Jackal III (2024) dismantled West African fraud networks, including Black Axe, across 21 nations on five continents. The operation resulted in the closure of 720 bogus bank accounts associated with online financial crime. This demonstrates law enforcement's capacity to organise complex international enforcement operations.
2. CBI Operation Chakra-V—Noida Call Centre Raid: On July 7, 2025, India's CBI dismantled a Noida-based contact centre, FirstIdea, involved in fraud schemes targeting the United Kingdom and Australia. The operation, in collaboration with the FBI, UK National Crime

Agency, and Microsoft, demonstrated real-time evidence collection and international cooperation in combating social engineering fraud.

3. Surat Police—Crypto-enabled Cross-Border Fraud: The Surat DCB exposed a fraudulent syndicate including China, Pakistan, and Myanmar. Perpetrators changed victim monies into cryptocurrency (USDT) through Binance, subsequently moving the proceeds overseas. The case illustrates contemporary fraudulent techniques employing cryptocurrency trails and international digital collaboration.

8. ETHICAL, OPERATIONAL, AND ORGANIZATIONAL CHALLENGES

8.1 Data Privacy and Ethical AI Concerns

AI-driven fraud detection systems have advanced functionalities; yet, they frequently necessitate huge quantities of sensitive data, which raises significant ethical and privacy issues. Many systems functions without obtaining fully informed permission. Individuals may be unaware of the collection and utilisation of their financial and behavioural data for AI-driven fraud analysis, which might act upon privacy rights and regulatory requirements such as GDPR and CCPA (ResearchGate, 2025). The lack of transparency in these systems destroys confidence and responsibility, as individuals are unaware of how their data is processed—or even that it is being processed at all. Ethical frameworks, such as those suggested by KPMG, emphasise the significance of data minimisation, transparency, fairness, accountability, and privacy-by-design throughout the AI lifecycle (KPMG, 2025). The European AI Act categorises fraud detection systems as high-risk, necessitating comprehensive documentation, bias testing, and oversight from development to implementation. Organisations must transcend mere compliance and adopt Ethics by Design proactively integrating ethical issues into system development. This includes privacy-preserving technologies such federated learning, differential privacy, safe multiparty computation, and homomorphic encryption, as recommended by ethical AI frameworks (B2Bdaily, 2024).

8.2 Algorithmic Bias and Fairness in Fraud Detection

Algorithmic bias continues to pose a substantial risk in AI-based fraud detection systems. Models trained on biassed historical data may perpetuate or intensify inequitable treatment among demographic groups, resulting in unjust bad results for specific populations, especially marginalised communities. Wikipedia, 2025. Research indicates that bias in fraud detection can be complex yet widespread. Pombal discovered that bias originates from the interplay between model architecture and data imbalances, indicating that fundamental bias reduction techniques, such as excluding sensitive features, can prove ineffectual (Pombal et al., 2022). Nuanced methodologies, such as fairness-aware algorithms and bias audits, are essential to integrate service excellence with equitable treatment.

Practical examples demonstrate the hazards: In the UK, the DWP's fraud algorithm mistakenly identified 200,000 housing benefit claims, two-thirds of which were valid, resulting in unwarranted investigations and distress among disadvantaged groups (FRPA, 2024). Similarly, Denmark's welfare surveillance system encountered criticism for including sensitive characteristics such as nationality, which raised worries regarding systematic profiling and insufficient transparency. Organisations must do algorithmic audits, create customised fairness indicators for skewed fraud data, and ensure human oversight in decision-making processes to establish equitable systems. Ethical AI frameworks advocate for iterative bias identification and correction, as well as the use of diverse training data to prevent systemic imbalance.

8.3 Organizational Silos and Coordination Issues

Technological and ethical systems can't survive in isolation. Fraud detection frequently encounters challenges due to the fragmentation of data, knowledge, and jurisdiction across departments, preventing comprehensive responses. Digital Ocean highlights that a successful fraud strategy requires a multidisciplinary fraud management team with experts from IT, data science, operations, compliance, and legal sectors (Lulka, 2024). In the absence of this structure, organisations face the danger of mismatch between detection logic and regulatory or operational restrictions. In addition, data silos restrict learning and decrease model efficiency. When behavioural, transactional, and risk data exist in various places, models lack the contextual information necessary to differentiate between harmful activities and anomalies. Addressing barriers may require investment in federated learning, enabling collaborative modelling while maintaining local data autonomy. When combined with a governance framework based on shared KPIs, audit policies, and cohesive workflows, federated systems can address functional and ethical differences within organisations.

8.4 Incident Response and SOC Integration

Efficient fraud operations necessitate the integration of AI detection with human-driven incident response, often located within Security Operations Centres (SOCs). SOC solutions, such as SIEM (Security Information and Event Management) systems, consolidate signals from various networks and systems, facilitating real-time incident triage and forensic analysis. Integrating fraud telemetry into SIEM solutions guarantees that financial irregularities are addressed with equivalent haste and coordination as cybersecurity risks. Still, integration issues endure. Many organisations utilise older systems that are incompatible with real-time risk feeds, and Security Operations Centre (SOC) teams are generally trained to address IT or cybersecurity issues rather than transaction-level fraud patterns. Addressing this gap necessitates training and architectural improvements to integrate transaction streams, behavioural signals, and risk assessments into SOC dashboards. Human analysts are crucial for analysing complicated fraud indicators and resolving false positives, as highlighted in debates of AI-human hybrid models for trust and oversight.

9. PROPOSED INTEGRATED GOVERNANCE & TECHNOLOGY MODEL

9.1 Conceptual Framework for AI-Powered Fraud Prevention

This architecture shown in Figure 3 combines strategic governance, legal compliance, and advanced AI to establish a resilient, adaptive fraud prevention ecosystem. The approach inspired by Awosika et al. (2023), integrates Explainable AI and Federated Learning for privacy-preserving fraud detection, prioritising data confidentiality, interpretability, and institutional trust. An institutionally orientated model, employed in financial environments such as the UAE and Qatar, includes seven fundamental constructs: transparency, algorithmic bias, fairness perception, trust, regulatory compliance, AI exposure, and AI adoption. Trust and fairness facilitate adoption, with regulatory compliance serving as a key driver.

Figure 3. Consolidated conceptual framework for AI-powered fraud prevention

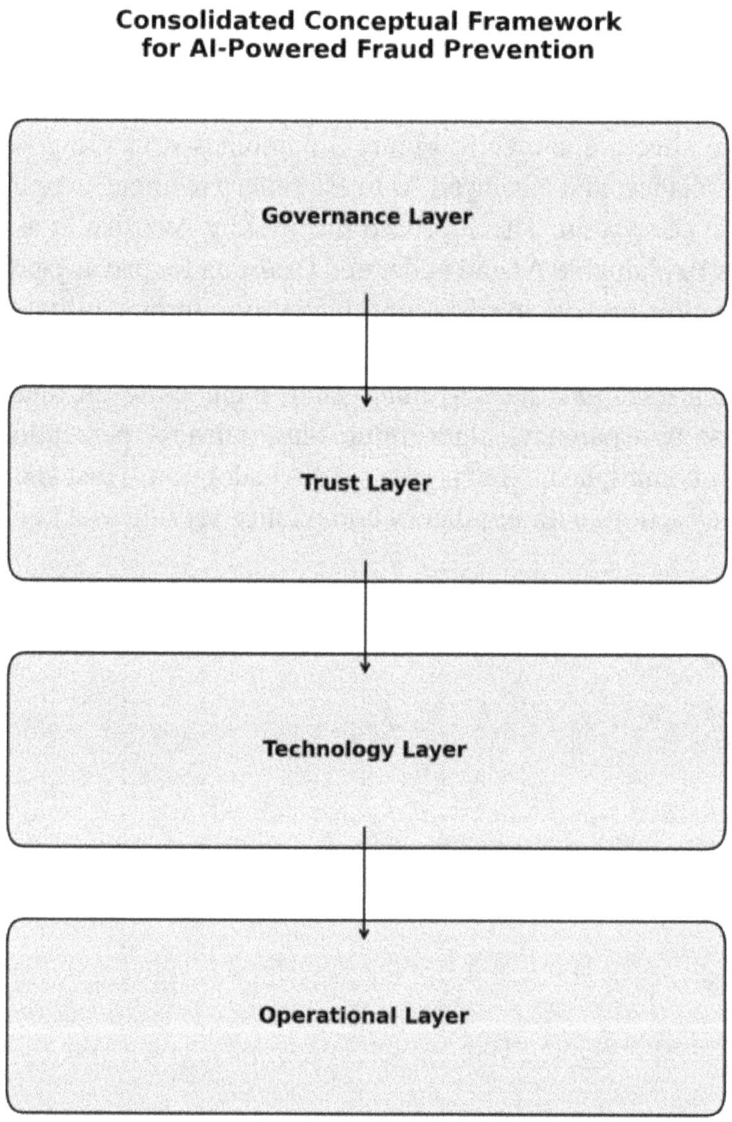

Consolidated Conceptual Framework:

1. **Governance Layer**: Emphasizes transparency, fairness, and regulatory compliance.
2. **Trust Layer**: Builds user and stakeholder confidence through explainable outputs and ethical design.
3. **Technology Layer**:
   - o Employs AI models (hybrid architectures like Mixture of Experts),
   - o Incorporates federated and explainable technologies,
   - o Ensures integration with real-time and early warning systems (e.g., streaming pipelines).
4. **Operational Layer**: Embeds real-time risk evaluation, SOC coordination, and multi-agency communication protocols.

This layered model ensures that AI is not just effective, but ethically anchored, regulated, interpretable, and aligned with cross-sectoral operational needs.

9.2 Multi-Agency and Cross-Sector Collaboration Strategies

An efficient anti-fraud ecosystem necessitates robust connections among public agencies, financial institutions, regulators, and technology vendors. The UAE–Qatar study highlights that regulatory compliance, openness, and equity promote AI adoption, suggesting that collaborative trust among institutions is essential for good governance.

Collaboration Techniques:

- **Federated Learning Across Entities**: Enables multiple institutions to co-train fraud models without sharing raw customer data preserving confidentiality while enhancing detection capabilities
- **Federated Graphs for Relationship Analysis**: Real-time contextual systems employ federated graph learning to map emergent fraud patterns across networks while respecting privacy.
- **Shared Early Warning Platforms**: Multi-sector institutions exchange risk indicators using structured standards such as STIX/TAXII—facilitating timely threat intelligence.

- **Joint Governance Forums**: Regular coordination, as seen in Chandigarh's stakeholder meetings, ensures practical issue resolution and aligns operational practices across sectors.

This collaborative design ensures that adaptive host detection systems are reinforced by collective learning, shared governance, and coordinated response.

9.3 AI–Human Teaming in Decision-Making

Despite the increasing complexity of AI, human judgement is important for monitoring, ethical decision-making, and contextual understanding. TechRadar underscores that although AI enhances detection accuracy and reduces false positives, hybrid systems that integrate AI with human expertise are essential for sustained resilience and trust.

Roles and Complementarity:

- **AI Systems**: Monitor vast data streams, flag anomalies, generate risk scores, provide real-time alerts.
- **Human Experts**: Investigate complex cases, calibrate AI rules, interpret system signals, and offer ethical context.
- **Explainability (XAI)**: Tools like SHAP or LIME facilitate human understanding of AI decisions, building confidence and accountability.
- **Feedback Integration**: Human decisions inform AI models through feedback loops, enhancing performance and transparency over time.

9.4 Integration and Synthesis of the Model

Table 1. Summary of the integrated model

Layer	Components
Governance	Transparency, fairness, compliance, multi-sector trust mechanisms
Technology	Hybrid AI models, federated learning, real-time pipelines, XAI
Collaboration	Cross-institution federated modelling, STIX/TAXII info sharing, forums
Human-AI Interaction	AI automated alerts + human investigation + feedback loops
Infrastructure	Unified real-time data platform, cloud-native CEP, early warning systems

This Table 1 promotes a comprehensive strategy that integrates governance, trust, technology, collaboration, and human oversight into an integrated framework for robust fraud prevention.

9.5 Real-Time Monitoring and Early Warning Architectures

Real-time capabilities are essential for detecting and responding to fast-moving fraud in digital finance.

Benefits of Real-Time Architectures:

- **Immediate Detection**: Identifies fraud during transaction execution.
- **Reduced False Positives**: Adaptive models calibrate thresholds dynamically.
- **Operational Agility**: Enables dynamic response (e.g., blocking, MFA prompts).
- **Regulatory Compliance**: Ensures governance workflows are embedded into real-time detection.

10. FUTURE OUTLOOK

10.1 Emerging Trends: Federated Learning, Quantum-Resistant AI, Synthetic Data

1. **Federated Learning (FL):** Federated Learning facilitates the collaborative training of AI models among several institutions while preserving the confidentiality of sensitive raw data. In fraud detection, federated learning improves model accuracy while maintaining privacy. Awosika et al. (2023) presented a federated learning architecture integrated with Explainable AI (XAI) that maintains privacy while ensuring transparency and effectiveness. This method promotes collaboration between institutions while complying with regulatory requirements.
2. **Quantum-Resistant AI and Quantum-Enhanced Models:** Quantum computing offers both risk and possibilities. A recent study presented FedRansel, a federated framework that includes quantum-enhanced Long Short-Term Memory (LSTM) models, resulting in a 5% performance improvement and increased resilience against poisoning and inference attacks (4–8% enhancement). The QFNN-FFD model integrates Quantum Machine Learning with federated training, attaining over 95% precision and a solid 80% accuracy in noisy situations, representing a substantial advancement in quantum-based fraud detection frameworks (Innan et al., 2024).
3. **Synthetic Data for Training and Modelling:** Synthetic data reconstructed or generated data that maintains statistical properties addresses data scarcity and privacy issues in fraud modelling. It facilitates model training among organisations without revealing actual transaction data. Also, digital twin methodologies employed in predictive analytics can simulate customer behaviour patterns and forecast fraud 6–8 weeks in advance, reportedly decreasing first-party fraud by 40%.

10.2 Policy Recommendations for Global Harmonization

10.2.1 Unified Definitions and Legal Harmonization

A mutual comprehension of the elements that define cyber-enabled fraud is essential. The World Economic Forum advocates for international agreement on restrictions, including ransomware, phishing, identity theft, and the operation of criminal infrastructure. World Economic Forum, 2025. The UN Convention against Cybercrime (2024) presents a revised international treaty featuring extradition and mutual aid clauses; yet, it has faced criticism over potential privacy concerns. Additional harmonisation initiatives such as uniform extradition statutes, efficient MLAT processes, and standardised sanctions can address enforcement deficiencies.

10.2.2 Global Institution for Cybercrime Enforcement

Experts advocate for the establishment of an International Cybercrime Coordination Authority (ICCA), a permanent worldwide entity facilitating intelligence sharing, coordinated investigations, collaborative operations, and exerting pressure on states that provide safe haven. IMPACT, the United Nations-supported cybersecurity alliance, facilitates cross-sector threat exchange and comprises 152 member governments as of 2025. Such initiatives could develop into institutional structures for strategic and timely responses to complex global fraud.

10.2.3 Multistakeholder Collaboration Platforms

Leaders in the private sector, such as Google, promote the facilitation of collaboration through shared platforms—such as the Global Signals Exchange legally endorsed rules, and incentives (e.g., safe harbour for good-faith defenders) (Erickson, 2024). Integration of policies among governments, technology companies, financial entities, and civil society fosters resilience through transparency and collective intelligence.

10.3 Building Resilient and Adaptive Anti-Fraud Ecosystems

10.3.1 Adaptive Metrics and Monitoring

Institutions have to switch from static KPIs to dynamic metrics, including the identification of emerging fraud types, the rapidity of model retraining, and the importance of alerts by 2025. Resilience stems from flexibility, demonstrated by a cryptocurrency asset management firm that integrated AI alert triage with expert research, minimising false positives and attaining a 24% revenue increase despite sector volatility.

10.3.2 Human-AI Synergy in Governance and Operations

AI systems have significant capabilities; still, they remain incomplete. According to TechRadar, the integration of optimised AI with human expertise is crucial for sustained resilience and trust. This hybrid methodology facilitates ethical governance, adaptive responses, and ongoing feedback mechanisms ensuring systems adapt to evolving dangers.

10.3.3 Institutional and Infrastructure Investments

Establishing adaptable ecosystems necessitates investments in federated infrastructure, quantum-capable artificial intelligence, and real-time monitoring systems. Collaborations like as IMPACT and consortia like the Global Fraud Brain, designed as encrypted networks for sharing fraud patterns among banks, telecommunications, and e-commerce, establish a foundation for future resilience through the exchange of data, technology, and governance.

CONCLUSION

The increasing complexity of fraud and cybercrime poses a significant challenge for modern governance, financial institutions, and digital environments. This chapter demonstrates that successful countermeasures cannot depend exclusively on technology, regulation, or politics in isolation. They require a comprehensive, multi-faceted approach that includes strategic policy frameworks, aligned legal tools, and innovative technical solutions rooted in ethical governance and operational resilience. The proposed analysis of developing threat landscapes and the examination of AI-driven detection architectures highlight that AI serves as both a powerful enabler and a possible weakness. Although machine learning, federated learning, and quantum-enhanced models have exceptional detection skills, they require protection from adversarial manipulation, algorithmic bias, and privacy violations. This requires Ethics by Design, ongoing bias checks, and explainable AI to uphold confidence among stakeholders and conform to changing regulatory frameworks. We have demonstrated that teamwork is a critical determinant of success. Collaborative relationships across several agencies, sectors, and nations—bolstered by secure exchanges of threat intelligence and federated model training improve collective defence while conforming to jurisdictional and privacy limitations. In conjunction with AI–human collaboration, where machine accuracy is enhanced by human discernment, this partnership guarantees operational flexibility and ethical supervision. The suggested Integrated Governance and Technology Model consolidates these ideas into a stratified architecture, integrating governance, trust, technology, and human oversight. Real-time monitoring, early warning systems, and integrated data frameworks constitute the technical base, whereas legislative integration, regulatory consistency, and international collaboration ensure structural integrity. In the future, emerging technologies quantum-resistant AI, synthetic data, and advanced federated learning will transform fraud prevention capabilities. However, their promise will only be actualised if supported by global policy consistency, strong governance frameworks, and flexible risk management strategies that react to the changing threat environment. Ultimately, establishing a robust and adaptive anti-fraud ecosystem is not a singular task but a continuous strategic commitment. It necessitates ongoing innovation, institutional flexibility, and steadfast collaboration across public, commercial, and civil society stakeholders. By integrating strategic foresight with technological innovation and ethical accountability, the global community can progress towards a future where digital trust becomes the standard rather than the exception.

REFERENCES

Alicia, M. (2025). *Fraud in the Modern Era and a Proactive Approach to Anti-Fraud Practices.* Connect on Tech. https://connectontech.bakermckenzie.com/fraud-in-the-modern-era-and-a-proactive-approach-to-anti-fraud-practices/

Aly Bouke, M., Alshatebi, S. H., Abdullah, A., Cengiz, K., & El Atigh, H. (2023). *African Union Convention on Cyber Security and Personal Data Protection: Challenges and Future Directions.* https://arxiv.org/pdf/2307.01966

Awosika, T., Shukla, R. M., & Pranggono, B. (2023). Transparency and Privacy: The Role of Explainable AI and Federated Learning in Financial Fraud Detection. *IEEE Access : Practical Innovations, Open Solutions, 12*, 64551–64560. DOI: 10.1109/ACCESS.2024.3394528

Belen-Saglam, R., Altuncu, E., Lu, Y., & Li, S. (2023). A systematic literature review of the tension between the GDPR and public blockchain systems. *Blockchain: Research and Applications, 4*(2). Advance online publication. DOI: 10.1016/j.bcra.2023.100129

Buckman, B. (2025). *The 2025 Cybercrime Report: 9 Emerging Trends + Statistics.* Huntress; huntress.com. https://www.huntress.com/blog/cybercrime-trends

Burgess, M. (2020). *MPs slam UK data regulator for failing to protect people's rights.* WIRED. https://www.wired.com/story/ico-data-protection-gdpr-enforcement/

Dahl, D. W., Noble, C. H., Schreier, M., & Toubia, O. (2025). Better Innovation for a Better World. *Journal of Marketing, 89*(6).

Daigle, B., & Khan, M. (2020). *United States International Trade Commission Journal of International Commerce and Economics The EU General Data Protection Regulation: An Analysis of* Enforcement *Trends by EU Data Protection Authorities.* https://www.usitc.gov/journals

Doherty, R. (2025). *GDPR is important but EU has turned privacy protection into a bureaucratic mess – here's why we need to sla...* The Irish Sun. https://www.thesun.ie/news/15040550/gdpr-privacy-protection-bureaucratic-mess-european-union-ireland/

Dubey, S. (2022). Artificial Intelligence in Financial Fraud Detection: A Case Study of Indian Banking Sector. *Innovative* Research. *Thoughts, 8*(4). Advance online publication. DOI: 10.36676/IRT.V8.I4.1503

Erickson, M. (2024). *A safer internet: policy recommendations for fighting scams and fraud together*. Google. https://blog.google/outreach-initiatives/public-policy/a-safer-internet-policy-recommendations-for-fighting-scams-and-fraud-together/

Eurojust (2020). *Challenges and best practices from Eurojust's casework in the area of cybercrime*. Eurojust. https://www.coe.int/en/web/cybercrime/glacyplus

European Data Protection Board. (2024). *Data protection benefits for you | European Data Protection Board*. Www.edpb.europa.eu. https://www.edpb.europa.eu/sme-data-protection-guide/data-protection-benefits-for-you_en

FRPA (2024). *DWP algorithm wrongly flags 200,000 people for possible fraud and error.* Frpafraudviewer.org.

Graff, G. M. (2024). *Anne Neuberger, a Top White House Cyber Official, Sees the "Promise and Peril" in AI.* WIRED. https://www.wired.com/story/anne-neuberger-cybersecurity-q-and-a/

Hoover, A. (2025). *I scammed my bank with just an AI voice generator and a phone call.* Business Insider. https://www.businessinsider.com/bank-account-scam-deepfakes-ai-voice-generator-crime-fraud-2025-5

How GDPR Is Failing | WIRED. (n.d.). Retrieved August 14, 2025, from https://www.wired.com/story/gdpr-2022/

Innan, N., Marchisio, A., Bennai, M., & Shafique, M. (2024). *QFNN-FFD: Quantum Federated Neural Network for Financial* Fraud *Detection*. https://arxiv.org/pdf/2404.02595

Jarugula, S. (2025). AI-Driven Real-Time Transaction Monitoring and Automated Threat Response: Revolutionizing Payment Security. *IJSAT-International Journal on Science and Technology, 16*(1). Pranto, T. H., Kim, S., Chen, L., & Hong, S. (2022). Hessian-Aware Training for Enhancing Model Resilience for In-Memory Computing.

Joshi, A., Goldstein, T., & Moschetta, G. (2025). Anticipatory Governance on Cybersecurity. In *Anticipatory Governance: Shaping a Responsible Future* (pp. 203-219).

Khadam, N., Anjum, N., Alam, A., Ali Mirza, Q., Assam, M., Ismail, E. A. A., & Abonazel, M. R. (2023). How to punish cyber criminals: A study to investigate the target and consequence based punishments for malware attacks in UK, USA, China, Ethiopia & Pakistan. *Heliyon, 9*(12). Advance online publication. DOI: 10.1016/j.heliyon.2023.e22823 PMID: 38076082

Kingston, J. K. (2018). Using Artificial Intelligence to Support Compliance with the General Data Protection Regulation. *Artificial Intelligence and Law, 25*(4), 429–443. DOI: 10.1007/s10506-017-9206-9

Kudriasova, Z. (2025). *Cryptologic Techniques and Associated Risks in Public and Private Security. An Italian and European Union Perspective with an Overview of the Current Legal Framework*. https://arxiv.org/pdf/2505.08650

Levy, L. (2025). *Inside the billion-dollar identity fraud ecosystem*. TechRadar. https://www.techradar.com/pro/inside-the-billion-dollar-identity-fraud-ecosystem

Li, X., Peng, Y., Sun, X., Duan, Y., Fang, Z., & Tang, T. (2025). *Unsupervised Detection of Fraudulent Transactions in E-commerce Using Contrastive Learning*. https://arxiv.org/pdf/2503.18841

Lulka, J. (2024). *Understanding AI Fraud Detection and Prevention Strategies | DigitalOcean*. Digitalocean.com. https://www.digitalocean.com/resources/articles/ai-fraud-detection

Lunghi, D., Molinghen, Y., Simitsis, A., Lenaerts, T., & Bontempi, G. (2025). *FRAUD-RLA: A new reinforcement learning* adversarial *attack against credit card fraud detection*. https://arxiv.org/pdf/2502.02290

Meda, K. (2024). *Unifying forces: The synergy of cybersecurity and fraud prevention teams*. Thomson Reuters Institute. https://www.thomsonreuters.com/en-us/posts/investigation-fraud-and-risk/cybersecurity-fraud-prevention-teams/

Niu, X., Wang, L., & Yang, X. (2019). *A Comparison Study of Credit Card Fraud Detection: Supervised versus Unsupervised*. https://arxiv.org/pdf/1904.10604

Note Transnational Cyber Offenses: Overcoming *Jurisdictional Challenges*. (n.d.). Retrieved August 14, 2025, from https://www.rand.org/pubs/researchmemoranda/RM3

Ostapowicz, M., & Żbikowski, K. (2019). Detecting Fraudulent Accounts on Blockchain: A Supervised Approach. *Lecture Notes in* Computer *Science (Including Subseries Lecture Notes in Artificial Intelligence and Lecture Notes in Bioinformatics), 11881 LNCS*, 18–31. https://doi.org/DOI: 10.1007/978-3-030-34223-4_2

Pelekis, S., Koutroubas, T., Blika, A., Berdelis, A., Karakolis, E., Ntanos, C., Spiliotis, E., & Askounis, D. (2025). Adversarial machine learning: a review of methods, tools, and critical industry sectors. Artificial *Intelligence Review 2025 58:8, 58*(8), 1–87. https://doi.org/DOI: 10.1007/S10462-025-11147-4

Pombal, J., Cruz, A. F., Bravo, J., Saleiro, P., Figueiredo, M. A. T., & Bizarro, P. (2022). *Understanding* Unfairness *in Fraud Detection through Model and Data Bias Interactions*. https://arxiv.org/pdf/2207.06273

Pranto, T. H., Hasib, K. T. A. M., Rahman, T., Haque, A. B., Islam, A. K. M. N., & Rahman, R. M. (2022). Blockchain and Machine Learning for Fraud Detection: A Privacy-Preserving and Adaptive Incentive Based Approach. *IEEE Access : Practical Innovations, Open Solutions*, *10*, 87115–87134. DOI: 10.1109/ACCESS.2022.3198956

Ryan, P., Crane, M., & Brennan, R. (2020). Design Challenges for GDPR RegTech. *ICEIS 2020 - Proceedings of the 22nd International Conference on Enterprise Information Systems, 2*, 787–795. https://doi.org/DOI: 10.5220/0009464507870795

Shastri, S., Wasserman, M., & Chidambaram, V. (2019). *GDPR Anti-Patterns: How Design and Operation of Modern Cloud-scale Systems Conflict with GDPR*. https://arxiv.org/pdf/1911.00498

She, K., Alexandridis, G., Tzouveli, P., & Taherdoost, H. (2023). Blockchain and Machine Learning: A Critical Review on Security. *Information 2023, Vol. 14, Page 295, 14*(5), 295. https://doi.org/DOI: 10.3390/INFO14050295

Sollitto, N. (2024). *What is the Payment Services Directive 2 (PSD2)? Complete Guide | UpGuard*. Upguard.com. https://www.upguard.com/blog/what-is-psd2

Sood, A. K., & Enbody, R. J. (2013). Crimeware-as-a-service—A survey of commoditized crimeware in the underground market. *International Journal of Critical Infrastructure Protection, 6*(1), 28–38. DOI: 10.1016/j.ijcip.2013.01.002

SuperAGI. (2025). *Real-Time Fraud Prevention: Case Studies of Businesses Using AI to Secure Online Payments in 2025 - SuperAGI*. SuperAGI. https://superagi.com/real-time-fraud-prevention-case-studies-of-businesses-using-ai-to-secure-online-payments-in-2025/

What are STIX/TAXII Standards? | Anomali. (n.d.). Retrieved August 14, 2025, from https://www.anomali.com/resources/what-are-stix-taxii

Compilation of References

Abdul Salam, M., Fouad, K. M., Elbably, D. L., & Elsayed, S. M. (2024). Federated learning model for credit card fraud detection with data balancing techniques. *Neural Computing & Applications*, *36*(11), 6231–6256. DOI: 10.1007/s00521-023-09410-2

Abraha, H. H. (2021). Law enforcement access to electronic evidence across borders: Mapping policy approaches and emerging reform initiatives. *International Journal of Law and Information Technology*, *29*(2), 118–153. DOI: 10.1093/ijlit/eaab001

Abrol, S., & Gupta, M. (2023). Role of big data analytics in financial fraud detection-a bibliometric analysis. *Corporate Governance Insight*, *5*(1), 82–111. DOI: 10.58426/cgi.v5.i1.2023.82-111

Adeyemo, K., & Obafemi, F. J. (2024). A survey on the role of technological innovation in Nigerian deposit money bank fraud prevention. *South Asian Journal of Social Studies and Economics*, *21*(3), 133–150. DOI: 10.9734/sajsse/2024/v21i3790

Admissibility of electronic record under Section 65B of the Indian Evidence Act vis-à-vis judicial interpretation. (n.d.). *ResearchGate*. Retrieved October 30, 2025, from https://www.researchgate.net/publication/380324562

Ahmed, S. F.. (2025). Forensics and security issues in the Internet of Things. *Wireless Networks*, *31*(4), 3431–3466. DOI: 10.1007/s11276-025-03942-2

Ajmal, A., Ibrar, S., & Amin, R. (2022). Cloud computing platform: Performance analysis of prominent cryptographic algorithms. *Concurrency and Computation*, *34*(15), e6938. DOI: 10.1002/cpe.6938

Alfian, A., Ritchi, H., & Adrianto, Z. (2023). Fraud analytics practices in public-sector transactions: A systematic review. *Journal of Public Budgeting, Accounting & Financial Management*, *35*(5), 685–710. DOI: 10.1108/jpbafm-11-2022-0175

Ali, A., & Eshete, B. (2020). Best-effort adversarial approximation of black-box malware classifiers. In *Lecture Notes of the Institute for Computer Sciences, Social-Informatics and Telecommunications Engineering* (Vol. 335, pp. 318–338). Springer. https://doi.org/DOI: 10.1007/978-3-030-63086-7_18

Alicia, M. (2025). *Fraud in the Modern Era and a Proactive Approach to Anti-Fraud Practices.* Connect on Tech. https://connectontech.bakermckenzie.com/fraud-in-the-modern-era-and-a-proactive-approach-to-anti-fraud-practices/

Aly Bouke, M., Alshatebi, S. H., Abdullah, A., Cengiz, K., & El Atigh, H. (2023). *African Union Convention on Cyber Security and Personal Data Protection: Challenges and Future Directions.* https://arxiv.org/pdf/2307.01966

Amnesty International. (2025). *India 2024.* Retrieved from https://www.amnesty.org/en/location/asia-and-the-pacific/south-asia/india/report-india/

Antoniuk, D. (2023). *Sri Lanka loses months of government data in ransomware attack.* The Record. Retrieved from https://therecord.media/sri-lanka-loses-months-of-government-data-in-ransomware-attack

Anvar, P. V. P. K. Basheer (Supreme Court on electronic evidence). (n.d.). *Information Technology Law.* Retrieved October 30, 2025, from https://www.itlaw.in/anvar-p-v-vs-p-k-basheer-supreme-court-on-electronic-evidence/

Apruzzese, G., Colajanni, M., Ferretti, L., Guido, A., & Marchetti, M. (2018). On the effectiveness of machine and deep learning for cybersecurity. *10th International Conference on Cyber Conflict (CyCon)* (pp. 371–390). IEEE. https://doi.org/DOI: 10.23919/CYCON.2018.8405026

Aryan, A. (2023, February 10). AIIMS cyber attack took place due to improper network segmentation: Govt in RS. ETtech, *The Economic Times*. Retrieved from https://economictimes.indiatimes.com/tech/technology/aiims-cyber-attack-took-place-due-to-improper-network-segmentation-govt-in-rs/articleshow/97805598.cms?from=mdr

Aslan, Ö., Aktuğ, S. S., Ozkan-Okay, M., Yilmaz, A. A., & Akin, E. (2023). A comprehensive review of cyber security vulnerabilities, threats, attacks and solutions. *Electronics (Basel)*, *12*(6), 1333. DOI: 10.3390/electronics12061333

Aw, C. (2019, January 15). *"Worst breach of personal data in Singapore's history" attracts highest penalties totalling S$1 million. Technology Law Dispatch*. Retrieved from https://www.technologylawdispatch.com/2019/01/privacy-data-protection/worst-breach-of-personal-data-in-singapores-history-attracts-highest-penalties-totalling-s1-million/

Awosika, T., Shukla, R. M., & Pranggono, B. (2023). Transparency and Privacy: The Role of Explainable AI and Federated Learning in Financial Fraud Detection. *IEEE Access : Practical Innovations, Open Solutions*, *12*, 64551–64560. DOI: 10.1109/ACCESS.2024.3394528

Ayinla, B. S., Asuzu, O. F., Ndubuisi, N. L., Ike, C. U., Atadoga, A., & Adeleye, R. A. (2024). Utilizing data analytics for fraud detection in accounting: A review and case studies. *International Journal of Science and Research Archive*, *11*(1), 1348–1363. DOI: 10.30574/ijsra.2024.11.1.0221

Belen-Saglam, R., Altuncu, E., Lu, Y., & Li, S. (2023). A systematic literature review of the tension between the GDPR and public blockchain systems. *Blockchain: Research and Applications*, *4*(2). Advance online publication. DOI: 10.1016/j.bcra.2023.100129

Bendiab, G., Haiouni, H., Moulas, I., & Shiaeles, S. (2025). Deepfakes in digital media forensics: Generation, AI-based detection and challenges. *Journal of Information Security and Applications*, *88*, 103935. Advance online publication. DOI: 10.1016/j.jisa.2024.103935

Benmalek, M. (2024). Ransomware on cyber-physical systems: Taxonomies, case studies, security gaps, and open challenges. *Internet of Things and Cyber-Physical Systems*, *4*, 186–202. DOI: 10.1016/j.iotcps.2023.12.001

Bentotahewa, V., Hewage, C., & Williams, J. (2022). The normative power of the gdpr: A case study of data protection laws of south asian countries. *SN Computer Science*, *3*(3), 183. DOI: 10.1007/s42979-022-01079-z

Bergman, D. (2016, March 15). *Bangladesh bank governor resigns after $81m hack. Al Jazeera.* Retrieved from https://www.aljazeera.com/news/2016/3/15/bangladesh-bank-governor-resigns-after-81m-hack

Bernardo, B. M. V., Mamede, H. S., Barroso, J. M. P., & Dos Santos, V. M. P. D. (2024). Mobile device forensics framework: A toolbox to support and enhance this process. *Emerging Science Journal*, *8*(3), 972–998. DOI: 10.28991/ESJ-2024-08-03-011

Bhardwaj, D. (2023, July 2). *AIIMS ransomware attack led to new SOP on cyber breaches: Ex-cybersecurity chief Pant. Hindustan Times.* Retrieved from https://www.hindustantimes.com/india-news/aiims-ransomware-attack-led-to-new-sop-on-cyber-breaches-ex-cybersecurity-chief-pant-101688321198625.html

Bhardwaj, G., Gupta, R., Srivastava, A. P., & Singh, S. V. (2021, April). Cyber Threat Landscape of G4 Nations: Analysis of Threat Incidents & Response Strategies. In 2021 2nd International Conference on Intelligent Engineering and Management (ICIEM) (pp. 75-79). IEEE.

Bhardwaj, A. (2024). *5G: The Emerging Cybersecurity Threat Landscape for India. In 5G and Fiber Optics Security Technologies for Smart Grid Cyber Defense.* IGI Global.

Bouke, M. A., Abdullah, A., Alshatebi, S. H., El Atigh, H., & Cengiz, K. (2023). *African Union Convention on Cyber Security and Personal Data Protection: Challenges and future directions*. arXiv. https://doi.org/DOI: 10.48550/arXiv.2307.01966

Bracken-Roche, D., Bell, E., Macdonald, M. E., & Racine, E. (2017). The concept of 'vulnerability' in research ethics: An in-depth analysis of policies and guidelines. *Health Research Policy and Systems*, *15*, 1–18.

Buckman, B. (2025). *The 2025 Cybercrime Report: 9 Emerging Trends + Statistics.* Huntress; huntress.com. https://www.huntress.com/blog/cybercrime-trends

Bukowski, M. (2023). Combating economic cybercrime using artificial intelligence (AI). *PRZEGLĄD POLICYJNY*, *151*(3), 339–365. DOI: 10.5604/01.3001.0053.9746

Bureau, E. T. (2025, January 16). India's internet user base to surpass 900 million by 2025, driven by rural growth: Report. *The Economic Times*. Retrieved from https://economictimes.indiatimes.com/industry/telecom/telecom-news/indias-internet-user-base-to-surpass-900-million-by-2025-driven-by-rural-growth-report/articleshow/117304976.cms?from=mdr

Burgess, M. (2020). *MPs slam UK data regulator for failing to protect people's rights.* WIRED. https://www.wired.com/story/ico-data-protection-gdpr-enforcement/

Butt, U. A., Amin, R., Aldabbas, H., Mohan, S., Alouffi, B., & Ahmadian, A. (2022). Cloud-based email phishing attack using machine and deep learning algorithm. *Complex & Intelligent Systems*, •••, 1–28. DOI: 10.1007/s40747-022-00788-9 PMID: 35668732

Butt, U. A., Amin, R., Mehmood, M., Aldabbas, H., Alharbi, M. T., & Albaqami, N. (2023). Cloud security threats and solutions: A survey. *Wireless Personal Communications*, *128*(1), 387–413. DOI: 10.1007/s11277-022-09754-1

Butun, I., Österberg, P., & Song, H. (2019). Security of the Internet of Things: Vulnerabilities, attacks, and countermeasures. *IEEE Communications Surveys and Tutorials*, *22*(1), 616–644.

Cath, C. (2018). Governing artificial intelligence: Ethical, legal and technical opportunities and challenges. *Philosophical Transactions. Series A, Mathematical, Physical, and Engineering Sciences*, *376*(2133), 20180080. Advance online publication. DOI: 10.1098/rsta.2018.0080 PMID: 30322996

Chakravarti, J. (2023, September 13). *Ransomware attack wipes out Sri Lankan government emails. BankInfoSecurity*. Retrieved from https://www.bankinfosecurity.asia/ransomware-attack-wipes-out-sri-lankan-government-emails-a-23075

Cheng, D., Xiang, S., Shang, C., Zhang, Y., Yang, F., & Zhang, L. (2020). Spatio-temporal attention-based neural network for credit card fraud detection. Proceedings of the ... AAAI Conference on Artificial Intelligence. AAAI Conference on Artificial Intelligence, 34(01), 362–369. https://doi.org/DOI: 10.1609/aaai.v34i01.5371

Cheng, X. (2024). The Gendered Impact of Deepfake Technology: Analyzing Digital Violence Against Women in South Korea. *Lecture Notes in Education Psychology and Public Media*, *75*, 80–85. DOI: 10.54254/2753-7048/75/20241102

Chennuri, S. (2024). Advancing fraud detection in banking: Integration of data pipelines, machine learning, and cloud computing. *International Journal For Multidisciplinary Research*, *6*(6). Advance online publication. DOI: 10.36948/ijfmr.2024.v06i06.29893

Chesney, R. M., & Citron, D. K. (2019). Deep fakes: A looming challenge for privacy, democracy, and national security. *California Law Review*, *107*, 1753–1819. https://www.californialawreview.org/print/deep-fakes-a-looming-challenge-for-privacy-democracy-and-national-security/

Choi, D., & Lee, K. (2018). An artificial intelligence approach to financial fraud detection under IoT environment: A survey and implementation. *Security and Communication Networks, 2018*, 1–15. DOI: 10.1155/2018/5483472

Council of Europe. (2001). *Convention on Cybercrime*. European Treaty Series No. 185. Council of Europe

Cull, R., Peria, M. M. S. M., & Verrier, J. (2017). *Bank ownership: Trends and implications*. International Monetary Fund.

CyberPeace Foundation. (2023) *National Cyber Security Reference Framework – Need of the hour*. CyberPeace. https://www.cyberpeace.org/resources/blogs/national-cyber-security-reference-framework-need-of-the-hour

Dabas, P. (2024, November 28). *The impact of deepfake technology: Legal risks and regulatory solutions*. Mondaq. https://www.mondaq.com/india/new-technology/xxxxx

Dahl, D. W., Noble, C. H., Schreier, M., & Toubia, O. (2025). Better Innovation for a Better World. *Journal of Marketing*, *89*(6).

Daigle, B., & Khan, M. (2020). *United States International Trade Commission Journal of International Commerce and Economics The EU General Data Protection Regulation: An Analysis of* Enforcement *Trends by EU Data Protection Authorities*. https://www.usitc.gov/journals

Dhirani, L. L., Armstrong, E., & Newe, T. (2021). Industrial IoT, cyber threats, and standards landscape: Evaluation and roadmap. *Sensors (Basel)*, *21*(11), 3901.

Doherty, R. (2025). *GDPR is important but EU has turned privacy protection into a bureaucratic mess – here's why we need to sla...* The Irish Sun. https://www.thesun.ie/news/15040550/gdpr-privacy-protection-bureaucratic-mess-european-union-ireland/

Douglas, S. (2025, March 26). *Bridging connectivity and collaboration gaps in Bangladesh.* APNIC Blog. Retrieved from https://blog.apnic.net/2025/03/26/bridging-connectivity-and-collaboration-gaps-in-bangladesh/

Doyle, K. (2025, June 3). *The Rising Tide: Understanding the Surge in Cyber Attacks in India.* Tripwire. Retrieved from https://www.tripwire.com/state-of-security/rising-tide-understanding-surge-cyber-attacks-india

Duan, M., Zheng, T., Gao, Y., Wang, G., Feng, Z., & Wang, X. (2024). DGA-GNN: Dynamic grouping aggregation GNN for fraud detection. Proceedings of the ... AAAI Conference on Artificial Intelligence. AAAI Conference on Artificial Intelligence, 38(10), 11820–11828. https://doi.org/DOI: 10.1609/aaai.v38i10.29067

Duarte, F. (2025, May 21). Countries with the highest number of internet users (2025). *Exploding Topics.* Retrieved from https://explodingtopics.com/blog/countries-internet-users

Dubey, S. (2022). Artificial Intelligence in Financial Fraud Detection: A Case Study of Indian Banking Sector. *Innovative* Research. *Thoughts, 8*(4). Advance online publication. DOI: 10.36676/IRT.V8.I4.1503

Du, X., Le-Khac, N. A., & Scanlon, M. (2017). Evaluation of digital forensic process models with respect to digital forensics as a service. In *Proceedings of the European Conference on Information Warfare and Security (ECCWS)* (pp. 573–581).

Ebers, M., Hoch, V. R. S., Rosenkranz, F., Ruschemeier, H., & Steinrötter, B. (2021). *The European Commission's proposal for an Artificial Intelligence Act—A critical assessment by members of the Robotics and AI Law Society (RAILS).* J, 4(4), 589–603. https://doi.org/DOI: 10.3390/j4040043

Economic Times. (2023, May 9). India sees sharp increase in cyberattacks in Q1 2023: report. The Economic Times Tech. Retrieved from https://economictimes.indiatimes.com/tech/technology/sharp-increase-in-cyberattacks-in-india-in-q1-2023-report/articleshow/100096450.cms?from=mdr

Ee, S. K. E. (2019, January). *Prevention is no cure: A case study of the 2018 SingHealth breach* (East–West Center Occasional Paper). Konrad Adenauer Foundation

EPAS. (2022, August). *Cybersecurity governance in South Asia: India and Pakistan*. European Foundation for South Asian Studies. 7. Retrieved from https://www.efsas.org/EFSAS%20Article-Cybersecurity%20Governance-India%20and%20Pakistan-August%202022.pdf

Erickson, M. (2024). *A safer internet: policy recommendations for fighting scams and fraud together*. Google. https://blog.google/outreach-initiatives/public-policy/a-safer-internet-policy-recommendations-for-fighting-scams-and-fraud-together/

Eurojust (2020). *Challenges and best practices from Eurojust's casework in the area of cybercrime*. Eurojust. https://www.coe.int/en/web/cybercrime/glacyplus

European Data Protection Board. (2024). *Data protection benefits for you | European Data Protection Board*. Www.edpb.europa.eu. https://www.edpb.europa.eu/sme-data-protection-guide/data-protection-benefits-for-you_en

Faizal, A., & Luthfi, A. (2024). Comparison study of NIST SP 800-86 and ISO/IEC 27037 standards as a framework for digital forensic evidence analysis. *Journal of Information Systems and Informatics*, *6*(2), 701–718. DOI: 10.51519/journalisi.v6i2.717

Farabi, S. F., Ro, M. P., Alam, M., Hossan, M. Z., Ariful, M., Islam, M. R., Uddin, A., Bhuiyan, M., & Biswas, M. Z. A. (2024). Enhancing credit card fraud detection: A comprehensive study of machine learning algorithms and performance evaluation. *Journal of Business and Management Studies*, *6*(3), 252–259. DOI: 10.32996/jbms.2024.6.13.21

Finkle, J., & Miglani, S. (2016, May 13). Bangladesh Bank heist similar to Sony hack; second bank hit by malware. *Reuters*. Retrieved from https://www.reuters.com/article/world/bangladesh -bank-heist-similar-to-sony-hack-second-bank-hit-by-malware-idUSKCN0Y40SF/

Finlay, A. (2024, October 17). Integrating policy, research and technical standards in gender approaches to cybersecurity: Key takeaways from a recent APC-hosted roundtable. *Association for Progressive Communications.* Retrieved from https://www.apc.org/en/news/integrating-policy-research-and-technical-standards-gender-approaches-cybersecurity-key

Frechette, K. (2023, February 14). *The history and impact of the ILOVEYOU Virus*. GoldSky Security. Retrieved from https://www.goldskysecurity.com/the-history-and-impact-of-the-iloveyou-virus/

FRPA (2024). *DWP algorithm wrongly flags 200,000 people for possible fraud and error.* Frpafraudviewer.org.

Gamboa, F. P. (2025, August 11). *The digital police state: Surveillance, secrecy and state power in Bangladesh* (Occasional Paper). Tech Global Institute. Retrieved from https://techglobalinstitute.com/research/the-digital-police-state/

Gamboa, F. P. (2025, August). *Observations on the state of cybersecurity in Southeast Asia* (East–West Center Occasional Paper). East–West Center.

Glasser, J., & Lindauer, B. (2013). *Bridging the gap: A pragmatic approach to generating insider threat data. IEEE Security and Privacy Workshops.* IEEE., DOI: 10.1109/SPW.2013.24

Goodfellow, I. J., Pouget-Abadie, J., Mirza, M., Xu, B., Warde-Farley, D., Ozair, S., Courville, A., & Bengio, Y. (2014). *Generative adversarial networks.* arXiv. https://arxiv.org/abs/1406.2661

Graff, G. M. (2024). *Anne Neuberger, a Top White House Cyber Official, Sees the "Promise and Peril" in AI.* WIRED. https://www.wired.com/story/anne-neuberger-cybersecurity-q-and-a/

Grobler, M. M., & von Solms, S. H. (n.d.). *A best practice approach to live forensic acquisition.*

Gupta, R. (2024, October 30). *National Cyber Threat Assessment 2025–2026*. Communications Security Establishment Canada. Retrieved from https://www.cyber.gc.ca/en/guidance/national-cyber-threat-assessment-2025-2026

Hamid, I., & Rahman, M. M. H. (2024). A comprehensive literature review on volatile memory forensics. *Electronics (Basel)*, *13*(15), 3026. Advance online publication. DOI: 10.3390/electronics13153026

Hamon, R., Junklewitz, H., Soler Garrido, J., & Sanchez, I. (2024). Three challenges to secure AI systems in the context of AI regulations. *IEEE Access : Practical Innovations, Open Solutions*, *12*, 61022–61035. DOI: 10.1109/access.2024.3391021

Hamza, A., Yonghong, D., & Ullah, I. (2025). Dynamic shifts in social media usage in pakistan: A comparative analysis across pre-, during-, and post-covid-19 periods. *Journalism and Media*, *6*(2), 59. DOI: 10.3390/journalmedia6020059

Haque, A. K. M. B. (2019, June). Need for critical cyber defence, security strategy and privacy policy in Bangladesh – Hype or reality? *International Journal of Managing Information Technology*, *11*(1). Advance online publication. DOI: 10.5121/ijmit.2019.11103

Hasan, K., Hosen, M. N., & Saha, K. (2024). Federated learning for telecom fraud detection: A privacy-preserving approach to overcoming data fragmentation and enhancing security. *European Journal of Theoretical and Applied Sciences*, *2*(6), 99–109. DOI: 10.59324/ejtas.2024.2(6).08

Henderson, R. (2020). Using graph databases to detect financial fraud. *Computer Fraud & Security*, *2020*(7), 6–10. DOI: 10.1016/s1361-3723(20)30073-7

Homoliak, I., Toffalini, F., Guarnizo, J. D., Elovici, Y., & Ochoa, M. (2019). Insight into insiders and IT: A survey of insider threat taxonomies, analysis, modeling, and countermeasures. *ACM Computing Surveys*, *52*(2), 1–40. DOI: 10.1145/3303771

Hoover, A. (2025). *I scammed my bank with just an AI voice generator and a phone call.* Business Insider. https://www.businessinsider.com/bank-account-scam-deepfakes-ai-voice-generator-crime-fraud-2025-5

How GDPR Is Failing | WIRED. (n.d.). Retrieved August 14, 2025, from https://www.wired.com/story/gdpr-2022/

Ikhsan, W. M., Ednoer, E. H., Kridantika, W. S., & Firmansyah, A. (2022). Fraud detection automation through data analytics and artificial intelligence. *Riset*, *4*(2), 103–119. DOI: 10.37641/riset.v4i2.166

Innan, N., Marchisio, A., Bennai, M., & Shafique, M. (2024). *QFNN-FFD: Quantum Federated Neural Network for Financial* Fraud *Detection*. https://arxiv.org/pdf/2404.02595

Islam, T., Islam, S. A. M., Sarkar, A., Khan, A. J. M. O. R., Paul, R., & Bari, M. S. (2024). Artificial intelligence in fraud detection and financial risk mitigation: Future directions and business applications. *International Journal For Multidisciplinary Research*, *6*(5). Advance online publication. DOI: 10.36948/ijfmr.2024.v06i05.28496

Ismaeil, M. K. A. (2024). Harnessing AI for next-generation Financial Fraud Detection: A data-driven revolution. *Journal of Ecohumanism*, *3*(7), 811–821. DOI: 10.62754/joe.v3i7.4248

ITU. (2024). *Global Cybersecurity Index 2024: Measuring global cybersecurity commitment* (GCI 5th ed.). International Telecommunication Union. Retrieved from https://www.itu.int/en/ITU-D/Cybersecurity/Documents/GCIv5/2401416_1b_Global-Cybersecurity-Index-E.pdf

Jain, N., & Patil, S. (2024). Artificial intelligence models for fraud detection: Advancements, challenges, and future prospects. International Journal of Global Innovations and Solutions (IJGIS). https://doi.org/DOI: 10.21428/e90189c8.6d8ab5f6

Jarugula, S. (2025). AI-Driven Real-Time Transaction Monitoring and Automated Threat Response: Revolutionizing Payment Security. *IJSAT-International Journal on Science and Technology, 16*(1). Pranto, T. H., Kim, S., Chen, L., & Hong, S. (2022). Hessian-Aware Training for Enhancing Model Resilience for In-Memory Computing.

Jayathilaka, R., & Udara, I. (2024, August 20). Security matters: Empowering e-commerce in Sri Lanka through customer insights. *Humanities & Social Sciences Communications*, *11*, 1054. Advance online publication. DOI: 10.1057/s41599-024-03585-2

Jobin, A., Ienca, M., & Vayena, E. (2019). The global landscape of AI ethics guidelines. *Nature Machine Intelligence*, *1*(9), 389–399. DOI: 10.1038/s42256-019-0088-2

John, N. (2020, November 25). Breach at Kudankulam nuclear plant may have gone undetected for over six months: Group-IB. *The Economic Times*. Retrieved from https://economictimes.indiatimes.com/news/politics-and-nation/breach-at-kudankulam-nuclear-plant-may-have-gone-undetected-for-over-six-months-group-ib/articleshow/79412969.cms?from=mdr

Joshi, A., Goldstein, T., & Moschetta, G. (2025). Anticipatory Governance on Cybersecurity. In *Anticipatory Governance: Shaping a Responsible Future* (pp. 203-219).

Joshi, A., Moschetta, G., & Winslow, E. (2025, January 13). *Global Cybersecurity Outlook 2025*. World Economic Forum.

Jung, S., Seo, S., Kim, Y., & Lee, C. (2021). Memory layout extraction and verification method for reliable physical memory acquisition. *Electronics (Basel)*, *10*(12). Advance online publication. DOI: 10.3390/electronics10121380

Kandias, M., Virvilis, N., & Gritzalis, D. (2010). The insider threat in cloud computing. In *Critical Information Infrastructure Security* (pp. 230–241). Springer., DOI: 10.1007/978-3-642-16806-2_21

Karie, N. M., Kebande, V. R., Venter, H. S., & Choo, K.-K. R. (2019). On the importance of standardising the process of generating digital forensic reports. *Forensic Science International. Reports, 1*, 100008. Advance online publication. DOI: 10.1016/j.fsir.2019.100008

Karki, R., Yu, J., Ashraf, A. A., Hogeveen, B., Jaffri, A., Mallick, P. K., Spidalieri, F., & Vidanage, H. (2023, February 23). *Cybersecurity governance in South Asia* (Thematic Brief; edited by A. Schnabel). Geneva Centre for Security Sector Governance (DCAF). Retrieved August 12, 2025, from https://www.dcaf.ch/cybersecurity-governance-south-asia-brief

Kaur, G. Emerging Trends in Cyber Crime in India.

Kemp, S. (2025, March 3). Digital 2025: Bangladesh. *Data Reportal*. Retrieved from https://datareportal.com/reports/digital-2025-bangladesh

Khadam, N., Anjum, N., Alam, A., Ali Mirza, Q., Assam, M., Ismail, E. A. A., & Abonazel, M. R. (2023). How to punish cyber criminals: A study to investigate the target and consequence based punishments for malware attacks in UK, USA, China, Ethiopia & Pakistan. *Heliyon, 9*(12). Advance online publication. DOI: 10.1016/j.heliyon.2023.e22823 PMID: 38076082

Khaitan, A. (2025, July 4). *Top 15 cyberattacks that rocked India*. The Cyber Express. Retrieved from https://thecyberexpress.com/top-15-cyberattacks-that-rocked-india/

Khasanova, L., & Simonyan, A. (2025). (Geo)politicizing international law of cyberspace in post-Soviet Eurasia. *Chinese Journal of International Law, 24*(2), jmaf016. Advance online publication. DOI: 10.1093/chinesejil/jmaf016

Kingston, J. K. (2018). Using Artificial Intelligence to Support Compliance with the General Data Protection Regulation. *Artificial Intelligence and Law, 25*(4), 429–443. DOI: 10.1007/s10506-017-9206-9

KPMG Assurance and Consulting Services LLP. (2024, August 20). *SEBI CSCRF – Our point of view*. KPMG in India.

Kudriasova, Z. (2025). *Cryptologic Techniques and Associated Risks in Public and Private Security. An Italian and European Union Perspective with an Overview of the Current Legal Framework.* https://arxiv.org/pdf/2505.08650

Łabuz, M. (2023). Regulating deep fakes in the Artificial Intelligence Act. [ACIG]. *Applied Cybersecurity & Internet Governance*, *2*(1). Advance online publication. DOI: 10.60097/ACIG/162856

Lakhani, N., Safi, M., Sabbagh, D., Walker, S., Kirchgaessner, S., & Ellis-Petersen, H. (2021, July 19). *NSO clients' spying disclosures prompt political rows & drop in Apple stock price; company founder "very concerned" about reports. The Guardian.* Retrieved from https://www.theguardian.com/news/2021/jul/19/nso-clients-spying-disclosures-prompt-political-rows-across-world

Lalani, F., & Shahani, S. H. (2025, February). *Digital governance and rights in South Asia, and the path forward* (White paper). Tech Global Institute.

Latham & Watkins LLP. (2023, August 16). *China's new AI regulations* (Client Alert No. 3110). https://www.lw.com/

Le, D. C., & Zincir-Heywood, A. N. (2019, April). Machine learning based insider threat modelling and detection. In *2019, IFIP/IEEE Symposium on Integrated Network and Service Management (IM)* (pp. 1–6). IEEE. https://doi.org/DOI: 10.23919/INM.2019.8719981

Levy, L. (2025). *Inside the billion-dollar identity fraud ecosystem.* TechRadar. https://www.techradar.com/pro/inside-the-billion-dollar-identity-fraud-ecosystem

Li, X., Peng, Y., Sun, X., Duan, Y., Fang, Z., & Tang, T. (2025). *Unsupervised Detection of Fraudulent Transactions in E-commerce Using Contrastive Learning.* https://arxiv.org/pdf/2503.18841

Li, H. (2024). Biometric-driven digital village governance: A SWOC-enabled model with fraud prevention. *Journal of Electrical Systems*, *20*(3s), 1929–1940. DOI: 10.52783/jes.1732

Li, J., & Yang, D. (2023). Research on financial fraud detection models integrating multiple relational graphs. *Systems, 11*(11), 539. DOI: 10.3390/systems11110539

Lin, D. (2023). An empirical analysis of machine learning for fraud detection in diverse financial scenarios. Advances in Economics. *Management and Political Sciences, 42*(1), 202–216. DOI: 10.54254/2754-1169/42/20232110

Liu, J., Feng, Y., Liu, X., Zhao, J., & Liu, Q. (2023). MRm-DLDet: A memory-resident malware detection framework based on memory forensics and deep neural network. *Cybersecurity, 6*(1), 1–22. DOI: 10.1186/s42400-023-00157-w

Livemint. (2024, November 29). Mint Quick Edit: Cyber cons go from digital arrests to wedding scams. LiveMint. Retrieved from https://www.livemint.com/opinion/quick-edit/mint-quick-edit-cyber-cons-go-from-digital-arrests-to-wedding-scams-digital-arrest-whatsapp-invite-malware-scam-crime-11732775304080.html

Lulka, J. (2024). *Understanding AI Fraud Detection and Prevention Strategies | DigitalOcean.* Digitalocean.com. https://www.digitalocean.com/resources/articles/ai-fraud-detection

Lunghi, D., Molinghen, Y., Simitsis, A., Lenaerts, T., & Bontempi, G. (2025). *FRAUD-RLA: A new reinforcement learning* adversarial *attack against credit card fraud detection.* https://arxiv.org/pdf/2502.02290

Macedo, P. S., Coelho Inácio, H., & Vieira, S., E. (2022). A model to detect financial statement fraud in portuguese companies by the auditor. *Contaduría y Administración, 67*(3), 346. DOI: 10.22201/fca.24488410e.2022.2987

Maheshwari, R. (2024). Development and evaluation of bioactive wound healing formulations containing medicinal plant extracts. *African Journal of Biomedical Research, 27*(6), 755–764. DOI: 10.63122/ajbr.v27i6.1163

Majumder, T. (2024). The evaluating impact of Artificial Intelligence on risk management and fraud detection in the commercial bank in Bangladesh. *International Journal of Applied and Natural Sciences*, *1*(1), 67–76. DOI: 10.61424/ijans.v1i1.75

Malik, A. A., Maheshwari, C., & Aggarwal, A. (2025, June 6). *A global comparative study on social media censorship: Regulating digital rights, privacy and surveillance*. In T. Teena, P. Avasthi, S. Yadav, & A. Dixit (Eds.), *Proceedings of the National Seminar on Enhancing Privacy Protection in the Digital Age: Legal Challenges & Innovations (NSEPPDA 2025)* (pp. 56–72). Atlantis Press. https://doi.org/DOI: 10.2991/978-2-38476-426-6_5

Massei, G., Kindberg, J., Licoppe, A., Gačić, D., Šprem, N., Kamler, J., & Náhlik, A. (2015). Wild boar populations up, numbers of hunters down? A review of trends and implications for Europe. *Pest Management Science*, *71*(4), 492–500.

Mazumder, S. A., & Rhaman, M. A. (2024). Patient care and financial integrity in healthcare billing through advanced fraud detection systems. Academic Journal on Business Administration. *Innovation & Sustainability*, *4*(2), 10–69593.

Meda, K. (2024). *Unifying forces: The synergy of cybersecurity and fraud prevention teams*. Thomson Reuters Institute. https://www.thomsonreuters.com/en-us/posts/investigation-fraud-and-risk/cybersecurity-fraud-prevention-teams/

Mehmood, R. (2023). Volatile data acquisition and analysis by using memory forensics techniques. *International Journal for Electronic Crime Investigation*, *7*(4), 81–90. DOI: 10.54692/IJECI.2023.0704169

Mehmood, R., & Ahmad, Z. (2024). Live memory forensic: Capture and analysing volatile data. *International Journal for Electronic Crime Investigation*, *8*(3). Advance online publication. DOI: 10.54692/IJECI.2024.0803208

Mirsky, Y., & Lee, W. (2021). *The creation and detection of deepfakes: A survey*. ACM Computing Surveys, 54(1). *Article*, *7*, 1–41. DOI: 10.1145/3425780

Mishra, A., Alzoubi, Y. I., Anwar, M. J., & Gill, A. Q. (2022). Attributes impacting cybersecurity policy development: An evidence from seven nations. *Computers & Security*, *120*, 102820. DOI: 10.1016/j.cose.2022.102820

Mittal, S., & Vetter, J. S. (2016). Reliability tradeoffs in design of volatile and nonvolatile caches. *Journal of Circuits, Systems, and Computers*, *25*(11), 1650139. Advance online publication. DOI: 10.1142/S0218126616501395

Mızrak, F. (2024). Integrating AI with aviation cybersecurity: The strategic role of human resources. *Business And Management Studies An International Journal*, *12*(3), 610–628. DOI: 10.15295/bmij.v12i3.2396

Mizrak, F., & Reyhan Akkartal, G. (2024). Prioritizing cybersecurity initiatives in aviation: A dematel-QSFS methodology. *Heliyon*, *10*(16), e35487. DOI: 10.1016/j.heliyon.2024.e35487 PMID: 39687858

Mohammad, N., Prabha, M., Sharmin, S., Khatoon, R., & Imran, M. A. U. (2024). Combating banking fraud with it: Integrating machine learning and data analytics. *The American Journal of Management and Economics Innovations*, *6*(07), 39–56.

Mookhey, K. K. (2022, December 27). *AIIMS ransomware attack: What it means for health data privacy*. ET CISO. Retrieved from https://ciso.economictimes.indiatimes.com/news/aiims-ransomware-attack-what-it-means-for-health-data-privacy/96538957

Munir, F. (2025, July 17). *Cybersecurity or suppression? Youth perspectives on the impact of emerging cyber laws in Asia-Pacific*. NetMission Asia. Retrieved from https://netmission.asia/2025/07/17/cybersecurity-or-suppression-youth-perspectives-on-the-impact-of-emerging-cyber-laws-in-asia-pacific-fatima-munir/

Murray, D., Fussey, P., Hove, K., Wakabi, W., Kimumwe, P., Saki, O., & Stevens, A. (2024). The chilling effects of surveillance and human rights: Insights from qualitative research in uganda and zimbabwe. *Journal of Human Rights Practice, 16*(1), 397–412. DOI: 10.1093/jhuman/huad020

Narooka, P., Arora, S., Srivastava, S., Tiwari, M., & Yadav, S. (2025). Adaptive machine learning system for cybersecurity threats. *Journal of Discrete Mathematical Sciences & Cryptography, 28*(5-A), 1611–1620. DOI: 10.47974/jdmsc-2161

Nassif, A. B., Talib, M. A., Nasir, Q., & Dakalbab, F. M. (2021). Machine learning for anomaly detection: A systematic review. *IEEE Access : Practical Innovations, Open Solutions, 9*, 78658–78700. DOI: 10.1109/access.2021.3083060

Nguyen, C. L., & Golman, W. (2021). Diffusion of the Budapest Convention on cybercrime and the development of cybercrime legislation in Pacific Island countries: *"Law on the books" vs "law in action". Computer Law & Security Review, 40*, 105521. Advance online publication. DOI: 10.1016/j.clsr.2020.105521

Niu, X., Wang, L., & Yang, X. (2019). *A Comparison Study of Credit Card Fraud Detection: Supervised versus Unsupervised.* https://arxiv.org/pdf/1904.10604

Note Transnational Cyber Offenses: Overcoming *Jurisdictional Challenges.* (n.d.). Retrieved August 14, 2025, from https://www.rand.org/pubs/researchmemoranda/RM3

Noto, G. (2024, May 17). *Scammers siphon $25M from engineering firm Arup via AI deepfake "CFO"*. CFO Dive. https://www.cfodive.com/

Novikava, A. (2024, July 4). *The evolution of cyber threats: Looking back over the past 10 years*. NordLayer. Retrieved from https://nordlayer.com/blog/evolution-of-cyber-threats-over-10-years/

Novita, N., & Indrany Nanda Ayu Anissa, A. (2022). The role of data analytics for detecting indications of fraud in the public sector. International Journal of Research in Business and Social Science (2147-4478), 11(7), 218–225. https://doi.org/DOI: 10.20525/ijrbs.v11i7.2113

Nurdiawati, A., Mir, B. A., & Al-Ghamdi, S. G. (2025). Recent advancements in prospective life cycle assessment: Current practices, trends, and implications for future research. Resources. *Environmental Sustainability*, •••, 100203.

Nyholm, H.. (2022). The evolution of volatile memory forensics. *Journal of Cybersecurity and Privacy*, *2*(3), 556–572. DOI: 10.3390/jcp2030028

Oberoi, P. (2017). Survey of various security attacks in cloud-based environments. *International Journal of Advanced Research in Computer Science*, *8*(9), 405–410. DOI: 10.26483/ijarcs.v8i9.5012

Odeyemi, O., Mhlongo, N. Z., Nwankwo, E. E., & Soyombo, O. T. (2024). Reviewing the role of AI in fraud detection and prevention in financial services. *International Journal of Science and Research Archive*, *11*(1), 2101–2110. DOI: 10.30574/ijsra.2024.11.1.0279

Oliveri, A., & Balzarotti, D. (2025). *A comprehensive quantification of inconsistencies in memory dumps*. arXiv. Retrieved October 30, 2025, from https://arxiv.org/pdf/2503.15065

Ostapowicz, M., & Żbikowski, K. (2019). Detecting Fraudulent Accounts on Blockchain: A Supervised Approach. *Lecture Notes in* Computer *Science (Including Subseries Lecture Notes in Artificial Intelligence and Lecture Notes in Bioinformatics), 11881 LNCS*, 18–31. https://doi.org/DOI: 10.1007/978-3-030-34223-4_2

Ottmann, J., Cengiz, Ü., Breitinger, F., & Freiling, F. (2023). *As if time had stopped: Checking memory dumps for quasi-instantaneous consistency*. arXiv. Retrieved October 30, 2025, from https://arxiv.org/pdf/2307.12060

Oyewole, A. T., Okoye, C. C., Ofodile, O. C., & Ugochukwu, C. E. (2024). Cybersecurity risks in online banking: A detailed review and preventive strategies application. *World Journal of Advanced Research and Reviews*, *21*(3), 625–643.

Palutke, R., Block, F., Reichenberger, P., & Stripeika, D. (2020). Hiding process memory via anti-forensic techniques. *Forensic Science International Digital Investigation*, *33*, 301012. Advance online publication. DOI: 10.1016/j.fsidi.2020.301012

Palvia, S., Aeron, P., Gupta, P., Mahapatra, D., Parida, R., Rosner, R., & Sindhi, S. (2018). Online education: Worldwide status, challenges, trends, and implications. *Journal of Global Information Technology Management*, *21*(4), 233–241.

Panadés, R., & Yuguero, O. (2025). Cyber-bioethics: The new ethical discipline for digital health. *Frontiers in Digital Health*, *6*, 1523180. DOI: 10.3389/fdgth.2024.1523180 PMID: 39839847

Pandey, B., Kumar, A., Acharya, D. B., Pandey, P., & Bakar, W. A. W. A. (2025). Memory forensic: Detecting unusual intrusion activity in dump of RAM memory using FTK imager. *International Journal of Information Technology : an Official Journal of Bharati Vidyapeeth's Institute of Computer Applications and Management*, *17*(7), 4209–4216. DOI: 10.1007/s41870-025-02567-0

Pan, E. (2024). Machine learning in financial transaction fraud detection and prevention. Transactions on Economics. *Business and Management Research*, *5*, 243–249. DOI: 10.62051/16r3aa10

Pankaj, V. (2025, April 25). *Cybersecurity Profile 2025: India.* Henry M. Jackson School of International Studies, University of Washington. Retrieved August 12, 2025, from https://jsis.washington.edu/news/cybersecurity-profile-2025-india/

Papakonstantinou, V. (2022). Cybersecurity as praxis and as a state: The EU law path towards acknowledgement of a new right to cybersecurity? *Computer Law & Security Review*, *44*, 105653. DOI: 10.1016/j.clsr.2022.105653

Parasnis, S. (2024, June 27). *China-backed hacker group behind 2022 AIIMS attack: Report. MediaNama*. Retrieved from https://www.medianama.com/2024/06/223-china-backed-hacker-group-behind-aiims-attack-report/

Parepa, L.-A. (2020). The Belt and Road Initiative as continuity in Chinese foreign policy. *Journal of Contemporary East Asia Studies*, *9*(2), 175–201. DOI: 10.1080/24761028.2020.1848370

Patil, S. (2022). India's cyber security landscape. In *Varying Dimensions of India's National Security: Emerging Perspectives* (pp. 75–90). Springer Nature Singapore.

Pelekis, S., Koutroubas, T., Blika, A., Berdelis, A., Karakolis, E., Ntanos, C., Spiliotis, E., & Askounis, D. (2025). Adversarial machine learning: a review of methods, tools, and critical industry sectors. Artificial *Intelligence Review 2025 58:8*, *58*(8), 1–87. https://doi.org/DOI: 10.1007/S10462-025-11147-4

Pendergrass, J. A., ... (2019). *Technical report: A toolkit for runtime detection of userspace implants*. arXiv. Retrieved October 30, 2025, from https://arxiv.org/abs/1904.12896

Peron, A. E. dos R., Almstadter Mattar de Magalhães, D., & Caetano, G. F. (2025). Beyond digital repression: Techno-authoritarianism in radical right governments. *Cogent Social Sciences*, *11*(1). Advance online publication. DOI: 10.1080/23311886.2025.2528457

PIB. (2024, August 2). *Universal connectivity and Digital India initiatives reaching all areas, including tier-2/3 cities and villages* [Press release]. Press Information Bureau, Government of India. Retrieved from https://pib.gov.in/PressReleasePage.aspx?PRID=2040566

Plumb, C. (2024, July 30). *Understanding the UN's new international treaty to fight cybercrime: Can it balance law enforcement, privacy, and human rights?* United Nations University – Centre for Policy Research. Retrieved from https://unu.edu/cpr/blog-post/understanding-uns-new-international-treaty-fight-cybercrime

Pombal, J., Cruz, A. F., Bravo, J., Saleiro, P., Figueiredo, M. A. T., & Bizarro, P. (2022). *Understanding* Unfairness *in Fraud Detection through Model and Data Bias Interactions*. https://arxiv.org/pdf/2207.06273

Powell, W. W., & DiMaggio, P. J. (Eds.). (1991). *The new institutionalism in organizational analysis*. University of Chicago Press.

Pranto, T. H., Hasib, K. T. A. M., Rahman, T., Haque, A. B., Islam, A. K. M. N., & Rahman, R. M. (2022). Blockchain and Machine Learning for Fraud Detection: A Privacy-Preserving and Adaptive Incentive Based Approach. *IEEE Access : Practical Innovations, Open Solutions*, *10*, 87115–87134. DOI: 10.1109/ACCESS.2022.3198956

Press Information Bureau. (2024, July 17). *India leads discussions on cybersecurity at Global Digital Summit 2024*. https://www.pib.gov.in/PressReleaseIframePage.aspx?PRID=2109192

Ptashkin, R. L., Hozhyi, O. O., Obruch, Y. Y., Pavlov, V. V., & Kalinichenko, R. A. (2021). Analysis of operational memory as one of the methods of conducting computer-technical forensic research. *Bulletin of Cherkasy State Technological University*, (4), 39–47. DOI: 10.24025/2306-4412.4.2020.214993

PTI. (2020, November 17). *India sees 375 cyberattacks everyday*. The Hindu. Retrieved from https://www.thehindu.com/business/india-sees-375-cyberattacks-everyday/article33110725.ece/amp

Quadir, S. (2019, January 30). Bangladesh to sue Manila bank over $81 million cyber heist: Cenbank governor. *Reuters*. https://www.reuters.com/article/technology/bangladesh-to-sue-manila-bank-over-81-million-cyber-heist-cenbank-governor-idUSKCN1PO19F/

Rakotondravony, N.. (2017). Classifying malware attacks in IaaS cloud environments. *Journal of Cloud Computing (Heidelberg, Germany)*, *6*(1), 1–12. DOI: 10.1186/s13677-017-0098-8

Ramakrishnan, U. P., & Tandon, J. K. (2018). The evolving landscape of cyber threats. *Vidwat*, *11*(1), 31–35.

Ramesh, A., Dhariwal, P., Nichol, A., Chu, C., & Chen, M. (2022). *Hierarchical text-conditional image generation with CLIP latents.* arXiv. https://doi.org//arXiv.2204.06125DOI: 10.48550

Rana, M. S., Nobi, M. N., Murali, B., & Sung, A. H. (2022). Deepfake detection: A systematic literature review. *IEEE Access : Practical Innovations, Open Solutions*, *10*, 25494–25513. DOI: 10.1109/ACCESS.2022.3154404

Ranković, M., Gurgu, E., Martins, O. M. D., & Vukasović, M. (2023). Artificial intelligence and the evolution of finance: Opportunities, challenges and ethical considerations. *EdTech Journal*, *3*(1), 20–23. DOI: 10.18485/edtech.2023.3.1.2

Ratcliffe, C., Bokolo, B. G., Oladimeji, D., & Zhou, B. (2022). Detection of anti-forensics and malware applications in volatile memory acquisition. In *Lecture Notes in Computer Science* (Vol. 13343, pp. 516–527). https://doi.org/DOI: 10.1007/978-3-031-08530-7_44

Ravikumar, A. S., & Mamadiyarov, Z. (2025). Mitigating risks through AI-powered fraud detection systems in digital banking. In Innovating Cost-Efficient and Scalable Business Models in the Digital Era (pp. 343–376). IGI Global Scientific Publishing. https://doi.org/DOI: 10.4018/979-8-3373-2120-2.ch011

Reghunadhan, R. (2018). Cyber threat landscape of digital India: A critical perspective. *Journal of Polity and Society*, *10*(1&2), 37–50.

Report, C. S. I. S. (2025, June). *Significant Cyber Incidents since 2006* [PDF]. Strategic Technologies Program. Centre for Strategic and International Studies. Retrieved from https://csis-website-prod.s3.amazonaws.com/s3fs-public/2025-06/250610_Significant_Cyber_Incidents.pdf/

Rout, S., & Jaiswal, K. (2024). Fraud detection using deep learning. International Journal of Electrical and Data Communication, 5(1), 07–11. https://doi.org/DOI: 10.22271/27083969.2024.v5.i1a.37

Roy, A. (2024, March 10). *How India is using the internet. The Economic Times – ETtech.* Retrieved from https://economictimes.indiatimes.com/tech/technology/how-india-is-using-the-internet/articleshow/108354854.cms?from=mdr

RSF (Reporters Without Borders). (2025, February). *Pakistan: instead of revising legislation that censors dissent, Sharif's government strengthened it.* RSF. Retrieved from https://rsf.org/en/pakistan-instead-revising-legislation-censors-dissent-sharif-s-government-strengthened-it

Rufat, S., Tate, E., Burton, C. G., & Maroof, A. S. (2015). Social vulnerability to floods: Review of case studies and implications for measurement. *International Journal of Disaster Risk Reduction, 14*, 470–486.

Ryan, P., Crane, M., & Brennan, R. (2020). Design Challenges for GDPR RegTech. *ICEIS 2020 - Proceedings of the 22nd International Conference on Enterprise Information Systems, 2*, 787–795. https://doi.org/DOI: 10.5220/0009464507870795

Rzepka, L., Ottmann, J., Stoykova, R., Freiling, F., & Baier, H. (2025). A scenario-based quality assessment of memory acquisition tools and its investigative implications. *Forensic Science International Digital Investigation, 52*, 301868. Advance online publication. DOI: 10.1016/j.fsidi.2025.301868

S, S. G., & K, S. H. (2023). Detecting financial fraud in the digital age: The AI and ML revolution. International Journal For Multidisciplinary Research, 5(5). https://doi.org/DOI: 10.36948/ijfmr.2023.v05i05.6139

Saba, L., Saam, T., Jäger, H. R., Yuan, C., Hatsukami, T. S., Saloner, D., & Wintermark, M. (2019). Imaging biomarkers of vulnerable carotid plaques for stroke risk prediction and their potential clinical implications. *Lancet Neurology, 18*(6), 559–572.

Saluja, S. (2024). Identity theft fraud- major loophole for FinTech industry in India. *Journal of Financial Crime, 31*(1), 146–157. DOI: 10.1108/jfc-08-2022-0211

Sánchez-Aguayo, M., Urquiza-Aguiar, L., & Estrada-Jiménez, J. (2021). Fraud detection using the fraud triangle theory and data mining techniques: A literature review. *Computers, 10*(10), 121. DOI: 10.3390/computers10100121

Sandoval, M. P., de Almeida Vau, M., & Solaas, J.. (2024). Threat of deepfakes to the criminal justice system: A systematic review. *Crime Science, 13*, 41. Advance online publication. DOI: 10.1186/s40163-024-00239-1

Sandvik, J.-P., Franke, K., Abie, H., & Årnes, A. E. (2022). Quantifying data volatility for IoT forensics with examples from Contiki OS. *Forensic Science International Digital Investigation*. Advance online publication. DOI: 10.1016/j.fsidi.2022.301343

Schilling, J., Hertig, E., Tramblay, Y., & Scheffran, J. (2020). Climate change vulnerability, water resources and social implications in North Africa. *Regional Environmental Change, 20*, 1–12.

Shafqat, N., & Masood, A. (2016). Comparative analysis of various national cyber security strategies. *International Journal of Computer Science and Information Security, 14*(1), 129–136.

Shakarian, P., Shakarian, J., & Ruef, A. (2013). Political cyber attack comes of age in 2007. In *Introduction to Cyber-Warfare* (pp. 11–22). Elsevier., DOI: 10.1016/B978-0-12-407814-7.00002-6

Shanker, A. K., & Usha, G. (2017, April). Cyber threat landscape in cyber space. In *2017 International Conference of Electronics, Communication and Aerospace Technology (ICECA)* (Vol. 1, pp. 375–380). IEEE.

Sharma, V., Jamwal, A., Agrawal, R., & Pratap, S. (2025). A review on digital transformation in healthcare waste management: Applications, research trends and implications. *Waste Management & Research, 43*(6), 828–849.

Shastri, S., Wasserman, M., & Chidambaram, V. (2019). *GDPR Anti-Patterns: How Design and Operation of Modern Cloud-scale Systems Conflict with GDPR*. https://arxiv.org/pdf/1911.00498

She, K., Alexandridis, G., Tzouveli, P., & Taherdoost, H. (2023). Blockchain and Machine Learning: A Critical Review on Security. *Information 2023, Vol. 14, Page 295, 14*(5), 295. https://doi.org/DOI: 10.3390/INFO14050295

Sipayung, E. S. N., Yanti, H. B., & Setya, A. B. (2023). Impact of anti-fraud awareness, fraud detection procedures, and technology to fraud detection skill. In Advances in Social Science, Education and Humanities Research (pp. 783–787). Atlantis Press SARL. https://doi.org/DOI: 10.2991/978-2-494069-49-7_132

Solanke, A. A., & Biasiotti, M. A. (2022). Digital forensics AI: Evaluating, standardizing and optimizing digital evidence mining techniques. *KI – Künstliche Intelligenz, 36*(2), 143–161. https://doi.org/DOI: 10.1007/s13218-022-00763-9

Sollitto, N. (2024). *What is the Payment Services Directive 2 (PSD2)? Complete Guide | UpGuard.* Upguard.com. https://www.upguard.com/blog/what-is-psd2

Sood, A. K., & Enbody, R. J. (2013). Crimeware-as-a-service—A survey of commoditized crimeware in the underground market. *International Journal of Critical Infrastructure Protection, 6*(1), 28–38. DOI: 10.1016/j.ijcip.2013.01.002

Statista. (2024). Cyber security in India. https://www.statista.com/study/85981/cyber-security-in-india/

Statista. (2025). Number of internet users in selected countries [Statistics]. *Statista*. Retrieved from https://www.statista.com/statistics/262966/number-of-internet-users-in-selected-countries/

Stuart, J. (2024). *Cybersecurity threats, vulnerabilities and resilience among women human rights defenders and civil society in South-East Asia*. UN Women Regional Office for Asia and the Pacific & United Nations University Institute in Macau. https://doi.org/DOI: 10.17605/OSF.IO/H38WZ

Stupp, C. (2019, August 30). *Fraudsters used AI to mimic CEO's voice in unusual cybercrime case*. The Wall Street Journal. https://www.wsj.com/

SuperAGI. (2025). *Real-Time Fraud Prevention: Case Studies of Businesses Using AI to Secure Online Payments in 2025 - SuperAGI*. SuperAGI. https://superagi.com/real-time-fraud-prevention-case-studies-of-businesses-using-ai-to-secure-online-payments-in-2025/

Supriyadi, H., Priyarsono, D. S., Achsani, N. A., & Andati, T. (2024). An integrated GRC approach to combating fraud in microloan services. *International Journal of Innovative Research and Scientific Studies*, *7*(4), 1580–1591. DOI: 10.53894/ijirss.v7i4.3457

Surakanti, S., Goundar, S., & Dwight, J. (2025). Countering anti-forensic tactics in cybercrime investigations: A systematic literature review. *International Journal of Information Security*, *24*(5), 1–24. DOI: 10.1007/s10207-025-01131-y

Tageldin, L., & Venter, H. (2023). Machine-learning forensics: State of the art in the use of machine-learning techniques for digital forensic investigations within smart environments. *Applied Sciences (Basel, Switzerland)*, *13*(18), 10169. Advance online publication. DOI: 10.3390/app131810169

Taheri, B., Hosany, S., & Altinay, L. (2019). Consumer engagement in the tourism industry: New trends and implications for research. *Service Industries Journal*, *39*(7–8), 463–468.

Tang, J., & Karim, K. E. (2019). Financial fraud detection and big data analytics – implications on auditors' use of fraud brainstorming session. *Managerial Auditing Journal*, *34*(3), 324–337. DOI: 10.1108/maj-01-2018-1767

Touqeer, H., Zaman, S., Amin, R., Hussain, M., Al-Turjman, F., & Bilal, M. (2021). Smart home security: Challenges, issues and solutions at different IoT layers. *The Journal of Supercomputing*, *77*(12), 14053–14089. DOI: 10.1007/s11227-021-03795-y

Tripwire. (2024, May 6). Rising tide: Understanding the surge in cyber attacks in India. The State of Security. https://www.tripwire.com/state-of-security/rising-tide-understanding-surge-cyber-attacks-india

Tru ă, F. (2018, July 24). *Hackers breach Singapore's largest healthcare provider; steal records of 1.5 million patients, including the Prime Minister*. Bitdefender. Retrieved from https://www.bitdefender.com/en-us/blog/hotforsecurity/hackers-breach-singapores-largest-healthcare-provider-steal-records-of-1-5-million-patients-including-the-prime-minister

Vaccari, C., & Chadwick, A. (2020). Deepfakes and Disinformation: Exploring the Impact of Synthetic Political Video on Deception, Uncertainty, and Trust in News. *Social Media + Society*, *6*(1). Advance online publication. DOI: 10.1177/2056305120903408

Vajiram Content Team. (2023, November 15). *Digital India Bill*. Vajiram & Ravi. https://vajiramandravi.com/current-affairs/digital-india-bill/

Vandezande, N. (2024). Cybersecurity in the EU: How the NIS2-directive stacks up against its predecessor. *Computer Law & Security Review*, *52*, 105890. Advance online publication. DOI: 10.1016/j.clsr.2023.105890

Villegas-Ortega, J., Bellido-Boza, L., & Mauricio, D. (2021). Fourteen years of manifestations and factors of health insurance fraud, 2006-2020: A scoping review. *Health & Justice*, *9*(1), 26. DOI: 10.1186/s40352-021-00149-3

Vishwanath, A. (2025, June 14). Protecting Critical Infrastructure in South Asia: Cyber Threats and Solutions. *South Asian Voices*. Retrieved from https://southasianvoices.org/sec-f-in-r-critical-infrastructure-cyber-06-14-2025/

Vömel, S., & Freiling, F. C. (2011). A survey of main memory acquisition and analysis techniques for the Windows operating system. *Digital Investigation*, *8*(1), 3–22. DOI: 10.1016/j.diin.2011.06.002

Wang, H., Wang, W., Liu, Y., & Alidaee, B. (2022). Integrating machine learning algorithms with quantum annealing solvers for online fraud detection. *IEEE Access : Practical Innovations, Open Solutions*, *10*, 75908–75917. DOI: 10.1109/access.2022.3190897

Werder, K., Ramesh, B., & Zhang, R. (sophia). (2022). Establishing data provenance for responsible artificial intelligence systems. *ACM Transactions on Management Information Systems*, *13*(2), 1–23. DOI: 10.1145/3503488

What are STIX/TAXII Standards? I Anomali. (n.d.). Retrieved August 14, 2025, from https://www.anomali.com/resources/what-are-stix-taxii

Yigitcanlar, T., Butler, L., Windle, E., Desouza, K. C., Mehmood, R., & Corchado, J. M. (2020). Can building "artificially intelligent cities" safeguard humanity from natural disasters, pandemics, and other catastrophes? An urban scholar's perspective. *Sensors (Basel)*, *20*(10), 2988. DOI: 10.3390/s20102988

York, J. C. (2024, June). The global suppression of online LGBTQ+ speech continues. *Electronic Frontier Foundation*. Retrieved from https://www.eff.org/deeplinks/2024/06/global-suppression-online-lgbtq-speech-continues

Yuhertiana, I., & Hadi Amin, A. (2024). *Artificial intelligence driven approaches for financial fraud detection: A systematic literature review*. KnE Social Sciences., DOI: 10.18502/kss.v9i20.16551

Zangana, H. M. (2024). Future trends in AI and digital forensics. In *Digital forensics in the age of AI* (pp. 347–380). IGI Global., DOI: 10.4018/979-8-3373-0857-9.ch013

Zetter, K. (2016, May 17). *That insane, $81M Bangladesh Bank heist? Here's what we know. WIRED*. Retrieved from https://www.wired.com/2016/05/insane-81m-bangladesh-bank-heist-heres-know/

Zhang, S., Hu, C., Wang, L., Mihaljevic, M. J., Xu, S., & Lan, T. (2023). A malware detection approach based on deep learning and memory forensics. *Symmetry*, *15*(3), 758. Advance online publication. DOI: 10.3390/sym15030758

Zheng, X., Feng, C., Yin, Z., Zhang, J., & Shen, H. (2023). Research on fraud detection method based on heterogeneous graph representation learning. *Electronics (Basel)*, *12*(14), 3070. DOI: 10.3390/electronics12143070

Zhou, J., Cui, G., Hu, S., Zhang, Z., Yang, C., Liu, Z., Wang, L., Li, C., & Sun, M. (2020). Graph neural networks: A review of methods and applications. *AI Open*, *1*, 57–81. DOI: 10.1016/j.aiopen.2021.01.001

Zou, S., Sun, H., Xu, G., & Quan, R. (2020). Ensemble strategy for insider threat detection from user activity logs. *Computers, Materials & Continua*, *65*(2), 1321–1334. DOI: 10.32604/cmc.2020.010563

About the Contributors

Ricardo Marcão, PhD, MBA, PMP, is a globally recognized expert in Project Management, Finance, Strategy, Grand Strategy, and Healthcare Innovation, with extensive experience in Pharma, MedTech, Medical Devices, IT, and Professional Services. Beyond corporate strategy, Ricardo's expertise extends into Grand Strategy, Democracy, and International Relations, with a particular focus on how geopolitics, economic strategy, and competitive intelligence shape global business dynamics. His knowledge in policy frameworks and transatlantic relations positions him as a thought leader in aligning business growth, technological innovation, and governance for long-term impact. Throughout his career, he has led major transformations, implementing gamification strategies to enhance engagement and sales, redefining Pharma and MedTech consulting through digital innovation, and introducing a risk control framework that improved project margins by 20%. From 2022 to 2023, he spearheaded global CRM projects for top pharmaceutical firms, optimizing commercial operations across international markets. An accomplished academic, editor, and international speaker, Ricardo has authored and edited multiple books on strategy, innovation, and performance evaluation. As a coordinator of MBA, Post-Graduate, Master's and Higher Technical programs at ISLA Santarém, he plays a key role in developing future business leaders at the intersection of business, technology, and governance. Actively engaged in SCIP Portugal, APMP NYC, and PMI, he continues to contribute to strategic intelligence, business consultancy, and global policy discourse.

Vasco Santos is an Adjunct Professor at the Polytechnic University of Tomar (IPT) and member of the Research and Innovation Support Office (GAII). He has a Habilitation in Management (European University, Lisbon), a PhD in Business Sciences (Fernando Pessoa University, Porto), a PhD in Tourism (University of Seville, Spain) and a Post-Doctorate in Innovation Management (University of Aveiro). Specialises in Hotel and Restaurant Management. Integrated researcher at NECE-UI and collaborating researcher at GOVCOPP (University of Aveiro), TECHN&ART (Polytechnic University of Tomar) and CITUR (Polytechnic of Leiria). Editor-in-Chief of the scientific journal 'International Journal of Digital Marketing, Management, and Innovation (IJDMMI)'. Author and reviewer for indexed scientific journals. Author of Book Chapters in IGI Global. Editor of Books in IGI Global.

Nuno Mateus-Coelho is a renowned expert in computer security, holding several academic positions and serving as a Cyber Security Adviser and CISO & DPO for several organizations. He holds a PhD in computer security and is a sought-after speaker on the topic. Nuno is also the CEO of NRMC.PT, author of numerous works on computer security, and winner of the Inncyber Innovation Award for "best European research" in 2021. His greatest work, the Vent2Life project, aimed to repair hospital ventilators

***

Abhilash Aggarwal is a distinguished legal scholar, educator, and researcher with a profound commitment to excellence in the field of law. Holding a B.A.LL.B (Hons.) from Jamia Millia Islamia, an LL.M (Gold Medalist) in Constitution & Administrative Law from NUSRL, Ranchi, and a Ph.D. (Thesis submitted) from Central University of Haryana, he has consistently demonstrated academic brilliance. His qualifications are further bolstered by UGC NET certification and multiple specialized certificate courses in Human Rights Law, Consumer Protection, and French Language. With over six years of extensive teaching and research experience, Abhilash has held prestigious positions such as Head of Department and Assistant Professor at Rai University, Ahmedabad, and

Guest Faculty at Jamia Millia Islamia, New Delhi. His expertise spans legal research, moot court training, competitive exam guidance, and NAAC accreditation assessment. As the founder of The Mendes Legal, an e-learning platform, he has also contributed significantly to legal education through innovative digital solutions. Abhilash is a prolific writer and thinker, with numerous publications in reputed journals and book chapters, including contributions to Springer Nature and UGC Care-listed journals. His research focuses on contemporary issues such as artificial intelligence in law, social media censorship, and human rights. He has presented papers at international and national conferences, including events at GNLU Ahmedabad, Banaras Hindu University, and Kerala Law Academy, earning accolades for his insightful analyses. A sought-after speaker and mentor, Abhilash has judged moot court competitions, chaired conference sessions, and delivered guest lectures on topics ranging from gender sensitization to constitutional law. His leadership roles include Director of Research at Better With Law and Editor-in-Chief of the CLRS Journal for Global Justice & Governance. His dedication to institutional development is evident through his coordination of workshops and national conferences on cutting-edge legal topics. Recognized for his contributions, Abhilash has been honored with awards such as the Gold Medal in LL.M, Best Research Paper Presenter at international conferences, and Best Presenter at forums like GNLU. His philosophy centers on diligence, innovation, and mentorship, aiming to bridge theoretical knowledge with practical legal challenges. Abhilash Aggarwal continues to inspire students and peers alike, shaping the future of legal education and research with his unwavering passion and expertise.

B. Sreedevi is a distinguished academician with a profound interest in Mobile and Wireless Networks, Soft Computing, and Computer Networks. With over two decades of teaching experience, she brings a wealth of knowledge and expertise to her role as a Senior Assistant Professor in the Department of Computer Science and Engineering at SRC, SASTRA Deemed to be University, Kumbakonam, TamilNadu. Her passion for these domains is evident through her extensive research contributions, including presentations at prestigious international and national conferences and publications in esteemed journals.

Ubaldo Comite was born in Cosenza, Italy, June 14 1971. He has a degree in Law (1994) and Economics (1996) at the University of Messina (Italy), and earned his Ph.D. in Public Administration at the University of Calabria, Rende (Cs) Italy, in 2005. Currently he is a professor of Budget and Business Organization at the Faculty of Economy, Department of Business Sciences, University of Calabria. Furthermore he is a professor of Business Administration and Health Management at the Faculty of Economy, University Giustino Fortunato (Benevento – Italy). His Research interests are: Private and Public Management, Non profit Organizations and Accounting, Health Management. E-mail, u.comite@unifortunato .eu Key words areas specialization: management, public administration, accountancy, health management

Kiranbhai Ramabhai Dodiya is an experienced Cyber Forensic Expert and Assistant Professor specializing in cyber security and digital forensics. He has taught at prestigious institutions and is currently pursuing a PhD in Biochemistry and Forensic Science. With a strong background in ethical hacking and malware analysis, Kiranbhai is passionate about educating students and contributing to the field of cyber forensics. His expertise includes malware forensic, computer forensics, and data recovery software. Kiranbhai's commitment to professional growth is evident through his participation in workshops, seminars, and research publications. He is dedicated to shaping the next generation of professionals in the field and combatting cybercrimes.

Ankit Kumar is an Assistant Professor at the School of Law, Sandip University, Sijoul, Madhubani, Bihar. He holds a Ph.D. in Law from the Department of Law and Governance, Central University of South Bihar, where he also obtained his LL.M. and B.Sc.LL.B. (Hons.) degrees. He has qualified the UGC-NET in Law. Dr. Kumar has an extensive academic and research portfolio, with multiple publications including research papers, articles, patents, and book chapters in edited volumes. His works have appeared in peer-reviewed journals and UGC CARE-listed and Scopus publications, and he has presented papers at numerous national and international seminars and conferences. He has also actively participated in various workshops and Faculty Development Programmes (FDPs) at both national and international levels. In addition to his teaching and research responsibilities, Dr. Kumar serves as an editorial member of the University Newsletter of Mangalayatan University, Jabalpur. He has been instrumental in organizing workshops, webinars, and other academic events. His areas of expertise and research interest include Constitutional Law, Arbitration Law, Sports Law, Cyber Law, and allied legal domains.

Kapil Kumar is currently working as an Associate Professor and Coordinator at the Department of Biochemistry and Forensic Science, Gujarat University, Ahmedabad. He has completed his Ph.D. and Master's degree in Forensic Science. He was a pioneer member in establishing the Department of Forensic Science at Gujarat University, Ahmedabad in 2006. He was an organizing secretary for the 24th All India Forensic Science Conference (2018) jointly organized by DFS, Ministry of Home Affairs, RSU, and Gujarat University. He served as a resource person at many RUSA-sponsored Faculty Development Programmes, Short Term Courses, and Refresher courses in various universities covering topics on several branches of Forensic Science and Nanotechnology. He is a lifetime member of Gujarat Science Academy and a member of the Board of Studies of Forensic Science at Parul University, Vadodara. He is also a member of the Board of Studies at Biotechnology, Biochemistry and Forensic Science at YCIS, Satara. He has numerous publications under his name in various National and International journals. He has also provided Consultancy activities in financial fraud investigation with various Banks and Police organizations.

Yunfei Li is General Manager of the Network Finance Department of a bank and a Senior Engineer. He obtained a Ph.D. from Rajamangla University of Technology Tawan-Ok in 2024. His main research directions include financial technology, financial risks, AI, digital currencies, etc. He is currently a Postdoctoral Research Fellow at the Department of Business Sciences, University Giustino Fortunato, 82100 Benevento, Italy, and has published more than 10 papers in international journals and conferences.

Shagufta Parween, Head & Assistant Professo, Department of English, Chaitanya Bharathi Institute of Technology, Hyderabad, is a highly qualified and competent educator with more than 16 years of experience in teaching and research. She holds a Gold Medal in M.A

English and a PhD in English Literature specializing in Indian English Novels, and is the author of many research papers in well-established and peer reviewed international journals. Dr. Parween has significantly contributed to the academic community as a reviewer of journal articles and provided best practices in English Language and Literature, Business Communication, Technical Writing Skills, Gender Sensitization, Soft Skills and Employability Skills at the undergraduate and post-graduate levels. In addition, she has presented her research in many prestigious conferences and is actively engaged in professional development programs. Dr. Parween is an accomplished and energetic learner-centered educator who is known for her expertise in teaching methods and actively tries to find new ways to create student engagement and success in her teaching.

Ravikumar R. N. is currently a Postdoctoral researcher at Universiti Malaysia Perlis, Malaysia. Also, working as an Associate Professor in the department of Computer Engineering at Marwadi University, Rajkot, Gujarat. He has 12+ years of national and international teaching experience. He completed his PhD at Amity University, Rajasthan, M.E at VMRF Deemed University, B.E at Anna University, Chennai. He is the co-founder of the Research Activities Club at Marwadi University and trains students on research activities, which leads to the publication of 7 Scopus/SCI journals, 20 Book chapters, 25 Conference papers, and 10 patents. His specialization is ML, DL, Federated Learning, Recommendation Systems, and Optimization Techniques.

Aarthi S is a dedicated Assistant Professor in Computer Science with over six years of teaching experience. She is currently pursuing her Ph.D. at Marwadi University, Gujarat, and holds an M.Phil. and MCA from Bharathiar University, Tamil Nadu. Throughout her academic career, Aarthi has specialized in programming languages such as C++, Java, and C, and contributed to research in recommender systems and AI-related data privacy. She has published journal articles, contributed to book chapters, and actively participated in technical workshops. Known for her student mentorship and engagement in academic events, Aarthi remains committed to fostering innovation and excellence in computer science education.

Barathi S is an assistant professor of English and Research supervisor at SRC, SASTRA Deemed to be University, KUMBAKONAM. She is a bilingual poet, translator and Critic. She has published her poems in various national and international anthologies. She has so far translated five poetry anthologies, two short story collections and a novel in Tamil language. Besides, she has published numerous research papers in numerous peer reviewed, UGC care and SCOPUS indexed journals of national and international repute. She had been a guest of honour, chaired sessions, delivered keynote address in many national and international conferences.

Kaveri Sharma, Professor & Dean, School of Legal Studies at K.R. Mangalam University, Gurugram has got an academic experience of more than 14 years. She is currently pursuing a Post Doctoral Research Program from University of Economics and Pedagogy, Uzbekistan and International Engineering and Technology Institute (IETI), Hong Kong, China on Artificial Intelligence and law. Previously she was associated with various prestigious Universities in Delhi/NCR like Guru Gobind Singh Indraprastha University, University Institute of Law and Management Studies, Gurugram & Manav Rachna University, Faridabad as Head of the Department. She has written and presented more than 25 research papers/ book chapters, which have been published in National and International Journals and Books. Recently, her edited book on "Artificial Intelligence, Robotics and Law" was published by Central Law Agency. She has done diploma courses in Intellectual Property Rights and Cyber Laws from Indian Law Institute, New Delhi and on 'Cyber Crime prosecution and Defence' from Asian School of Cyber Laws. She has two published patents on "A Novel Method for Real-Time Autonomous Vehicle Traffic Management" & "Artificial Intelligence based Humanoid Robot for Security". She has also adjudged various National Moot Court Competitions organized by different Universities.

Parvesh Sharma is an Assistant Professor in the Department of Biochemistry and Forensic Science at Gujarat University. His research focuses on digital forensics, forensic document examination, microscopy, and cybercrime investigation. He has published widely on memory forensics, dark web drug trading, hyperspectral imaging, non-destructive document analysis, and AI applications in forensic science. Dr. Sharma has contributed book chapters in Forensic Microscopy and Artificial Intelligence in Forensic Science and has presented his work at major national forensic science forums. His interdisciplinary work advances modern investigative techniques and strengthens the scientific foundation of forensic practice.

Index

A

Adversarial AI 218, 239
AI-Driven Detection 161, 164, 165, 172, 175, 179, 182, 189, 198, 257
AI-driven Fraud Analytics 97, 100, 103, 105, 120, 125
AI Fraud Detection 261
AML 218, 232, 239, 240, 241
Anomaly Detection 2, 32, 47, 97, 102, 103, 106, 110, 115, 116, 130, 133, 136, 137, 143, 144, 146, 150, 153, 237, 242, 244

C

CCPA 218, 246
Cyberattacks 55, 56, 65, 72, 74, 81, 90, 93, 198, 199, 201, 203, 208, 211, 214, 218, 222, 224
Cyber Attacks 75, 209, 213, 216
Cybercrime Prevention 110, 219
Cyber Resilience 38, 72, 84, 93, 104, 208, 227, 245
Cyber Security 57, 68, 77, 78, 83, 84, 87, 88, 199, 206, 207, 213, 214, 215, 227, 228, 259
Cybersecurity Law 178

D

Deepfake Fraud 161, 162, 163, 165, 166, 167, 174, 176, 179, 181, 183, 184, 186, 189, 191, 192, 193, 219
Digital Forensics 1, 2, 3, 27, 35, 38, 43, 45, 47, 50, 53, 187, 190
Digital Governance 91, 102
Digital Transformation 55, 82, 102, 197, 198, 199, 200, 204, 208, 211, 215, 222

E

Email Analysis 135
Ethical AI 113, 120, 122, 123, 133, 191, 192, 246, 247
EU AI Act 104, 113, 122, 124, 174, 218, 233, 243
Evidence Preservation 16, 37

F

Financial Fraud 106, 109, 127, 128, 129, 131, 132, 134, 162, 163, 168, 171, 179, 183, 184, 221, 240, 259, 260
Fraud Prevention 98, 101, 102, 104, 105, 114, 116, 120, 121, 124, 126, 127, 129, 133, 134, 225, 229, 231, 244, 245, 249, 253, 257, 262, 263

G

GDPR 22, 78, 83, 84, 87, 104, 113, 124, 134, 175, 177, 178, 218, 219, 230, 231, 232, 234, 235, 236, 239, 242, 246, 259, 260, 262, 263
Generative AI 32, 162, 164, 166, 192
Governance 36, 38, 44, 45, 55, 56, 60, 63, 64, 65, 66, 72, 73, 74, 76, 77, 78, 79, 80, 82, 83, 86, 89, 90, 91, 102, 103, 105, 107, 110, 119, 120, 122, 123, 124, 125, 126, 127, 129, 133, 165, 166, 169, 170, 173, 178, 181, 182, 183, 186, 188, 189, 192, 193, 194, 197, 198, 207, 212, 219, 220, 225, 229, 230, 233, 235, 248, 249, 251, 252, 253, 256, 257, 261

I

Insider Threat Detection 141, 159

L

Law 2, 5, 7, 9, 27, 31, 41, 43, 44, 46, 48, 50, 64, 65, 78, 83, 87, 91, 92, 93, 94, 113, 166, 171, 174, 177, 178, 187, 188, 194, 201, 205, 207, 217, 221, 224, 229, 232, 233, 236, 245, 261
Legal Challenges 26, 91, 161
Legal Compliance 122, 220, 249
LightGBM 135, 136, 138, 140, 141, 142,

143, 146, 150, 152, 156

M

Machine Learning 20, 32, 97, 98, 100, 105, 106, 107, 109, 111, 112, 114, 116, 117, 125, 128, 129, 130, 132, 133, 135, 136, 137, 138, 140, 142, 143, 144, 145, 146, 150, 152, 156, 158, 162, 164, 176, 218, 220, 236, 237, 238, 239, 240, 243, 254, 257, 262, 263
Malware Analysis 207

P

Phishing 57, 59, 60, 67, 68, 69, 74, 75, 84, 97, 98, 103, 112, 115, 117, 134, 137, 158, 166, 187, 218, 221, 222, 223, 225, 244, 245, 255
Policy 2, 26, 37, 38, 50, 60, 63, 64, 65, 66, 70, 71, 72, 77, 78, 84, 85, 89, 90, 91, 93, 98, 104, 109, 120, 123, 124, 166, 173, 177, 180, 189, 190, 207, 208, 213, 219, 220, 221, 225, 228, 229, 230, 255, 257, 260
Privilege Escalation 135, 136, 137, 138, 139, 140, 142, 143, 144, 145, 147, 148, 150, 152, 154, 156

R

Random Forest 107, 111, 135, 136, 137, 138, 140, 143, 146, 150, 152, 156, 238
Ransomware 9, 28, 55, 59, 60, 61, 66, 70, 71, 72, 73, 74, 75, 78, 79, 84, 86, 87, 88, 91, 98, 103, 134, 197, 199, 201, 202, 205, 211, 218, 222, 223, 228, 255

S

SVM 111, 135, 136, 138, 140

T

Threat Intelligence 85, 211, 221, 238, 239, 251, 257

V

Vectorization 135
Volatile Memory 2, 3, 4, 5, 7, 9, 18, 19, 20, 22, 28, 29, 30, 34, 43, 45, 47, 48, 51, 52

X

XGBoost 135, 137, 138, 140, 143, 146, 150, 152, 153, 156, 237, 238

www.ingramcontent.com/pod-product-compliance
Lightning Source LLC
LaVergne TN
LVHW081525300926
849161LV00006B/1307